CREATING
A SEASON TO REMEMBER

THE NEW YOUTH-SPORTS-COACHING LEADERSHIP HANDBOOK

JACK PERCONTE

Second Base Publishing

Jack Perconte/Second Base Publishing
6197 Hinterlong Ct.
Lisle IL 60532
www.baseballcoachingtips.net

Ordering Information:
Quantity sales. Special discounts are available on quantity purchases by corporations, associations, and others. For details, contact the "Special Sales Department" at the address above.

Creating a Season to Remember/Jack Perconte—1st edition
LCCN 2016917857
ISBN 978-0-9981709-0-9
    1. Youth sports coaching
    2. Sports for children – Social aspects
    3. Adults and children – relationship building

Dedicated to Kelly.

Best roommate ever.

You have been an inspiration to so many.

Always playing the game hard for the whole 9 innings, the way it should be.

Acknowledgements

I would like to thank my family - Linda, Matthew, Kristin, Michal, Julie Jackie, Cora and Paul - for their support. They had to be sick of hearing me say my book was almost finished for the last three and a half years.

Much appreciation to Coach Bill Vasko for setting the scene in the foreword for the youth sports environment, and this book. We have similar philosophies and desires to help provide better experiences for athletes and coaches.

I am extremely thankful to my editor, Joanna Ellis-Escobar, for bringing things to life with her dedication and interest in helping youth, too.

To all the dedicated players, coaches and parents I have dealt with – "Thank *You!*"

Contents

"The time has come to put the sense and integrity back into youth sports"
Jack Perconte

Foreword

I started in the coaching profession in 1992 because I wanted to work with young people, both from an athletic standpoint, and an educational standpoint. I wanted to help young athletes develop the same passion for athletic competition that I had, while also learning such virtues as character, teamwork, discipline, and resiliency.

Since I first started my coaching career, youth sports has unfortunately, or fortunately depending upon your perspective, become a big business. There is a lot of money at stake in youth sports – personal instruction, high tech facilities, club/travel teams, tournaments, showcases – all with two main goals in mind: the almighty dollar and the college scholarship.

There is no putting the genie back in the bottle at this point, so how do we ensure that the focus of youth sports is where it should be – on the KIDS? Coach Perconte has developed some tremendous ideas in this handbook that will certainly help coaches at all levels. However, it is our responsibility as coaches to internally evaluate our roles in the development of young athletes.

When we step back from our position as a coach, we must realize that whether we are a youth, club, high school, college, or professional coach, our primary role is one of developing relationships. While we have to develop relationships with a variety of groups of people when we are a coach, the most important relationship is the one that we have with our players.

Throughout my career, I have served as a coach at a variety of levels, from youth, to middle school, to high school, to the college level. I have found the experiences to be both enjoyable and very rewarding. When I first began my coaching career 25 years ago, my primary objective as a young coach was to win championships. While I have always enjoyed the competitive and strategic aspects of coaching, the bonds and relationships that are created and the young lives that you become involved with are the aspects that provide the greatest rewards in coaching. Being a coach, you can help shape and influence the lives and futures of so many young people. Not only are you a coach, but also a teacher, counselor, guide, disciplinarian, and most important of all, a companion in life.

The role of a coach in an athlete's life is an important one, and should not be taken lightly. The coach should always strive to provide a proper example of how one should conduct themselves in our society. While it is not the coach's responsibility to be the only, or even primary, role model for an athlete, a coach is an ideal person for setting a good example through his or her actions.

Many people believe that athletics is one of the few areas in today's society that can develop a person's character in a positive manner. Character is a broad term and participation in athletics can develop many aspects of a particular person's character. Some of these include, for example, discipline, respect, teamwork, cooperation, loyalty, faith, and trust. I feel that this is where the real satisfaction in coaching comes from – knowing that you have, to the best of your ability, helped prepare a young person for life beyond their athletic career. As a coach, it's easy to get caught up in the moment, but years later, when you look back, it's the young people you've worked with that you will cherish the most, not how many wins you got.

In order to put the focus of youth athletics back on the KIDS, each of us, as coaches, must reflect upon why we are involved in this profession. This includes the mom, dad, college student, etc., who may just be volunteering their time to help coach a youth team. Are we coaching because of the money? The fame? Because we think we can do the job better than someone else? Or are we sincerely trying to help kids become better athletes and even better people? Coach Perconte will be able to spur some further introspection while you read this handbook......our youth are counting on it!

Bill Vasko - Assistant Coach UMass Lowell, Owner and Writer for mycoachbook.com and maxxathletes.com

Introduction

THE STATE OF PLAY

"What do you mean you're not playing anymore?"
"It's not fun."
"You're playing."
"The coach stinks and I'm not going anymore."
"Well, I've spent a lot of money for you to play, so you're going."

If you're a parent of a young athlete, you've probably had, or will have sometime in the future, a similar conversation with your child. It's disappointing for everyone, because kids are out for fun and parents have high hopes for their children in sports.

THE GOOD OL' DAYS

There's always been a certain loss of common sense and perspective in youth sports. Competition is an encounter between two opposing forces, which automatically invites a higher-than-average intensity. The combination of kids, passion, and adults can bring out the worst in people. Although the youth sports' experience was never entirely without problems, the times were simpler back in the day.

Years ago, kids had less sporting options and plenty of free time to play in neighborhoods. That local play involved less structure and parental involvement. It led to kids figuring things out for themselves, and more often than not, the result was fun. In organized sports, coaches had the freedom to manage their players with little parental involvement. Bad coaches were around then, too, but fewer other concerns existed.

But now, because of many new factors, a troubled, degenerating state is upon us. The landscape has vastly changed since today's coaches played. Youth sports have sadly evolved into little or no free play at home, with organized leagues taking over. It's become big business. Travel and club sports with higher expenses are now the norm. Specialization, year-round play, and the intense pursuit of college scholarships are undeniably on the scene. Showcase events for young athletes are widespread, and the televising of youth sports is more abundant, too.

Along with these changes, teams with players as young as 10-years-old strive for national championships and rankings. The focus on winning at the youth levels now rivals the intensity of the professional ranks. One could argue that today's youth rosters change as much as, or more than, professional ones. Further complicating the situation is the movement into an exclusive system that's now only for elite players and those who can afford the high cost of play. Another concern is that many school districts have had to limit extra-curricular activities because of budget deficits. The kids in these areas have little chance to receive the benefits of sports play and the physical activity that others have.

All of these changes have created a high-anxiety era, for both the youth and the adults alike. The current environment for youth sports is one made up of the over-stressed athlete from the extreme adult demands for excellent play and winning. Today's athlete feels the pressure to not only play well, but to work harder than the rest and to outperform the neighbor's kid. Many parents want stars and winners, and too often, they'll stop at little to meet those ends. The most discouraging fact is that the fun seems to have diminished a great deal for the athletes from years past.

Stuck in the middle of it all are the youth coaches. The pressures parents lay on coaches today have made coaching a dubious proposition. Many youth coaches get into the season and begin to wonder why they ever even wanted to coach. They move from one headache to another. One day the players do not want to practice, the next day a parent complains of their child's role, and the following day an assistant coach "*goes off*" on a player. Coaches may begin to realize, were it not for the players and parents, coaching would be the enjoyable experience they envisioned. I'm making a joke here, but there is some merit to what I'm saying.

Of course, sometimes it's the coaches who are the problem. Some have the wrong perspective and coaching methods, which can lead to team turmoil. Whatever the case, the result can end up being athletes, coaches, and parents wondering: "*Is participation even worth it?*" Not only are they wondering this, but many kids are actually dropping out, and more than ever before, parents are unwilling to enroll their children in team sports simply because of the massive emphasis on winning, the quest for notoriety and the high costs that's entered the scene. Many adults considering coaching are unwilling to commit after observing the current youth sports environment.

DETERIORATING CONDITIONS

"*Did you see the news today? A coach chased an umpire with a bat during the game. No, wait, that was yesterday; today it was a parent punching his child's coach.*"

Sports headlines like these occur daily. It may be hard to believe, but some events are even more startling than these. Litigation surrounding a youth sports situation is a regular occurrence, too. These days, it seems everyone around the games has a horror story to tell.

I won't go on and on about these stories in this book, because that would be the same as reading or watching the news. But the sad reality is, fewer games than ever happen without unfortunate incidents occurring. Of course, most head-shaking sports accounts are much less severe than the examples I mention, but for many, the minor incidents take the enjoyment out of the game, too.

THE DILEMMA

There aren't many alternatives for parents who want their children in sports. It's either the ultra-competitive world of travel sports for the elite athletes and those who can afford it, or it's the only-slightly competitive recreational leagues where participation is the primary objective.

Many people believe that the less-intense recreational leagues can be an answer to the high-anxiety problem. But many non-competitive leagues provide little competition, inadequate training, and less knowledgeable coaches. For even mildly competitive parents and players, the casual atmosphere simply doesn't cut it.

Such is the paradox – people must now decide: *do they want the extreme, the less competitive, or to not play at all?* Unfortunately, we are seeing this last option more often, and I suspect this will continue with the now-high expense that's involved with competitive travel teams. Often, the fees to play travel ball are 5 times or more than the cost to play in local recreational leagues. Many club teams cost upwards of $1000 a year to play. Understandably, many parents cannot afford this, or they're just aren't willing to shell out those amounts.

THE ALL-TOO-OFTEN RESULT: QUITTING

Issues like burnout, pressure, overuse injuries, unmotivated athletes, cheating, and over the top adults still have no solutions. These, along with other circumstances, cause many children to stop playing at younger ages. A poll from the National Alliance for Youth Sports shows that around 70% of kids in the United States stop playing organized sports by the age of 13.

Reasons for Quitting Include:
- ✓ Lost interest.
- ✓ Too much pressure from parents.
- ✓ Felt winning was the only reason for playing.
- ✓ Inadequate coaching.
- ✓ The coaches were unfair.
- ✓ No confidence.
- ✓ Too little success for the amount of effort given.
- ✓ Lack of improvement.
- ✓ Grown weary from disappointing mom and dad too often.
- ✓ Boredom.
- ✓ Injury.
- ✓ Little playing time.
- ✓ Feeling demoralized after losing.
- ✓ Inability to get along with teammates or coaches.
- ✓ Friends stopped playing.
- ✓ Insufficient funds to play.
- ✓ Not enough time to devote to the year-round play.

Often, players package these reasons into the *"It just wasn't fun anymore"* rationale. Some children realize they aren't cut out for sports, and quitting is understandable. But for most athletes, the stoppage of play is troublesome and avoidable. Kids' desire to play is dissipating at younger ages than ever before. A chief reason for this exodus is the emphasis on sports being only for achievement and advancement. The stress and the lack of enjoyment that results have changed the games for kids. Of course, the lack of family funds to play is a troubling issue that needs addressing by our society, too.

WHY EVEN HAVE KIDS PLAY?

Youth sports can and should be one of the best avenues for developing children into mature teenagers and responsible adults. When at its best, youth sports can instill significant life values and lessons. Sports keep kids active and help them learn to compete and socialize. Many friendships, some lifelong, come from the playing fields.

Many research studies, both old and new, show the benefits of physical activity and sports play. Some of these findings are outlined in the *True Sport Reports – Why We Play Sport and Why We Stop* and *What Sports Mean to Us*. The findings are eye openers that all coaches and parents of athletes should read.

Research studies show the possible and real benefits of physical activity.

Athletes:
- ✓ Have higher test scores and grades.
- ✓ Have lower school absence rates.
- ✓ Graduate at a higher rate and are more likely to attend college.
- ✓ Show fewer signs of depression.
- ✓ Demonstrate less social anxiety and risk-taking behavior.
- ✓ Are less likely to commit suicide or become delinquent.
- ✓ Have better employment opportunities.
- ✓ Sleep better.
- ✓ Have better concentration skills.

Sports activity also can do the following.

Sports Can:
- ✓ Develop flexibility and balance.
- ✓ Help prevent child obesity.
- ✓ Aid in the social, emotional, and psychological maturation.
- ✓ Provide ready-made friendships and group membership.
- ✓ Help kids overcome social inadequacies.
- ✓ Facilitate kids' understanding of others.
- ✓ Help young people to follow rules, solve problems, and develop self-control.

✓ Make it more likely kids will remain physically active in their adult years.

All the above are staggering reasons and provide a compelling argument for why youth should play and keep playing sports. Few other youth activities give kids the chance to develop their bodies, confidence, and self-worth like sports can. When kids quit playing at young ages, they lose friends, group membership and the opportunity to learn valuable life skills. Maybe one of the best benefits of all, and no study is needed to convince parents of this, sports get kids out of the house and away from the TV, video games, and the internet.

WHY COACH IF IT SEEMS LIKE A NO-WIN SITUATION?

With the current problems and anxiety that come with coaching at the youth level, why would anyone choose to coach in the first place? Here is why.

A while back, I received two unsolicited letters from childhood friends after they saw I was doing some writing.

The first letter:

Jack,

Your dad was a great leader, coach, and gentleman. I can remember him from Joliet Little League, along with your fastball. Please write about him.

The second letter:

Jack,

I read what you post[ed] on here, and I can tell that your passion for sports and drive to help kids has a lot of your dad's influence in it. What a great man. I remember him with a lot of love and respect.

To know that two people remember my father in that way, some 45 years later, is remarkable. Knowing that my dad made such a memorable, positive impact on people's lives is powerful stuff. I cry every time I read these letters. I must believe that if my dad made that impression on three players, myself included, there are probably more. The chance to be remembered as great, a leader, a gentleman, with love and respect is worth it all. It's *fascinating* to think of the potentially tremendous influence that youth coaches have on impressionable young people.

Coaches change lives and make a difference. For people who have the time and knowledge, why wouldn't they want to shape kids' lives? Better yet, imagine the pride a dynamic parent coach can build in and the influence they can have on their child – priceless.

WHAT'S THE SOLUTION?

The situation is not all dire, despite what much of the above suggests. Many youth athletes have positive experiences with well-intentioned coaches. I see and work with many of both. Unfortunately, the good times are becoming more of an exception. Too many kids are not enjoying sports, getting much out of them, or even just having the opportunity to play them. Despite the tremendous possible benefits, the number of contented athletes and coaches decreases daily.

Maybe it would be best if the current youth sports system could revert to the way it once was, but that isn't going to happen any time soon. The big business that youth sports have become now prohibits going back to the simpler times. Therefore, we must deal with the present situation. Kids of all competition levels deserve the benefits playing provide and the fees to play should not deter parents from giving their kids the same opportunities others have.

The crux of it is this – most athletes' loss of desire and lack of fun comes about because coaches fail to inspire both youth and parents alike. The time has come to bring the enjoyment back to youth sports for everyone involved. This change must come from the only logical source, the coaches. Coaches can, *and must*, change the current youth sports culture before the enjoyment disappears for many more athletes. If it takes one coach at a time, so be it. One coach affects many, and now, more than ever, young people need inspiring role models.

In defense of coaches, most simply don't know how to make a difference. This lack of knowledge causes disillusionment for them, too. Coaches often have little training on how to deal with the modern athlete and the issues that pervade youth sports today. The unfortunate results are athlete, coach, and parent disappointment.

Parents would never send their children to a school with teachers who had little or no training, yet they are willing to let their kids be coached by someone without adequate experience. The endless negative news stories indicate that youth coaches do not have the wherewithal to deal with the prevailing state of affairs. Even sports leagues that offer coaching training usually don't provide acceptable solutions to the problems.

The fact is, the playing experience could be a lot better for all, even for those who are having fun. Dynamic coaching can deter athletes from quitting as a result of high anxiety. Most urgent, a youth sports coach should never be the reason players stop playing or leave a team.

WHY THIS BOOK?

Initially, I set out to write a book that would help the *"jerks,"* those 10% or so of coaches who give youth sports a bad reputation. They take away an athlete's desire to play with their demeaning coaching actions.

But then I realized, those types of coaches are probably unwilling to learn or change their ways, so a book like that would likely be a waste of time.

Instead, this book is for the countless, kind-hearted people coaching, or those who are thinking about giving it a try, who just want to help youth. It's for all the people who wish to have an enjoyable experience themselves. Better-trained coaches will make all levels of play beneficial, exciting, and less stressful for everyone involved.

The coaching techniques in this book will motivate and inspire coaches, young people and parents. That last thought, *inspiring parents*, is essential to-day. Parents with unreasonable ambitions for their children have become a significant issue. Some leagues have gone so far as to ban fans from youth games to avoid the unpleasantness created by the attending parents. Other organizations do not allow talk of any sort at events, creating silent games.

It's a shame things have come to this. Maybe the day will come when parent education programs for youth sports become mandatory and make a difference.

Until then, **coaches are on the hook** for that guidance.

Coaches must know ways to influence parents if they are going to have any chance of maintaining the pleasure of the game for all. Better coaching can turn overbearing parents into less demanding ones.

Additionally, coaches must learn to work with the kids of today, who are different than they were. Coaches cannot treat kids the same today as they did many years ago – they now must have a better game plan for educating the kids they're coaching.

All of the causes, cited previously, for kids leaving athletics are under a coach's control. Coaches have a direct bearing on keeping sports vital and exciting. According to a report by the U.S. Government Accountability Office, the quality of coaching is a major factor in *maximizing* all the possible benefits of playing.

Of all the reasons for quitting, the most common one is *"The joy is missing because the achievement level does not reflect the amount of effort given."* The best coaches focus on the fundamentals that bring the needed accomplishment. This book shows coaches ways to develop the skills that brings the progress that keeps players coming back for more. When the desired progress doesn't show up, this guide gives coaches ways of helping players handle failure. This handbook provides the answers and specific points to keep the excitement in and the stress out of games.

Some of the solutions found here may cause you to say, *"That's just common sense."* Sure, but many of the problems come about because practicality disappears in the heat of the moment. Common sense does not always turn into common practice in competition. The information here gives coaches the means to keep the necessary perspective.

It's not enough anymore to just show up, run practices, and manage games. The high number of concerns about today's game demands the case for new and better training. A new youth-sports-coaching-leadership formula is needed. This book contains the forward-thinking techniques that solve past and new concerns.

This book will help coaches seize the opportunity to *create that season to remember.* Most volunteer coaches have a short coaching window, so time is of the essence.

WHY ME?

Since my major league baseball career, I have worked with young athletes, coaches, and parents. For the past 27 years, I have partaken in, observed, and heard a great number of stories. Some of the conditions I've witnessed have become more upsetting and beyond belief each passing year. The stories tend to raise the standard questions:

"The coach did what?"
"Where was the coach when all this happened?"
"Why are you calling the coach an idiot?"

These questions are not surprising because coaches are the central figures in youth sports.

I have experimented over the years to come up with many suggestions to the issues surrounding the youth sports scene. Even the best-intentioned coaches can use the help. I'll share my encounters and pass on the coaching strategies I've used and have seen work. I recognize, as all coaches should, that I don't have all the answers. For that reason, I draw on the coaching lessons of many great coaches. Of course, I also know that people should never treat youth games as professional ones. However, as you'll read, the issues college and professional coaches face relate to all levels of sports. The coaching greats have leadership skills and methods of coaching that can inspire us all.

I know coaches can't do everything in this book, but learning new relationship techniques, teaching skills, and ways of inspiring others can make all the difference. Also, I know effective coaching brings the life-shaping experiences that athletes deserve.

When athletes look back to their playing days, their memories should be pleasant ones. But too often, they're not. Legendary coach Amos Alonzo Stagg once answered a question about whether a team was his best one. He responded with "*I won't know for 20 years or so.*" Stagg recognized that his job performance was dependent on how players' lives would end up years after their time together. His response attests to just how powerful a coach's influence can be, not only for sports, but for players' lives, too.

No sweeter words exist for me besides hearing "*Hi, Dad,*" than hearing "*Hi, Coach Jack.*" It's also a fantastic feeling to hear from former players who tell me about the valuable life experiences we shared years ago. Little did I know at the time that I was helping shape my players' lives for the better.

"*That feeling can be for every coach!*"

HOW TO READ THIS HANDBOOK

Before the season, you should read this book cover to cover. You will learn ways of inspiring you, players, parents, and in all situations. It gives a step-by-step plan that will help you reach your coaching potential. During the season, when needing to learn about a distinct issue, you can look up a topic in the table of contents to see how to handle it. It's important to keep in mind that not every suggestion will work for every situation, as all kids and teams differ.

Coaching is a trial and error process, but this book will help prevent much of the indecision that often comes with that process.

Also, sports' play and coaching depends on repetition. Coaches say it again, and players do it again. In this book, you'll come across occasional repetitive ideas for helping. The reiteration is necessary because some suggestions apply to many areas and bear repeating.

Finally, the terms kids, youth, players, children, team members, and athletes represent all ages below the high school level. Although the book's focus is on youth coaching, coaches of all levels of play, parents and teachers can benefit from the strategies in this book.

CHAPTER I

~

Creating the Mindset to Coach

People must examine their personal goals and life situations before making the commitment to coach. Self-introspection helps to know if you're cut out for the job and can handle today's parents and athletes.

Here is a letter I received from one of my former students, which relates to the impact coaches can have on athletes.

Dear Jack,

I read your article that you wrote about your Dad and wanted to let you know that the apple did not fall far from the tree. Speaking personally, you had an equal effect on my life as others were impacted by your Dad. Having the opportunity to learn from and work for you were some of the best times of my life. I remember as if it were only yesterday, opening up the place, watching you give lessons, taking swings in-between appointments, and having some great conversations. My kids are now beginning their sports careers, and I only hope that I can pass on the love of sports to them as it was passed on to me from my mentors growing up. I believe that we are the product of our environments and a culmination of the events in our lives and the influences which surround those events. I'm thankful every day for having mentors like you in my life.

MY COACHING LEGENDS

Besides my parents, wife, and kids, the biggest influences in my life were 3 of my sports coaches. They may not fall into as famous a category as many of the other coaches I'll write about, but they were incredible role models for me. Each of them came along at different points in my career.

In high school, Coach Gordie Gillespie was there, in college, Coach Johnny Reagan, and in professional baseball, Coach Del Crandall. Each shaped my life for the better, and none did it with earth-shaking actions, but rather in simple ways.

The first thing that comes to mind about these men is they all had the same way of inspiring – with just a look. They looked me in the eyes, and their eyes shouted, *"I believe in you."* To know and feel that someone believes in you as an athlete and as a person is a powerful experience. *"The look"* you give an athlete can be the best form of motivation possible.

Each of my mentors had different coaching personalities. Coach Gillespie was boisterous and made players believe they could move mountains. Coach Reagan was calm, but even with his quiet dignity, team members were aware of what he expected. Coach Crandall's personality was between the two, easy-going and fiery, depending on the situation.

With a word or two at the appropriate time, coaches can change lives, often without even realizing it. Coach Gillespie, so powerful an individual, had a way of making someone feel like they were the most important person in the world. He would ask me, *"What do you think we should do?"* when confronted with a decision for the intramural program he put me in charge of running. The finest leader I had ever known was asking *me*, a high school

18

student, what I thought we should do. The self-assurance I gained from that experience was immeasurable.

Coach Reagan was a communicator. He would walk up to players on the field and ask them what went wrong on a play. After the player would answer, he would respond with, "*You know, we can go into any dormitory on campus and find someone who can do the ordinary, we chose you for a reason.*" It was his way to motivate players to be better than average. On my last day of my freshman year, he said, "*Make sure you come back the next year, we have plans for you.*" He went on to say they planned to move our best player off of second base the next year to make room for me, a walk-on player. That meant so much after having played little my freshman year. I had no plans to go elsewhere, but that statement was the best self-esteem builder I could have received, one that I rode to the major leagues. Letting players know where they stand is crucial, no matter how insignificant it may appear.

Coach Crandall was there for me at various times in my professional career. It felt comforting when he said, "*Don't worry, you are my second baseman,*" after a struggling time in the major leagues. A coach's trust is critical for athletes. After a disappointing career moment, he consoled me, "*If that's the worst thing that comes in your life, that's not so bad.*" Helping players maintain perspective is another crucial coaching task.

Lessons Learned from Coach Gordie Gillespie, Coach Johnny Reagan, and Coach Del Crandall.

1. A coach's trust is empowering to athletes.
2. The best coaches allow communication to flow both ways.
3. Coaches motivate with a look of acceptance and belief.
4. Helping athletes through difficult times is a top leadership goal.
5. Effective leadership comes from various personality types.

KNOWING THE MODERN ATHLETES AND PARENTS

*"**Leadership, like coaching, is fighting for the hearts and souls of men and getting them to believe in you.**"*

– Coach Eddie Robinson, Football

Preview – Problems arise when coaches do not understand the parents and athletes of the contemporary age.

"Sure, athletes have changed over the years, but not nearly as much as their parents have."

– Coach Jack Perconte

When I began teaching ballplayers, the parents were interested in their children's progress but were silent, willing to let me work with their child. Now, many parents are directly involved. Many can't go more than a few minutes without adding their 2 cents worth. I don't know who to feel worse for, the parent who feels they have to speak up for their son or daughter to understand, or the player, who can't get away from their parent's intervening.

It always amazes me that some parents are so willing to get so immersed in their child's every move. They pay me a substantial amount to coach their child – I'm a former major league ballplayer with many years of coaching experience, but still, many parents today do not hesitate to intervene with my instruction and give their opinion of what's wrong with their child's play. If *I'm* getting this treatment as a professional, I can just imagine how much parents are in their child's coach's ear, as the coach likely has much less experience than I do.

In my previous book, *Raising an Athlete*, an illustration depicts a common situation in today's youth sports scene. The graphic shows many upset parents after a game, while the players quiz each other as to why their moms and dads are so distraught. It is not uncommon for present day parents to take the games more serious than their kids do. Some even follow up with regrettable acts that take the enjoyment away from the games that should be about the youth.

I enjoy helping ballplayers improve both their mental and their physical skills, but almost just as rewarding is having an effect on the parents. Often, when I begin working with players and teams, the parents expect more than they should. They can be unforgiving with their demands on their kids to work harder. Sometimes, my time with their children changes their demeanor into an understanding and sympathetic one. I have seen many moms and dads change their attitudes towards their son or daughter's performance. At the end of the day, that parental mindset change is as meaningful to me as their child's improvement. I know that attitude change leads to happier kids and a better chance of playing longer.

Many people think that players today are less skilled, and that the games aren't played as well. They believe all athletes from *their* era were dedicated, motivated, and gave 100%. This is not true. The kids of long ago had the same various personalities and dedication levels as those today do. The one thing that makes athletes different from the past is the amount of pressure on them today. Parental involvement, hopes, and demands are a big reason for this change.

A new parent is upon us and shows up in this way.

Many Parents Today:

- ➢ Put kids in competitive programs at earlier ages, sometimes as young as 3-years-old.
- ➢ Expect expert coaches.
- ➢ Have athletes specialize before the teenage years.
- ➢ Want their sons and daughters on the elite teams only.
- ➢ Use political maneuvering to get kids on teams.
- ➢ Have rude sideline behavior and act without regard for others.
- ➢ Give excessive scrutiny of players and coaching moves.

> ➤ Believe winning is the main reason for play.
> ➤ Demand excellence from kids without giving a voice to their concerns and desires.
> ➤ Expect coaches to turn players into stars.
> ➤ Spend a lot of money for their child to play and improve.
> ➤ Push for and expect scholarships.

The 2 Types of Parents

Parents today tend to fall into 2 camps. Some believe their child can do no wrong and have the stance, *"My son or daughter is great no matter how they do."* Their kids may develop a lazy attitude because they feel special and confident that they have it made. The second group believe their offspring is the next superstar in the sport. They expect way too much of their kids. With those beliefs, it's no wonder their kids become afraid to fail. More often than not, they have little or no confidence. They develop the belief that *"I'm no good"* quickly, with little willingness to think of the long-term goal. Without immediate results, these players move to another sport or quit altogether. Whatever the case, most kids feel the strain of playing and often have little or no say in decisions about their future in sports.

The one group of parents do not want coaches to critique or even yell at young players. The other parents believe kids today generally get the baby treatment and want coaches to push players until they succeed. With both types, excessive emphasis on their child's sports life is apparent, as is the coach's treatment of their children. Parents are not in the background like they were years ago. They are present and speak up more.

All of this has led to more than a healthy number of anxiety-ridden athletes. These kids have the same worries that professional athletes do, and they have less time and freedom to just be kids. Because of the pressure, players are sensitive, more emotional, and stressed out. Performance anxiety is a common result in today's youth sports culture.

The Reasons Kids Play

Kids today have the same motivation to play sports as they did years ago. They are out to have fun, spend time with friends, do things they are good at, and exercise. Many become motivated by other benefits of play like doing their best, physical tests, feeling good about themselves, and learning skills. Very few athletes have the goals of winning, fame, excellence, and gaining life lessons as reasons for playing sports.

The Consequence

Parents feel like they have to be the voice for their kids. They do not hesitate to speak their mind to their kids or to the coaches. Often, the message that coaches get is really just the parents' desires, not necessarily the athletes'.

Many parents want players to self-motivate, work harder, and win, or want the coaches to make those happen. The result is that tension grows between the parent, coaches and child, and the expressions of that disconnect makes everyone uncomfortable.

That parental involvement may even lead to less respect for coaches. The result is players who are harder to coach and less likely to want to please their coaches.

The Answer

Because of the changing player feelings and parent outlooks, you must treat athletes differently from years ago. Today's coaches need some psychological expertise for dealing with the modern athlete. Where once you could constructively criticize your players and it was acceptable, now it's likely to cause trouble. One critical statement or (in the eyes of the parent) questionable move by a coach can lead to upset players and parents. Both are now willing to confront the coach and even move teams over seemingly small issues.

Following are some measures coaches should know to help the stressed athlete of today.

Today's Coaches Should:

➢ Know that pleasing everyone is impossible. You should stay true to your personality, as long as you train athletes with integrity, enthusiasm, and patience.

➢ Know that kids value fun, opportunity, and fairness.

➢ Analyze each player's psyche to know how to help them best.

➢ Communicate with kids one-on-one, especially when you have players with anxiety due to parental pressure. You can help children recognize their emotions and help them find ways to deal with them.

➢ Give players enough of your time. Parents want more for the higher price they're paying for their kids to play. Just letting kids play without many practices was once common, but it's not sufficient anymore because the increased fees set a higher expectation of the coaches.

➢ Keep the ratio of praise to constructive criticism at about 4 to 1. Kids today need and respond to approval more than in the past, and many despise disapproval in any form.

➢ Shape the critiques in ways that do not attack an athlete's character. Any words that kids perceive as an attack may get them and their parents upset, leading to bigger problems.

➢ Remind players often that your critiques are not to be taken personally but as a means to improvement.

➢ Not challenge player toughness as coaches did years ago.

➢ Not use any demanding physical activity as punishment.

➢ Be politically correct. Many sayings that were once common in sports are not OK anymore. For example, "*You throw like a girl*" is inappropriate.

➢ Build up player self-assurance because it's often torn away at home by over-expectant parents.

➢ Not let an athlete's ego become too big because of parents who think their kid is the next superstar.

Final Thoughts

Today's parents often make every decision for their kids. The kids play and have no voice in anything. Coaches are frequently in the middle, trying to placate the parents' desires, with a child who's only playing because mom and dad want them to.

Having their child on an elite team is a sign of status for some parents. They revel in being able to tell their friends that their son or daughter plays for the best team in all the land. It's an unfortunate situation for many kids, because it's not always the best fit for them. They play while their parents bask in the supposed glory. As the parents soak up the admiration of others about how good their child is, many of them are willing to overextend their finances year after year to get the acclaim.

It's important to keep in mind that not all parents expect too much of the coaches. You shouldn't become pessimistic about all parents just because of the actions of a few bad apples. Unfortunately, the few bad ones tend to dominate your time and take the joy out of coaching.

Later in this book, I examine different player personality types and give proven tips for working with them.

MAKING THE DECISION TO COACH

"That's the beauty of coaching. You get to touch lives, you get to make a difference."

- Coach Morgan Wooten Basketball

Preview – At the lower levels of sports, a shortage of coaching volunteers often exists. Most adults who want to volunteer get the chance. This is both good and bad news. Many qualified and determined people get the opportunity, but some incompetent ones do, too.

"I played college ball; I know what I am doing."

— Volunteer coach who thinks this alone justifies them coaching.

This is a conversation I had with one of my hitting students.

"How have you been hitting?"
"I haven't been."
"Oh, that's too bad. Is it too many groundballs, fly balls, or strikeouts?"
"No, I don't get to hit."
"Why is that?"
"I'm a P.O."
"What's that?"
"A pitcher only."

I mentioned the conversation with his parent later, and the dad added, *"Yes, he plays for an elite team, and they treat it like the major leagues."*

That was an eye opener for me, seeing how this was an 11-year-old kid we were talking about. I admired him for continuing to work on his hitting skills. It was very disturbing to see such a young athlete having to play so little and being used for specialty spots only.

When I began coaching, I found I had a knack for working with kids. I soon figured out that coaching is more than just teaching the skills. There is *much* more to it than that. I found out that coaching included handling many situations that did not exist when I grew up. Along with teaching the game, I had a role in imparting life lessons. Coaching is about connecting with young people and inspiring them to do their best. Often, in subtle ways, I was helping kids mature into hard-working and happy adults.

At the same time, youth coaching is about adults – parents and other coaches. I began to understand that *this* is often the most difficult part. You must realize that before beginning to coach. I realized I had a role in influencing the adults, too.

Prospective coaches don't need to have been exceptional players. They do not need to have previous coaching experience or to be an expert in the sport. In fact, just because one played for a long time actually doesn't mean they'll even be adept at coaching. Some of the best players have trouble relating to athletes and are not skilled instructors. The ability to be a great coach doesn't automatically come from having played. Regardless of one's background, some things *are* required. You should only volunteer after careful self-analysis.

You Should Be Able to Answer "*Yes*" to the Following Questions:

✓ **Do I have an adequate background in the sport?**

Some experience is necessary, and you should have played when growing up. Without some background in the sport, credibility issues can lead to dysfunctional communication. People will hold your lack of knowledge and experience against you and feel they have the right to impose their advice on you. Those impositions usually lead to turmoil.

✓ **Do I have the time to devote to games and training?**

Parents and kids deserve a fair amount of training and consistency. Unless unforeseen circumstances arise, you must commit to the time.

✓ **Am I open to interacting with others?**

In coaching, no place exists for the "*My way or highway*" type person. Youth sports are not professional or college sports, where players may have to adapt to the coach. At the youth level, as a coach you should adjust to your players.

✓ **Do I understand parent wishes for the level of play?**

Parent demands are the source of many coaching headaches. You must be aware of and do your best to meet parents' expectations.

✓ **Am I willing to devote time to furthering my knowledge of the sport and to finding ways of working to better the team?**

You may or may not have much coaching experience, but you should strive to learn more. Training is easy to find on the internet, so little reason exists for you to not find coaching knowledge and teaching methods.

✓ **Am I committed to equal playing time?**

A big reason kids play is for opportunity. You have to find a way of making it fair for all, and that means the same amount of action for every player. That standard should apply to all levels, including travel team sports. A lack of fairness with playing time is, rightfully so, a top complaint in youth sports. You should schedule and use game substitutions so playing time is the same for all players over the course of the season.

A Few Other Things to Consider:

✓ **How important is winning to me?**

If your primary goal is attaining victories, you should think twice about coaching. Coaches must have the cognizance that winning is not a high priority or main reason why youth play. Only at the high school, college and professional levels should prevailing be *"the main goal."* Winning should never be a top priority for youth coaches. Very competitive people, who've had trouble handling losing in the past, should pass on the opportunity to coach kids.

✓ **Am I volunteering because I need the attention?**

Many people may not want to admit this is the reason they want to coach, but coaching because you need attention in your life is wrong. When helping kids is not at the top of your list for why you want to be a coach, trouble follows.

Final Thoughts

Other individual factors come into play for each person. But, as long as you feel comfortable with the above answers, you should feel free to give coaching a try. Use your answers to look for any red flags to consider before making the commitment.

The level of experience volunteers reached in their careers is more significant at the advanced club levels. Coaches should be careful of coaching top tier teams without a solid background in the sport. The more money people pay to have their child play, the higher the expectations of everyone, so a solid background in the sport is best.

One possible exception to the issue of equal playing time is when players miss games and practices for non-health reasons. Fairness can be tricky then. That issue needs to be addressed with parents at the beginning of each season.

Most volunteer coaches are parents of players. They should also ask, *"Is it the best thing for my child that I coach?"* That answer may not come until giving coaching a try.

IMPLEMENTING - NO MATTER YOUR INTENTIONS

"There is another side [to ego] that can wreck a team or an organization. That is being distracted by your own importance. It can come from your insecurity in working with others. It can be the need to draw attention to yourself in the public arena. It can be a feeling that others are a threat to your own territory. These are all negative manifestations of ego, and if you are not alert to them, you get diverted and your work becomes diffused. Ego in these cases makes people insensitive to how they work with others and it ends up interfering with the real goal of any group efforts."

– Coach Bill Walsh, Football

Preview – It's OK to have some selfish reasons to coach. The implementation of coaching methods is what makes the difference.

"I am not going to let another person screw up my son's potential."

– A common reason for coaching

The above quote is often an indictment against volunteer coaches. Many coaches volunteer to coach or start a team to make sure not only that their child plays, but that he or she plays the best positions. They don't want anyone to get in the way of their child's chance of stardom. Despite the fact that many people agree this is a dubious reason for coaching, it's natural to want to help your child, and coaching may be the way to do that.

Also, it's important to keep in mind that coaching to win and the desire to be the best team doesn't necessarily make you completely unsuited to coach. Volunteering adults deserve the benefit of the doubt about their intentions. Every volunteer should get the chance to prove they are more than just out for their child and victories.

Less Than Ideal Reasons to Coach

Some less than ideal motives for coaching exist. The most common of them is a coach trying to relive his or her glory days through their child. Coaching with a *"this is about me"* rationale, rather than it being about the players, is wrong.

Unacceptable Reasons to Coach

There are some flat out unacceptable reasons to volunteer, like the desire to be around youth for predatory reasons. It's unfortunate that this even needs mentioning, but rarely does a day go by without news coming out about sexual, emotional, or physical abuse by a coach. It's stories like these that, as implied in the introduction, are the worst case youth sports scenarios. Parents and coaches should insist that leagues have background checks for all coaching candidates. A national database of abusive coaches is an essential next step for youth sports to help prevent abuse.

The Best Reasons

In a perfect world, every volunteer would have the same intentions - the goals of influencing all youth in a positive way and of giving something back to the sport they love. But, if those were the main criteria, there may be too few coaches to go around.

In most cases, the problems arise because most volunteers do not have the training to coach and give fair treatment to all. Regardless of their original intentions, all coaches can become revered and qualified.

Coaches can overcome any debatable intentions and earn people's admiration. They can begin that process by doing these from the start.

Coaches Must:

➢ **Teach.** Making athletes' education a top priority leads to happy kids and satisfied parents most of the time.

➢ **Make every player's improvement a priority.** A significant reason kids play and parents enroll children is for training and development. Coaches must meet that desire to the best of their ability. Every player deserves equal consideration from the staff. Favoring your own child or a select few children is simply unacceptable. At the higher levels of sports, players may have to earn their coach's time, but that's not appropriate at the youth levels.

➢ **Give equal opportunity for players.** Along with committing to equal playing time for all, giving every player the chance to audition for spots is your responsibility as coach. Your son or daughter should not get the most desirable positions without earning them. The giving of something unearned is another cause of player and parent discontent. Earning their place helps athletes learn about the value of hard work and achievement.

Final Thoughts

Sports associations must also help people learn to recognize the signs of physical or sexual abuse. Leagues are responsible for making sure adults understand that they're required by law to report any suspected or knowledge of mistreatment.

Coaches must display objectivity with selection of positions, which is not always easy.

CHAPTER 2

$\sim$

Creating a Coaching Perspective

Once deciding to coach, coaches must prepare to be the best coaches they are capable of being. That preparation begins with knowledge, having the core principles of leadership, and using them to earn trust.

Following is a letter I received from concerned grandparents, which relates to a typical lack of perspective in today's games.

Dear Jack,

We are the grandparents of a 16-year-old grandson who has played baseball since he was small. His father played in college, and has coached at the high school level for over 10 years. His father's coaching record has been very good, taking his team to the state playoffs twice. My husband and I realize he has shown a great deal of knowledge in getting his team to the playoffs, but unfortunately his entire life is about baseball and sports. Our grandson has played on numerous teams, including a travelling team that includes most of the junior classmates he is playing with now on the high school varsity team. My husband and I have supported our grandson by attending his games throughout the years, including many of the travelling team games. We have come to know many of the players and their parents. We have noticed in the past that when our son-in-law was in charge of the lineup on the travelling team, he would pull his son out of the game if he struck out just once. He didn't do that with the other boys on the team. It is extremely upsetting to us that our son-in-law is so much harder on his own son. This past summer while at a travelling team game, our grandson sat on the bench more than any other kid on the team (with only 2 extra players). Our heart just broke for him. His father put him in a game in the 5th inning with a 6 to 6 tie, 2 on base, and 2 outs. Our grandson hit a home run with the first swing of the bat. He was back on the bench the rest of the game. During another travelling team game which his father didn't attend, he did excellent at outfield, pitched part of the game that took them into the finals, and didn't have a strike out the entire tournament. He played so well that he received the MVP award for the entire tournament. We have never understood why our son-in-law treats his son the way that he does – he deserves to be on the field. Our grandson also deserves a father who has faith in him.

Over the years, my husband and I have heard a great deal of negative comments made by our son-in-law to our grandson about how he needs to improve. We feel that our son-in-law puts way too much pressure on his son, and treats him differently than other kids on the team. Our grandson was named outstanding male athlete in middle school, played every game on JV, and works harder at practice and in the off season than any other kid on the team. We have complete faith in his ability as a player, but feel his dad is destroying his confidence.

JOE MADDON

There's a reason people get to the top of any profession, and sports coaching is no exception. The select few who get there have leadership qualities and knowledge that others simply do not. Major league manager Joe Maddon is one of those at the pinnacle. After listening to him discuss his coaching style, it's easy to see why he is where he is. The day Joe became the new manager of the Chicago Cubs, he talked about his coaching plans in his initial press conference.

"I have to earn the trust of the players on the field."

You may think that his players' trust would be a given after so many years of being a winning big league manager. But, it's clear that he doesn't take trust for granted.

The elite managers appreciate that leadership is about earning respect. It's not a given just because you're in charge.

Joe Maddon went on to give all the ways he planned to earn respect. He talked about sports being about connections with people, and about having the right goals. He explained that patience, simplifying things, and player development were indispensable ingredients for his plan. He also talked about the importance of accepting challenges and having optimism. He spoke of how imperative learning to react to failure and pressure is.

"So for me it's about getting to Spring Training, getting to know everybody, building relationships, developing trust...It's more about people and connections...Believe me I am really patient...I understand development. I love development. I love the young players, I do. I really like just trying to understand what's making this guy tick." – Joe Maddon, November, 3, 2014 press conference.

Joe gives terrific coaching lessons for all, from professional sports on down. In one line, he sums up the key to the sports experience:

"Don't ever permit the pressure to exceed the pleasure."

When coaches have that attitude and teach from that viewpoint, the result is *fun*. Too often, this is just not the case in youth sports. The tension overwhelms people until the enjoyment is no longer there. At the youth level of sports, earning the respect of the players and the parents is the goal. Without that trust, team and parent unrest can arise, leading to an unpleasant experience for many.

Joe Maddon also recognizes that victory is a byproduct of doing all these things he talks about. Because of that, he does not discuss triumph first. He expects to win, but doesn't feel the need to preach about the necessity of it.

Another solid idea, Joe tells his players to enjoy their victories for 30 minutes after a win, or feel bad for 30 minutes after a loss, then to move on. This is a great lesson for youth players, too. It's OK to celebrate after winning and it's OK to struggle after a loss, but only for a short while. Finally, Joe believes players should have a life beyond baseball and encourages them to experience many things.

Lessons Learned from Coach Joe Maddon

1. Coaches must earn the trust.
2. Patience with player progress is a must.
3. Enjoy the journey and do not dwell on the outcomes.
4. Stay optimistic through the inevitable challenges.
5. Sports are just one part of a player's life.

WINNING THE CREDIBILITY GAME

"Every leader needs to remember that a healthy respect for authority takes time to develop. It's like building trust. You don't instantly have trust; it has to be earned."

— Coach Mike Krzyzewski, Basketball

Preview – It's difficult to earn people's trust without knowledge of the sport. Knowing the basics and how to teach them is the key to player advancement. Coaching credibility comes by staying ahead of what the parents know about the game.

"He was a pro; he will be a great coach."

— Parent to son or daughter

Having played major league baseball, I thought coaching the game would be easy. Nothing was further from the truth. It was hard enough correcting my own habits, let alone trying to help *others* figure it out. I had an impressive rapport with the kids, but knew I had limited knowledge of the fundamentals. I could *do* them, but I had no clue of what I was doing and little knowledge of how to teach others. Only after much study and experience did I begin to actually *help* players. Having a solid background of playing buys coaches time to prove themselves, but that is all it does.

Many all-star caliber players have no clue how they do things. They cannot relay what they do not know to players. A coach's playing background is largely irrelevant after a while. The time comes when every coach has to convince everyone that they can actually develop players. Coaches must earn credibility because their playing background alone is just not enough.

Many of today's parents demand more than just setting up the lineups. Additionally, fun, what kids play for, is about impossible without signs of achievement. Having insufficient knowledge of the game does not cut it in the current youth sports culture. Even at the beginner levels, coaches have parental expectations on them that need meeting and the kids must feel a measure of advancement to have the joy they seek.

Having sufficient aptitude in the sport is the first step to developing kids and coaching success.

Coaching Credibility and Player Development Begins with:
- ✓ Knowing the basics, why they work, and developing them in others. Impressing everyone of their necessity is crucial, too.
- ✓ Developing an eye for right and wrong implementation of the mechanics.
- ✓ Transferring what you see and know into a working game plan.
- ✓ Displaying to all that you know more than the players' parents do.

Here are things coaches can do to ensure player development.

Coaches Must:

- ➢ Attend preseason coach's clinics.
- ➢ Take available coaching certification classes for the sport.
- ➢ Find an admired high school or college coach who will allow you to hang around team practices for a day or 2 and then, if there's time, pick their brain about teaching tactics.
- ➢ Study film online – with all the free video instruction available on the internet these days, this process is an easy task. The ability to analyze fast-moving actions is not an easy thing, and it takes a lot of time to develop an eye for it.
- ➢ Learn the most common fixes for the core competencies – nothing gives credibility more than helping athletes improve and get out of slumps.
- ➢ Know and use the lingo of the sport – using the wrong terms is a dead giveaway of an inexperienced coach.
- ➢ Watch upper-level games and observe new coaching strategies to try.
- ➢ Observe opposing teams' coaches' methods to ascertain both effective and bad coaching techniques.
- ➢ Discuss situations with other coaches as much as possible.
- ➢ Stay focused on the basics the whole season.
- ➢ Listen when people have things to say; this includes your young players. It's easier to gain trust through a back and forth exchange than it is through demands.
- ➢ Read articles and books about teaching techniques and the outstanding coaches of the past and present.

Final Thoughts

Convincing players and parents a coach knows his or her stuff is half the battle. The coaches who know and focus on the littlest of details get the most out of players. Later in this book you will read about how to impress everyone with the opening talks of the season, which are vital to your coaching credibility.

Coaches should not feel intimidated by their lack of knowledge but continue to seek information that builds their understanding. A continual desire for improvement is as necessary for coaches as it is for players. Once again, a quick search on the internet can usually produce some new teaching techniques that can help you stay ahead of the credibility game.

The best coaches have the ability to assess intricate moves and fast actions in crowded areas. Those that can do that have the best chance of making the right coaching moves and winning everyone's trust.

Coaching training is essential. Parents should demand that leagues provide education for their coaches.

DISPLAYING ANOTHER CRITICAL INGREDIENT OF COACHING

"Maybe one of the qualities of being a great coach is being [a jerk]. There are quite a few of them around."

– Coach Larry Robinson, Hockey

Preview – Ever wonder why jerks and bullies coach, and why they do so for such a long time?

"Coach is just being coach."

– Player resigned to the coach's behavior

I have played for and been around coaches who many consider to be *"big jerks."* Outsiders shake their heads and wonder why people put up with their antics. They can't fathom how these coaches last in the coaching profession.

Stories of offensive and over-demanding coaches are regularly in the news. The most remarkable aspect of these reports is that often some people actually defend the coach, to the amazement of many. Why is this?

Coaches, who know the finer details of the game and **care that each player improves, can survive being a jerk.**

Determined athletes and parents follow and appreciate coaches who develop players. When results come, athletes of over-demanding coaches have enough satisfaction that they put up with them. Parents tolerate assertive and discouraging coaching behavior in exchange for an athlete's betterment.

Extremist coaches exist and prosper because they know their stuff and display a caring attitude even though their methods are over the top. The coaches, who get the most out of their players' abilities, are valued. It is unfortunate they can act anyway they want, but it is a sign of how twisted some people's views are in sports. The coaches who win despite intimidating means end up getting the honor and respect from parents who only care that teams win and players flourish. Some parents seek out those coaches because player advancement is all they want. They hope the pleasure follows, but they're out for results, not fun. Many parents want stardom for their child and the means to that end are irrelevant to them.

The above is not to excuse or condone bullies and jerks coaching our youth. Rather, it *attests* to the importance of caring that athletes improve.

All volunteers go into coaching thinking they will be good at it. However, some don't care enough about all the players or fail to show it. They do not get the player development results that are satisfactory to parents and maybe not to players, either.

Coaches must have enough passion to satisfy most parents and kids.

You can show kids you care by:

➢ Telling kids you value their desire to play and that every player is crucial to the team's advancement.

➢ Thanking them for attending and allowing you to coach them.

➤ Teaching every player and never stop doing it. Caring coaches talk a lot and believe in players' chances of improving no matter what. Also, they express that sentiment to players in work and words. Looking players in the eye and saying *"I know you will figure this out,"* is mandatory.

➤ Understanding the main reasons kids play – fun, friends, exercise, playing well, and respect from adults.

➤ Allowing them to be kids.

➤ Giving them that look of acceptance.

➤ Telling each player you see potential in them as people and athletes.

➤ Sharing their pain when they struggle.

➤ Guiding them through their self-doubts and parental pressures.

➤ Bringing out the best in their abilities and personalities without resorting to demands and threats.

➤ Setting your ego aside by not making winning the result of your doing.

➤ Getting at their level. It helps kids to feel comfortable when speaking to them eye to eye. At the times when you want to give extra importance and motivation, kneel down when talking to them. Players will recognize the special significance when you do something different like that.

You can show parents you care by:

➤ Setting your ego aside so the games are not about you.

➤ Doing one's best to make decisions that are best for the players' well-being.

➤ Explaining why players are in the playing positions they are in.

➤ Asking parents for their opinion from time to time and consider what they say.

➤ Working equally with each player.

➤ Not accepting mediocrity. Working to help kids realize they can do better is a constant coaching chore, and one that parents want to see.

> ➢ Pulling them aside and telling them what you are working on with their son or daughter. You should make suggestions of things players can practice at home.
> ➢ Giving periodic updates of player improvement.

Final Thoughts

Many good-natured coaches with the best of intentions don't get the outcomes parents want, and as a result they lose their approval. Without convincing parents they can get more out of their kids, nice guy coaches may get an unfair reputation from intense parents.

The pushy, browbeating coach has always been around in youth sports. Those that used harsh tones and pushed players beyond practical means had little or no consequence years ago. Their style may be more objectionable now, but still accepted by those who believe the only goal of youth sports is success.

The best way to keep parents satisfied is through player development. When parents see their child improve, they usually will not rock the boat. Of course, that is a big coaching challenge.

What insistent parents and insensitive coaches do not understand is that the *ends do not justify the means*. What the bully coach and many parents don't see at the time is that sooner or later, their behavior affects kids in a detrimental way. You should not tolerate bullying behavior by other coaches. You must speak up when someone displays over the top anger, even if it's the opposition coach. Harsh physical movement of players, verbal abuse, obscene language and throwing things at kids are inexcusable conduct that demands your attention.

Done the right way, coaches can get the best out of kids without resorting to intimidation. Caring must involve a coach's commitment to thinking of a child's life *twenty years* hence, not just what players can do for coaches and parents in the present. Coaches, who work to get the best out of each player in a compassionate way, can sleep soundly at night no matter what parents or players think of them.

Later in this book, I explain the consequences of demeaning and punitive coaches. This book shows you how to express concern and get the most out of athletes, without resorting to intimidating methods.

GRASPING THIS ABSOLUTE OF QUALITY COACHING

"There are 3 secrets to managing. The first secret is to have patience. The second is to be patient, and the third and most important secret, is patience."

– Coach Chuck Tanner, Baseball

Preview – Patience is crucial if you want to help youth and enjoy the ride.

"I am sick of watching you play! Everyone line up! We are going to run sprints until you are ready to do what I say."

– Aggravated coach

I would hate to think that I was the reason a player decided they didn't want to continue playing. When I look back on my 27 years of coaching, I know I may have discouraged a few. Discouragement set in because they felt I lost patience with their progress. I regret this because that was never my intention.

Recently, I was hanging around the batting cage before a ball game as a coach was pitching to his team. What did I hear him say most? After a player made a solid hit, I would hear: *"Why don't you ever do that in the game?"* The second thing I heard him often say was, *"I don't want to ever see you do that again."* At another game I attended, the most positive words from the coach were *"Hey, wake up out there."* I can't believe these teams were having fun and could only imagine the lecture the players heard after the games. My guess is not many of the players of either coach would play again the next season, or at the very least, they probably wouldn't return to *his* team.

Unfortunately, this is a common occurrence at the youth sports level. It's one reason why players choose to not continue playing - the coach zapped the fun out of the game.

Coaching sports includes working with all types of players – from the most skilled to the least. Additionally, all athletes have different interests and motivation levels. From the most to the least attentive player, patience is imperative and is another pivotal ingredient of coaching. Intolerant coaches take the desire out of the kids. That loss, because of a lack of adult patience, is a shame because many athletes would be able to find pleasure and figure out how to succeed in time with a considerate coach.

Patience Begins with Coaches Acknowledging That:
- ✓ Performing movements with speed and consistency is challenging, even for the best athletes.
- ✓ It takes an exorbitant amount of time to get even close to skill-perfection and strategy understanding.
- ✓ The athletes who keep trying do so because they have coaches who display faith in them. Intolerant adults lead to irritated players who give up early without giving it their best shot.

Understanding the nature of sports and athletic performance is essential for educating young athletes. With the above in mind, coaches should help players and parents develop patient attitudes, too. Coaches can increase their patience levels by doing the following.

Coaches Should:
- ➤ Repeat to themselves often, *"These are 9, 10, 11-year-olds, etc."* You must recognize it's never as easy as it looks and that it's not about you – it's about the players.

➢ Leave the work day behind. Being annoyed with kids because of a long work day is common, but that doesn't make it right.

➢ Get enough rest and food before training and games.

➢ Understand players' effort and interest levels vary, so you can keep expectations reasonable.

➢ Never assume players know what to do.

➢ Never overload players with instruction.

➢ Not believe slow developing players are a waste of time.

➢ Think before speaking.

Final Thoughts

You can buy time for players' development with a complementary style and give hope through encouraging words and actions.

Having patience with player development is a key coaching ingredient, but, it must be honest patience. Honest patience includes persistence on doing things the right way and it holds players accountable, too. Coaches must emphasize they will not sympathize with players after bad games when their practice habits were inadequate. The idea of equating hard work with success is what honest patience is about and that reality must come for players and coaches to feel satisfied.

When adults are prone to outbursts at work or home, they should let others coach.

BRINGING IT WITH THE FINAL ESSENTIAL

"When you are enthusiastic, you are a catalyst to those around you."

– Coach Mike Krzyzewski, Basketball

Preview – People will recognize coaches who don't want to be there.

"They don't want to play."

– Coach to an observer

When I work with athletes who appear to be going through the motions, it's upsetting. But I've learned that before I ask them what's up, I look at my own actions and demeanor. Sometimes, I realize that *I'm* the one who needs a kick in the rear. I've been doing the same thing for 27 years. It would be easy to act like it doesn't matter if I coast a day or 2. When I think that way, I must do something to reenergize myself. My players deserve it, and it's not right for me to ask more from them than I'm willing to give of myself.

So how can you get into *"Coaching Mode?"* Find what works for you. One way I try to pick myself up is by listening to my favorite music in the car before arriving to the field. The music pumps me up and gets me in an energized mood. Another method I use to invigorate myself before the next session is to read about or watch movies of *"genius"* individuals. Their brilliance inspires me to work harder.

This final "must have" ingredient coaches must have, along with, knowledge, patience, and caring is enthusiasm. When you lack energy, you must find some. Many coaches complain about players' attitudes with comments like *"They don't care,"* or *"They don't want to play."* Another common complaint is *"They'd rather play video games than practice."* But a closer look at the situation will often reveal that it's the coaches who are the real problem. They do little to excite or inspire athletes, which results in despondent-looking players.

Teams reflect their coach, and when you show no excitement, the team will do the same. You must bring the energy to get the energy. You should look inside yourself and muster up the enthusiasm. Then, you will see a change in players' efforts and attitudes.

Which of these openings do you think kids will respond best to?

"Gang, we must plug away at the things we haven't been doing well. I know it may be boring, but we have no choice."
Or
"Gang, I like our progress lately, and we're close to getting things right. I have some new things we can try today, and I believe it'll be the last piece to the puzzle."

The second message is not some inspirational *"rah-rah"* speech, but it provides players with hope and encouragement. You don't have to go overboard with motivational speeches, but you should understand that effort grows when they *feel* the excitement. The passion that displays a genuine joy of the sport inspires others to act with the same joy. Enthusiasm has many benefits like the following.

Enthusiasm:
- ✓ Is infectious. It inspires others to meet the same level of vitality and brings out a better effort. Words and actions can resonate with others when they are tinged with excitement.
- ✓ Gives initial respect and the benefit of the doubt to the coaches during arduous times.
- ✓ Does not allow others to get too down on themselves.

So how do you keep up the excitement?

Coaches Can:
- ➤ Do things beforehand that are enjoyable and inspirational. Possibilities include physical activity, prayer, yoga, meditation, music, relaxation, eating, reading, or talking with friends. Whatever gets you in a terrific mood and ready to fire up your team is the goal.
- ➤ Use different voice levels and facial expressions. It's OK to act a little and let bystanders hear your elation.

> ➤ Get involved with the play, too. Physical action gets the heart pumping and picks up your spirit. Consider taking the initial warm-up jog with your players to get your energy level up.

> ➤ Encourage the other coaches to *"bring it"* and ask them to do the same for you.

> ➤ Keep gathering and delivering new material.

> ➤ Never forget to relate and show how proud you are to coach the team.

> ➤ Use inspiring and empowering words. Examples of these are: focus, vision, brilliance, discovery, growth, strength, quality, and solutions.

> ➤ Be creative and don't be afraid of some experimentation.

> ➤ Use an awe reaction. Display a look of surprise when a player does something they haven't done before. Then, look at others and say, *"Did you see that?"* Next, look back at the performing player with a smile and say, *"Where did that come from?"* or *"Look who's been holding out on us!"* Players will feel a satisfying sense of accomplishment from the wonderment.

> ➤ Model yourself after a person who loves what they do, whether it be in sports or another field. Walking around and acting like you're Joe Maddon is an amusing thing to try.

> ➤ Try not to dwell on the *"haters,"* those people who say harmful things just to say them. Passion can diminish quickly if you give too much thought to the downbeat talk.

Final Thoughts

If you don't have an energetic personality, you should try to get an assistant who does. It's OK to have coaches with different personalities.

You'll feel better at the end of the day when you have the view of, *"This is important stuff"* and *"You guys (girls) are worthy of my time."* Rarely will a coach lose the high opinion of their team when they bring constant energy to the table.

The remainder of this book talks of many other major necessities for coaching effectiveness. Honesty and fairness are high on that list.

SEIZING THE COMPLIMENT TO STRIVE FOR

"*Our emphasis is on execution, not winning.*"

— Coach Pat Summitt, Basketball

Preview – Being a winner and having a well-coached team are different things. The latter is the one under a coach's control.

"*They play the game the right way.*"

— Parent comment to another parent about the opposing team

As a coach, it always felt better to win. Winning gives you a comforting sense of accomplishment. But some victories come after teams underperform, and the win feels shallow. The one thing that always felt awesome was when people said they liked the way we ran our team or when other teams said they enjoyed competing against us. That compliment always provided a satisfying feeling.

It's OK to play to win, because that's a measure of achievement and improvement. But, even better than being on top is creating an outstanding atmosphere that others recognize. Teams with the most talent frequently win, and having the most talent is often beyond coaching control. But, having a well-coached team is *always* possible. Coaches should strive for this.

Well-Coached Teams Have Players Who:
  ✓ Wear their uniforms in the right manner to show pride in playing for the names on the front and back of the jersey.

✓ Hustle on and off the field.

✓ Listen to their coach.

✓ Display a consistent, no-nonsense pre-game routine, whether watched by coaches or not.

✓ Know the correct positioning before plays begin.

✓ Are in a ready position when play begins.

✓ Pay attention and are not out roaming around when not in the game.

✓ Cheer for their teammates and encourage struggling players.

✓ Have a perfect idea what to do when the action comes to them.

✓ Do not make the same mistakes as the game and season progress.

✓ Never question the officials.

✓ Look at the coach for suggestions rather than to their parents in the stands.

✓ Do not hang their head or swear when things don't go their way.

✓ Know when to look and receive coaching signals without stopping the game or affecting their play.

✓ Never cheer against, ridicule, or deride other teams.

✓ Help clean up after games.

✓ Congratulate and shake hands with the opposition afterward.

✓ Don't make excuses for losing.

✓ Look forward to their next practice and game.

✓ Give off signs that they enjoy playing the game.

Final Thoughts

These things don't happen overnight, but they will come with the right coaching methods.

Well-coached teams make it clear to observers that they enjoy playing for their coaches, too.

Well-run teams are not afraid of congratulating good play and wishing good luck to the opposition.

GAINING RESPECT

"Afford each person the same respect, support, and fair treatment you would expect if your roles were reversed. Deal with people individually, not as objects who are part of a herd – that's the critical factor."

– Coach Bill Walsh, Football

Preview – Knowing how to gain the respect of all, and then how to keep that respect, can be a challenge. The coaches who earn the respect have the best chance of bringing out the best in their players and are a role model to many.

"I don't know why that upset parent called me; it wasn't their child who was involved."

– Coach's comment

I remember the day my son's demeanor was different after practice. *"Did the coach say something that upset you?"* I asked. *"Yes, but not to me, he said something to Joey."* The strong effect it had on him surprised me. Later that night I pursued the conversation. My son felt like his coach's treatment of his friend was unfair and mean. It was clear that he did not regard his coach the same as he did before the incident.

With the youngest athletes, the trust may be present because they tend to look up to their coach at the start. That faith may change as they get older and parents get more involved. It may take time to earn players' approval, especially for first-time coaches. At any level, once the connection disappears, it rarely comes back.

Coaches must understand that degrading and unfair treatment to any player can and likely will affect everyone. Unfair coaching behavior towards any player risks losing the endorsement of the entire team. You need to be

51

able to realize that teammates will side with and feel sorry for their friends. Beyond that, athletes are more aware of your actions than you may think, even young kids. The best way to keep a player's trust is to never lose it in the first place.

Coaches can lose support a number of ways.

Coaches Should Never:

> Tell a player they will get an opportunity and then not follow up on it.
> Berate or ignore players.
> Talk behind players' backs.
> Favor the best, or "*hot*" players, with less concern for others.
> Blame individuals for losses.
> Take the credit for wins and player progress.
> Fail to have the same discipline for all.
> Have a "*Do it this way or sit on the bench*" approach.
> Fail to listen when kids have something to say.
> Deliver messages in a roundabout way. Coaches often say things to a certain player, knowing the word will get back to another player. Indirect messaging is more likely to alienate players, as the meaning often changes during the cycle.

Final Thoughts

All kids desire attention and approval. Coaches must not only give both of these to each player, but they also need to apply the right amount of each. Some kids require more self-esteem and confidence-building than others.

Fairness and honesty are virtues that earn and maintain respect. Coaches can display this through empathetic explanations for decisions.

Gaining players' admiration goes a long way with keeping parents satisfied. Parents are less inclined to complain about minor things when they know their child admires the coach.

It's natural for coaches to give more time and approval to the more dedicated players. But, coaches must not forget to tend to all players over time.

AVOIDING COACHING NAIVETY - THINGS TO PREPARE FOR

> *"Leadership is a matter of having people look at you and gain confidence, seeing how you react. If you're in control, they're in control."*
>
> – Coach Tom Landry, Football

Preview – Coaches must be ready for the current youth sports environment.

> *"Why are you are taking Johnny off the team? We are in first place, and we have a huge game this weekend."*
>
> *"Yea, sorry about that. We found him a team that better suits his enormous ability and one where he can play the position he should be playing."*
>
> – Coach and parent talk

Of all the phone calls I get, the most come from coaches looking for players because they're shorthanded. Players jumping teams at any moment is a sign of the new sports generation.

Youth sports are more competitive and unpredictable than ever. A lack of loyalty, sportsmanship, significance, and fairness are typical. Coaches must be ready for any number of surprising things. They must be willing to accept the challenges that come when people are confrontational. Otherwise, they may act in ways they regret. Players with a lack of interest, mean-spirited opposing coaches, and poor umpiring are at the top of that challenge list. Here are typical situations you should be prepared for and suggestions for how you can handle them when and if they do come up.

Common Scenario 1

This story came to me from a friend. He was coaching his baseball team and after the game, a parent asked if he could have a word with him. *"Sure,"* was his reply. The dad proceeded to ask, *"Why is my son not batting 3rd in the order?"* *"Excuse me?"* was the coach's response. The dad repeated his question. The coach just shook his head and walked away. That's probably not the best way to communicate with parents, but it's hard to fault the coach in this instance. The team consisted of 4-year-old players.

Unfortunately, parents today often become the complainers. Being a friendly, fair, and competent coach is not enough to appease all parents. Most kids are happy just to be playing and to be with their friends; they're largely oblivious to coaching moves. Often, those happy players change, believing the coach has become the enemy. What happened to the athlete?

Athletes usually change because their parents became unhappy. Many parents have illusions of fame for their sons and daughters. They get to thinking the coach is hindering their child's star potential. Then, they express their discontent in front of or to their kids about how their coach treats them. Kids' postures can change. Soon, both may begin to believe another team offers more opportunity, so parents make the decision to send the once-happy child to another team.

In this age of competitive travel organizations, people are always looking for better situations. The switching of teams at any time is a common occurrence. People have little regard for friendships, timing, and previous commitments when opportunities arise. Even good friends of the coach will jump ship for their perceived child's advancement. Losing a team member at any time becomes a significant disruption for the coach and season. A bigger dilemma comes when an assistant coach and his son or daughter leaves a team mid-season.

What to Do?

You shouldn't take things personally, as there's just no pleasing some parents. Having enough players from the beginning is best, so if needed, teams can absorb a lost player or two. You shouldn't look to raid other teams of players when you lose one. That just creates the same problem for another team. You may be able to find a qualified player from a recreational league or one who has finished their season. You should keep contact information on all players who tried out for the team but did not make it. This may give you a pool of possibilities to fill open spots later.

Familiar Situation 2

Opposition coaches tend to be likable before games and out for the players, but that may be the problem. They're out for their players, not all players. Once games begin, some coaches behave as if they're a coach for a professional team. They are out to win regardless of what it takes.

What to Do?

Operate with class and do not let opposing coaches drag you down to their level. You should do your best to keep the kids' minds on the game. Keeping things civil during games is a tall order, but it's crucial when dealing with a "win-at-all-cost" opponent.

Typical Occurrence 3

Some players just won't care. Many kids are there only because their parents want them to play, not because they have much interest. You must prepare for all types of dedication levels.

What to Do?

You should bring the enthusiasm, patience, and effort every day. These ingredients may motivate the less caring kids in time. As long as you continue to teach, you can take comfort in knowing you've done your job.

Probable Scenario 4

Bad refereeing is a distinct possibility. Officiating can be questionable at the highest levels of sports, so youth coaches should be aware that it will be shaky at the lower levels. Often, the judges are just teenagers, who have little experience officiating.

What to Do?

Questionable officiating is a teachable moment when you can explain the situation to the team. Poor officiating is not a reason for arguing or making a scene. Badgering officials in any way is never acceptable youth coaching behavior. You should prepare your team and parents for the likelihood of inadequate officiating.

Final Thoughts

When coaches act with integrity in any of the above instances, they earn high regard from most people. Coaches should make all decisions with the best interest of the players in mind.

At the end of the day, losing a disgruntled player or parent can be a blessing in disguise.

Coaches who prepare for questionable moves beforehand can avoid regrettable actions later. Detailed information for dealing with all of the above issues come later in this book.

HAVING OWN ROLE MODEL

"My father gave me the greatest gift anyone could give another person, he believed in me."

– Coach Jim Valvano, Basketball

Preview – The best leaders are those who are aware they don't know it all and continue to learn as they go. Just as players need inspiration, coaches need it too. Finding a mentor is a good start, and it's not as hard as you might think.

What would Coach John Wooden do?

— What I ask myself before making a tough decision

The thing that comes to my mind when thinking about coaching is a picture of basketball coach John Wooden. He's another reason I went into coaching, along with the influence of coaches from my past. I have read many books by and about Coach Wooden over the years. Just as kids are encouraged to have role models, coaches should have them as well. These esteemed persons provide guidance and a description of what coaches should be. Your role model may be someone in any profession.

Some people had the opportunity to play for an excellent coach when growing up. That chance provided a priceless resource. Those who played for role model-worthy mentors have first-hand knowledge of what it takes to coach. Others may not have had that luck and only had below-average teachers. They can read about esteemed people and their techniques to learn about quality coaching.

Here are suggestions for youth coaches to find inspiration.

Inspiration Can Be Found by:
- ✓ Writing down the things you admire about coaches from your past and then modeling those character traits.
- ✓ Thinking of people from your past in other fields whom you thought highly of. Write down the character traits, mannerisms, and words that were so efficient and memorable. Then, incorporate all those into your training methods.
- ✓ Recalling back to your playing days and remembering the things you liked and disliked about training procedures. Use the better techniques and come up with ways to alter the annoying ones.

✓ Reading up on the current athlete's point of view. You have to learn that some methods from your past may not work the same way today.

✓ Typing in the name of an esteemed coach on the internet and reading about them. Inspiring coaches, coaching quotes, and strategies are easy to find.

✓ Reading books about successful people to explore their leadership tactics.

✓ Finding a local college or high school known to have a valued coach and see if he or she would be willing to answer your questions. At the least, you can go watch higher level teams practice to find the best ways to run them. Knowing how to run effective practices is critical to creating motivated players.

There are also things that you can learn from the best coaches.

Experienced Coaches:

✓ Set realistic targets for themselves and their team, and then work to exceed them.

✓ Lead by example with a strong work ethic, a never-ending belief in players, and a love of the game.

✓ Recognize that things are always a work in progress and that perfection is impossible, but that should not diminish the effort for it.

✓ Get all the facts and search for answers before making difficult decisions.

✓ Give a lot of consideration to detail. Coaches who attend to the little things help players flourish and teams succeed.

✓ Play to win in a manner that rarely speaks of triumph and never with a win-at-all-cost outlook.

✓ Keep the spotlight on player development and team improvement. The real winners are the coaches who keep players interested. They have done a good job when players decide to keep playing the following season.

✓ Never let pressure, insecurity, or losing lead them in a pessimistic or cynical direction

✓ Encourage, listen, and answer questions. You'll know your players feel comfortable when they're willing to ask you how to do things.

✓ Have a sense of humor. Knowing when to lighten up situations is priceless in this age where many things are taken too seriously.

Final Thoughts

It bears repeating that a role model does not have to be a sports' coach. Even a teacher or parent who made a positive impact on your life can become a powerful influence. The ability to talk to and bounce ideas off someone is ideal.

Differences exist between youth coaching and upper-level sports when it comes to the amount of commitment. However, all can strive to achieve some of the above goals to make the season memorable for all.

CHAPTER 3

———————⟋⟍———————

Creating a Philosophy

Once committed to coaching, people must have values. That process begins with having the right goals and beliefs to implement the strategies needed for working with young athletes. Those beliefs are easier when a coach understands the realities of today's youth sports atmosphere.

Here is a letter I received which attests to the extent some parents will go to have their child achieve success.

Coach,

Since my son turned 2.5, I've had him on a routine of 500 swings per week Nov - Feb and 1,000 swings from Mar - Oct. He's hit off a tee since he was 2 and I don't mean chicken swinging, no leg movement, bat sagging. NONE of that... I've stressed perfect form since early on, reasoning as he ages, no pitcher will be able to break his sound fundamen-

tals. I use a mix of Bob Knight and Mike Agassi, and he understands that it must be the correct way. I realize I might need a softer approach, but reason that it must be hard for him to have success, and I want a professional coach to work with him. Would you be willing to do so? I'm an all or nothing guy, and I've said this before that I'd rather have him win the batting title or tell me at age 10 I'm burnt out, but nothing in the middle. Do you think this is a good routine??? Don't think I'm crazy but nobody his age has worked harder I can promise you that, and if you work with him, you won't be disappointed as he's used to 1 - 2 hour practices.

TONY DUNGY

I read a fascinating story about one of the superior coaches of this generation. ESPN's Paul Kuharsky asked legendary football coach Tony Dungy if every once in a while he aired out his team as a form of motivation. He said, "No." It's amazing to think that Tony's calm style worked even at the highest level of football, a sport that encourages aggressiveness.

Tony Dungy doesn't feel that's a way to motivate teams. He went on to say that he appreciated his coaches who were not "yellers." He noted the calm demeanor of Hall of Fame coach Chuck Noll of the Pittsburgh Steelers. Coach Dungy loved the calm explanations and felt that was the way to motivate.

Dungy doesn't find that screaming, humiliating, and threatening are effective coaching strategies. Like the incomparable Coach John Wooden, Dungy believes in treating players the way he wants people to treat him. He is one of the few coaches who, unlike most coaches, never swears to make his coaching point. He reminds us that respect comes from remaining faithful to your philosophy. He shows us that leaders don't have to be tyrants to get players to respond. They only have to be educators who want to and do help.

Lessons Learned from Coach Tony Dungy:

1. Treat athletes the way you would like others to treat you – with respect.
2. No matter the nature of the sport, using thoughtful ways to motivate, not ranting and raving, is best.
3. Swearing is not necessary or acceptable.
4. Threats and humiliation have no part in sports.

UNDERSTANDING THE TWO COACHING STYLES

"At Boston University I motivated negatively and I found that although it can work at first, by the end of the year everyone is dying for the year to end and you have lost them. The last 2 years at BU, I motivated positively and got much better results."

– Coach Rick Pitino, Basketball

Preview – Coaches must know the definitions and the representations of the two coaching styles.

"You are a bunch of chokers!"

– Coach of a 10-year-old team after a game

I will never forget my coach who walked far from the dugout, so he didn't have to pass by the players. He wanted to avoid acknowledging us, as a way of showing his disgust with our recent play. He felt this would get the message across that he was not happy. He thought this action would make us do better.

When I began my coaching career, I chose to adopt a low-key, patient manner. Having played to the highest level, I understand how hard the game can be and know the commitment it takes to succeed. Also, this is just my personality. I believe a pleasant demeanor is the best way to get young people to respond. My philosophy of coaching comes from a quote by Maya Angelou. It applies as much to coaches as anyone. She said, *"I've learned that people will forget what you said, people will forget what you did, but people will never forget how you made them feel."*

When I grew up, the most accomplished coaches were John Wooden, Tom Landry, Vince Lombardi, and Bobby Knight. The first two seemed to go about their business in a gentlemanly manner. The latter two had more of what could be interpreted as a bullying style. I assume there was some middle ground with them all. The point is, all were effective leaders. Some coaches disperse information in non-threatening and encouraging ways. Others lead players with harsh words and little encouragement.

Two words permeate the youth sports culture, positive and negative. No other terms describe possible coaching methodology as accurately as these. Knowing what makes up both is crucial when working with young athletes. Simply put, positive coaching has a beneficial effect and negative has a damaging effect.

The problem is that in general, adults don't often understand the impact that negativity and aggressive coaching can have on youth. The effects are difficult to gauge, and they appear at different times and in different ways for each player.

Another problem is that people have different baselines about what standard coaching tactics are. Some adults think coaches should "toughen kids up." Others do not believe coaches should even raise their voices to yell. What seems like abusive coaching behavior to some may be perfectly acceptable to others. No clear-cut philosophies exist.

A more definitive description of the two styles of coaching is needed. Then, coaches can decide how to go about their business and people can recognize one style from the other.

Positive Coaching

Positive coaches have a hopeful outlook, and this is reflected in how they deliver information to their team. It's relating to players in a manner that doesn't take the satisfaction out of the sport. It does not damage players' self-esteem. Affirmative coaching works with each player individually, encourages interaction amongst players, and focuses on long-term progress. Upbeat coaches ask players questions, listen to answers, and make the warranted changes. They encourage questions from players.

Positive Messages Come in Ways That Express:

- ✓ **Optimism**. A never-ending belief that athletes will find a way to improve. *"I know you can do it."*
- ✓ **Inspiration**. A message that appreciates kids playing. *"I am proud of you. I enjoy coaching and watching you play."*
- ✓ **Constructive analysis**. Looking for the skilled things players do, rather than just focusing on the negative. *"I like the way you did this, but I think this can be even better. Let's try this next time."*
- ✓ **Togetherness**. The dispersion of knowledge employs a *"we"* expression. *"Hang in there; we will figure it out."*
- ✓ **Encouragement**. Using faith building words. *"Yes, you can."*
- ✓ **Affirmation**. Giving praise when earned. *"Awesome! I knew you could do it."*
- ✓ **Enthusiasm**. Showing players you want to be there. *"Basketball is such a great game and I am looking forward to teaching it."*
- ✓ **Honesty**. Telling it like it is, in an empathetic manner. *"I know it's hard, but I also know you can do this if you work at it."*
- ✓ **Obedience**. Using discipline in ways that help kids learn lessons without humiliating them. *"It's important that you stop playing when you hear the whistle, or someone may get hurt."*

Negative Coaching

Discouraging coaching communicates in a manner that attacks a player's character. It makes playing more important in a child's life than it should be. Information comes in harsh tones and attacks on the athlete's character. Negative coaching can include vulgar language, taunting, pushing, or degrading athletes. Negative coaching is about control over others. It rules in overbearing ways and is more concerned with today's score only. Coaches demand things be their way, and they tend to not listen to suggestions.

This coaching style harms emotional well-being. Destructive consequences will show up eventually, and players usually end up loathing the offensive coach more often than not.

Off- putting coaches give advice with a condescending voice and slant that expresses a harsh view with words like:

"*Do you want to be here?*"
"*I'm not sure I [the coach] want to be here.*"
"*You will never be any good doing it that way.*"
"*You better win today.*"
"*It's embarrassing watching you play like that.*"
"*How many times do I have to tell you the same thing?*"
"*You better get your head screwed on straight.*"

All of the above question players' hearts and minds. They do not reflect a player's effort, but rather attack their self-image.

Final Thoughts

Positive coaches learn to say things with compassion. They understand that sports success is hard to come by and they relate with empathy, so players understand they are not "how they perform" on a sports field.

Positive coaching doesn't mean kids can to do whatever they desire. It also is not to say coaches have to become "*buddy, buddy*" with players. Holding kids accountable is an essential aspect of helping youth mature. The easy-going manner I have does not mean I fail to correct, discipline, or give an honest analysis of my players' efforts.

Supportive coaching also doesn't mean you should settle for mediocre play if a player isn't putting in his or her best effort. Coaches have the right to expect an honest effort from their athletes. If that means you need to give a mental boost to let them know they're not giving it their all, that's OK. You can be stern in a way that doesn't intimidate. *"It's time to pick it up, everyone."*

If you have to speak frankly, it's best to deliver the message out of the earshot of others. In some cases this is a whole-team discussion, and in that case, keeping it amongst just the team and other coaches is fine. This way, players don't feel like you're embarrassing them and it may encourage feedback from the players.

Nothing is more degrading than the gender suggestion – *"You guys are playing like a bunch of girls."* There is simply **no** place for this type of statement in sports today.

MAKING THE REASONABLE CHOICE

"You have to do something in your life that is honorable and not cowardly if you are to live in peace with yourself."

– Coach Larry Brown, Basketball

Preview – Negative coaches push players to win in the short-term, but lose the athletes in the end. Coaches have a choice as to how they go about dealing with people.

"I can't believe he is the son of a big league player."

– Coach's comment about my son

The quote above about my son did not make him feel supported when word got back to him. Sometimes it only takes *one* statement to completely change a youth's career. I don't need the recent studies to prove, even though they do, what I know from my experience.

One: Most athletes leave the sport soon after being around critical coaches.

Two: Negative coaching style tends to pass from generation to generation.

I'm not clairvoyant – sometimes I'm fooled by the results too, but usually, I'm right with my predictions. I can often predict whether a young player will play for a long time or not, or at least if he or she will continue to play as a teenager. Rarely do I base my prediction on talent, although that is part of the process too. Early success is also not the most important thing, as it doesn't always show a player's love for the game.

I've known many young ballplayers who have lots of success, but deep down, their hearts just aren't in the game. They quit before their talent falls short. On the other hand, many players love the game, but aren't very good at it. They stop because of a lack of talent.

Most young players fall somewhere in between – they've got some talent and some love. One thing makes a difference on whether they'll continue to play or not. It's as simple as *"How encouraging are the parents and coaches?"* When coaches fall into the cynical trap and expect too much, nag at players, or are never satisfied with a child's results or effort, kids quit before they know if they like playing or not.

The extreme end of coaching negativity is when coaches use physical or verbal abuse. Those actions drive athletes away from sports long before kids would have left on their own.

The effects of negativity may not immediately appear because kids don't always voice their real feelings. And a lot of times, the athletes who *do* speak up get little consideration from parents at the time. When players reveal their sentiments later, it may be too late to change their minds about playing. They've had enough and quit.

You may think that the detrimental coaching style wouldn't even be an option in youth sports. Wrong! Objectionable coaching often abounds because a coach:

- ✓ Experienced a similar coaching style when he or she was a young player.
- ✓ Has a demanding personality with everything, not just coaching.
- ✓ Believes kids respond better to intimidation.
- ✓ Thinks the games are about them.

Some coaches don't know of the dangers of pessimistic coaching. Others choose to ignore it because they believe their way works. And still others aren't even aware of their behavior and that how they come across is questionable.

What coaches need to understand is that current research shows that without a doubt, over-demanding coaches:

- ✓ Damage kids' desire and ego immediately or later in life.
- ✓ Chase kids away from sports more than anything else.
- ✓ Perpetuate the problem by acting out the same detrimental behavior they themselves experienced. In turn, athletes often begin to believe the negative way is acceptable and the norm, so they may go on to behave this way too. The discouraging line of attack moves from generation to generation.
- ✓ Cause kids to lose regard for adults. Any attack on a player's character can be enough to turn them off and destroy their regard for the coach *and* the game. Kids may associate a connection between how they're treated and trust. When adults treat them in an uncivil way, they may learn to distrust all authority figures.
- ✓ Cause sleepless nights and a loss of appetite. Enormous anxiety builds up in some cases, which can affect players' lives both on and off the fields.

Insensitive adults should either get out of coaching or turn their demeanor around in the following ways.

Coaches Should:

➤ Be aware that kids today thrive more on affirmation than criticism.

➤ Use supporting statements before critiquing players' actions.

➤ Say things that describe actions, without judging a player's intentions.

➤ Use the 3 second rule: wait a few seconds before giving out corrective information. This gives you a chance to organize your thoughts, calm down, and say things in a considerate manner.

➤ Praise effort, even when failure and loss ensue.

➤ Avoid accusatory statements that intimate a lack of caring.

➤ Steer clear of swearing. Cuss words and derogatory language have no place in the youth sports environment. Once a coach uses it, players will do the same and believe it is acceptable.

➤ Read and recommend to other coaches the helpful information put out by the *Positive Coaching Alliance*, the *Changing the Game Project,* and the *National Alliance for Youth Sports.*

Final Thoughts

A few kids can take a verbal berating, but most cannot. Negativity inspires few, if any, and it doesn't work for very long, even when it appears to be effective in the beginning. Much of the problem is the unfortunate inherent belief that you can only coach with the *"tough guy"* philosophy for some sports, like football. Tony Dungy proves that this does not have to be so.

You shouldn't buy into the culture that you have to be Mr.-or-Ms. Enforcer to be effective. If you can only act in intimidating ways, you shouldn't be a youth coach.

Not only have times changed in sports, but society has changed. Better treatment of young athletes is now expected. The *"I'm here to toughen up the athletes"* style of coaching youth is less tolerable now, as it should be. Often, leagues and parents demand the removal of menacing coaches. Unfortunately, this course correction comes too late for some kids, who've had enough before a coach is forced out or quits.

None of this means you have to pamper your athletes or let them do whatever they want. Coaches can be fair and honest. It's OK to point out when effort is lacking. There's a right way to do that, which gets the most out of athletes, without using negativity.

Coaches shape better futures for all by developing talent and motivating in positive ways. Outstanding character and the love of sports in all players is possible with the right philosophy.

Many people equate negative coaching with an intense coaching style. Coaching with a raised voice or with intensity does not take away self-esteem. It's the tone, purpose, and context of words that determine what is hurtful. Some of the best coaches give honest analysis and constructive advice in a booming, passionate voice. That's their style, but they are still affirmative coaches.

Every coach has a different coaching personality. Whether their style is blaring, calm, or somewhere between, it's OK as long as they do not coach in an offensive style.

ESCAPING THE WIN-AT-ALL-COST LABEL

"I want my team to be more detached from the wins and losses and be more focused on doing the little things well. When you focus on getting the win, it can suffocate you, especially during the playoffs when the pressure gets thick."

– Coach Sue Enquist, Softball

Preview – A high emphasis on winning can wear kids down. Many quit because of it.

"No pain no gain; you can play through it."

— Demanding coach to injured player

My teammates and I always valued the coaches who treated players with respect. The coaches we admired wanted to win as much as the next guy, but they managed people with class, integrity, and compassion. Some of my other coaches treated players as if they didn't exist when they weren't playing well. With others, all hell would break loose when the team didn't win. Players see right through coaches who make it about them and not the players. Athletes lose the desire to play for them.

By definition, competition involves a winner and a loser. After all, sport *is* competition, so of course there will be a winner and loser. The problem comes when adults believe victories are the ultimate and only purpose of the games. The demands of winning can create stress for everyone. The unfortunate result is when players and teams feel like losers, even after playing well and giving their all. The *win or else* coaches demoralize others and often lead to disengaged players.

Adults must understand that for most kids, winning just isn't a priority, and to make it so isn't healthy. Making winning the top priority adds more urgency to the game, and most young athletes don't want it to be this way. The effects of this approach may take some time to show up, but sooner or later, it usually will. Putting the emphasis on winning leads to anxious and burned out athletes.

People use phrases in youth sports like *"Keep it in perspective"* and *"Have fun,"* but few actually go on to define what this actually means. The win-at-all-cost coach is another one of those terms with little definition. Most people can agree that the philosophy is not right for young players. The problem is people don't know or recognize the signs of it.

Following are signs of the win-at-all-cost mindset.

A Win-at-All-Cost Coach Will:

- ✓ Over schedule kids by thinking *"more"* is the only means to better.
- ✓ Take losses much harder than their players do.
- ✓ Schedule teams that are not even close to the caliber of their team to pile up the wins.
- ✓ Insist and force players to play despite having injuries.
- ✓ Make it personal with the other team by insisting it is an *"us against them"* philosophy.
- ✓ Play fatigued players, which often leads to overuse injuries.
- ✓ Rush players back from injuries, which put them in danger of re-injury.
- ✓ Not substitute players even when leading by a significant amount.
- ✓ Bend or break the rules to get an edge.
- ✓ Ridicule and place struggling players on the bench.
- ✓ Berate the team and call out individuals when they lose or don't produce.
- ✓ Encourage players to injure the opposition and praise players when they knock an opposing player out of the action.
- ✓ Treat players differently after losses than after wins.
- ✓ Threaten players with or actually using excessive physical exercise after poor play.
- ✓ Take away something as punishment for failing to win.
- ✓ Convince teams to have an elitist mentality.
- ✓ Encourage under-performing players to look for another team.

Final Thoughts

Doing many of the above things goes beyond common sense at the youth level. Coaches should never forget that youth sports do not have the same purpose as college and professional sports.

Coaches should never believe they are defined by the scoreboard. When your ego takes a hit because of a team loss, you have the wrong perspective of youth sports.

It bears repeating that playing to win at all levels is OK, as long as you stay within the written and common sense rules. It's never right when trying to win comes at the expense of allowing bad behavior from anyone.

Any time you lose compassion for others, you've gone too far.

Many programs have coaches who win year after year with a stop-at-nothing approach in order to win. The *"everyone likes a winner"* mentality deters others from rocking the establishment and calling them out about their methods. The non-recognition or unwillingness of leagues and other coaches to speak up when a win-at-all-cost mentality is used allows these coaches to continue coaching.

TEACHING RESPECT FOR THE GAME

"*I won't accept anything less than the best a player's capable of doing, and he has the right to expect the best that I can do for him and the team!*"

– Coach Lou Holtz, Football

Preview – Respect for the game is more than sportsmanship. It's a valuable lesson about integrity that applies beyond sports.

"That's not how we play the game."

– Coach to out of line player

I cringe when I see some of the things that go on with athletes and sports. Excessive celebrations, taunts, and trash talk are a regular part of the games, now.

It's common for the older generation to take issue with the way players conduct themselves today. The thing to note is that times have changed, and they'll continue to change. How much expression of joy athletes can display without seeming like they're *"showing up"* the opposition is still something that's up for discussion. Unfortunately, it's not only athletes doing this. It's more common every day that the embarrassing actions are coming from the coaches and parents. The following 3 things must apply for everyone:

1. Embarrassing the opposition is unacceptable.
2. Expressing themselves in offensive ways is unacceptable.
3. Understanding that behavior at the professional levels does not make it automatically appropriate for youth sports.

Hall of Fame baseball player Joe DiMaggio explained why he gave 100% each game. He said, *"There is always some kid who may be seeing me for the first time. I owe him my best."* This sums up what respect for the game is from the players' perspective. Players owe it to themselves and others to give their best. They should represent themselves in ways others want to emulate. Respect for the game is how a player approaches playing and relationships.

This action also includes how people behave when watching games and role model conduct should begin with the adults. It's about having class, and it extends to everyone. Teammates, opposing players, coaches, fans, and officials are all accountable for their behavior.

Coaches have the responsibility of making sure everyone acts in ethical ways. That assurance starts with the coach's example. You can do this by knowing what respect is, showing it yourself, and passing that knowledge to others. We can keep honor in the game when adults make sure the games are about the players and by never drawing negative attention away from the action. Ethical sports conduct starts with recognizing when it breaks down.

Coaches must know the signs of disrespect.

Coaching Insolence Is:
- ✓ Kicking or throwing objects.
- ✓ Arguing with umpires.
- ✓ Berating a player before, during, or after games.
- ✓ Playing to win at any cost.
- ✓ Bringing the attention to themselves and away from players.

Signs of Rudeness by Parents and Fans Are:
- ✓ Yelling at referees' calls.
- ✓ Showing disgust with a team.
- ✓ Making disparaging comments to anyone.
- ✓ Negative actions that bring attention to the stands during games.
- ✓ Confronting coaches, officials, or the opposing team before, during or after games.
- ✓ Demeaning words or actions towards any player, including their own son or daughter.

Coaches must speak up when athletes or adults humiliate anyone. Youth coaches should help players learn what respect means and how to go about displaying it. Coaches must also hold parents accountable for respecting the game, too.

Here are things you must insist upon with team members in order to display a sense of honor for the game.

Players Should:
- ➢ Wear the uniform properly.
- ➢ Never question game officials.
- ➢ Never show disgust through demonstrative acts about their or another player's actions.

➢ Not be allowed to tell other players what they should have done; this is the coach's job.

➢ Give their best effort without resorting to dirty play. Dirty play is actions intended to injure or cheat another.

➢ Show hustle during play and enthusiasm before and after it.

➢ Treat opponents in a considerate manner. Being sincere with the post-game congratulatory comments and handshake is a must.

➢ Display happiness without rubbing victory into the other team's face.

➢ Play for the team and not just personal statistics.

➢ Address adults respectfully: Kids should use *"Coach"* with you and *"Mr."* or *"Ms./Mrs."* when addressing parents.

➢ Only address the referee with *"Hello or thank you Mr./Miss. Referee (Umpire)"* as a greeting. This is the only reason players should ever talk to a ref or ump.

Final Thoughts

A fine example of respect for the game came from an umpire friend of mine. She mentioned a catcher, no older than 10-years-old, who would wish each hitter *"Good luck"* as they walked into the batter's box. This good luck wish wasn't the insincere type that's meant to imply the pitcher is so impressive the batter would be lucky to get a hit. It was genuine, and a beautiful display of playing with class.

Part of having respect is showing gratitude for the opportunity to play. I often ask my players to thank their mom and dads for the chance to play.

Sportsmanship is inherent for honoring the game. You must explain what goes into sportsmanship rather than assume players and parents know what it is. Once explained, you should inform everyone that you expect it and that consequences will result when anyone is unsportsmanlike.

People should never leave a game talking about anything but the match itself. Coaches must do their best to limit adults taking the attention from the games.

Dealing with a lack of sportsmanship and discourteous adults comes later in this book.

IDENTIFYING THE FUN-KILLERS

"People thrive on positive reinforcement. They can take only a certain amount of criticism and you may lose them altogether if you criticize them in a personal way...you can make a point without being personal. Don't insult or belittle your people. Instead of getting more out of them you will get less."

— Coach Bill Walsh, Football

Preview – Coaches do not have to be experts at making things fun, but they should never take the joy out of the game.

"The coach never tells me what I am doing wrong."

— Words from a discouraged athlete

My worst coaching fear is that I'm the reason an athlete quits. I've had many students over the years that have had little or no interest in baseball. Baseball was not pleasant for them, and they were only there because mom and dad wanted them to play. No matter how fun I tried to make things, they just didn't enjoy it.

Enrolling a child in a sport they don't enjoy doesn't make people bad parents. Parents narrow down children's pursuits in that way. Just because there was no joy, that doesn't make one a bad coach, either. Coaches cannot guarantee fun for all. But, you should never contribute to kids disliking the play, either.

Fun should be a part of all education, but nothing is fun all the time. Poor play and losing are not pleasant. Hard work, having friends change teams, and failing to make teams are not usually joyful. If parents and athletes only want enjoyable things, sports are not that avenue. The reality is, sometimes sports will have unhappy moments for all athletes, and coaching leadership is crucial for these times.

Differences exist between making sports fun and never taking the joy out of the games. When adults don't contribute to the erosion of the joy, then it's the kids who decide the activities and games they enjoy. Kids will gravitate to the things they like in due time. Coaches should **never** be the reason a sport is not enjoyable. You can avoid taking the fun out of the game by knowing what can ruin the excitement.

Coaches Should Not:
> **Ignore players**. Weak skill sets, casual looking players, and bad games are no reason to stop working with your players. Neglected children may feel worse than those who receive criticism.
> **Have unrealistic plans**. Unreachable goals for your team can cause players to feel like failures.
> **Resort to threatening behavior**. Punishing athletes for poor play sends the wrong message. This punishment usually comes in the form of benching players or having exhausting exercises.
> **Use ridicule**. Motivation rarely comes from belittling players and nagging. Any initial benefits from these methods will end as athletes grow weary of those tactics.
> **Have dull practices**. You need to engage players, especially during practice time.
> **Make kids feel like they are disappointing themselves or others**. The wrong definition of success can lead kids to believing they are losers.
> **Hassle kids to work harder**. Putting fear in players about their future playing prospects is never OK.

> ➤ **Put too much emphasis on achievement and winning, instead of on the process and improvement**. Be sure to acknowledge players when they improve, not just when they win.

Final Thoughts

Topnotch coaches know ways of making things more exciting for all players.

There is an *upside* to failure. In what seems to be an effort to eliminate players not having fun, some sports' organizations have gone to a non-competitive atmosphere. Unfortunately, these leagues may be giving kids a false sense of life. The impression that the score is irrelevant, and how you play doesn't matter, may actually hurt kids' psychological growth. When it's all about the fun, kids fail to learn that disappointment is a part of life and even worse, they don't get the chance to deal with it. Kids need to learn how to deal with the things that come with competition, the good *and* the bad, the wins *and* the losses. A valuable part of playing, even if just out to have fun, is knowing that sports are a challenge and everyone has to deal with setbacks at one time or another in their lives. Topnotch coaches know ways of making things more exciting for all players.

Coaches should help their organizations find a balance between overly-competitive and non-competitive leagues. Having coaching evaluations at season's end may help find the right state of play.

ELUDING OTHER COACHING TRAPS

"Over coaching is the worst thing you can do to a player."

— Coach Dean Smith, Basketball

Preview – Besides a negative style, two other unfavorable techniques exist. Some coaches *over manage* and others *don't do enough*.

"Her coach never lets them just play." "They are not learning anything."

— Familiar parent comments

I often hear these parent complaints. Providing just the right amount of coaching for the age and level played is essential. Coaches must know the signs of doing too little and the signs of doing too much, so they can find that balance. It takes an astute coach to know which players to push a little and which ones to give some space to. Taking the wrong approach can lead people to lose respect for the coach.

The underachieving coach sets the lineups and manages games only. They believe those are their only responsibilities. They have little enthusiasm, which does nothing to inspire players.

Other Signs of Under Coaching Include:
- ✓ Not being prepared for team sessions and just winging it.
- ✓ Believing they know enough already without further study of the sport.
- ✓ Giving everything they know, or all that they just learned at a coaching clinic on the first day. They stop teaching soon after, believing they have done their part.
- ✓ Impressing players with words, but not reinforcing those words with any technical know-how.
- ✓ Instructing only a few players or just their own child.
- ✓ Having too few practices because they believe games are the prominent thing.
- ✓ Only coaching when parents are around.

At the other end of the spectrum are coaches who micromanage every detail or treat the players as if they're a professional sports team. They do not allow input from players and make all decisions for them. They seem unaware that knowledge and learning comes from communication.

Signs of Over Coaching Include:

- ✓ Overwhelming players with information, especially right before plays. Too much last minute instruction confuses players more than it helps them.
- ✓ Yelling instructions at players as action is occurring. Hearing voices during games distracts players. When athletes are not allowed to make their own decisions, it slows their comprehension.
- ✓ Giving long speeches. Some coaches believe people are there to watch them coach or hear how much they know about the game.
- ✓ Using language and terminology that is over players' heads.
- ✓ Failing to allow the other coaches to have a voice of their own and believing they have all the answers.

The following tips can help coaches find the right amount of balance.

Coaches Should:

- ➢ Have a rough draft of weekly material to cover at practice. This information often comes from what has occurred in recent games.
- ➢ Consult with the coaching staff about team plans and allow them to give their advice.
- ➢ Have an appropriate number of training sessions during the season. Only playing games without practicing is not beneficial for player or team progress.
- ➢ Take written notes of game mistakes. The memory of gaffes and the involved players is often fuzzy by the next practice.
- ➢ Reenact game missteps in drills with the same players in the games. Do the same with any players who might be in those positions in the future.
- ➢ Allow athletes to make their own decisions during play by remaining quiet. Players learn quicker and better by making their game decisions.

➤ Limit before and post plays instructions during games. Practices are the time to teach.

➤ Never be so demonstrative on the sidelines that it takes away attentiveness from the match itself. Some coaches try too hard to impress others with their coaching abilities and moves.

➤ Keep terminology simple and explanations short as possible.

Final Thoughts

The signs of both doing too little or too much are the same – player confusion and frustration. Under coaching leads to disenchanted parents and unprepared teams, while over coaching leads to confused and indecisive athletes.

Experience is the best teacher, but youth coaches may only coach a year or two. They must search for the right balance quickly.

You must remember that practice is your time to stand out, and the games are the players' time.

Two other coaching traps are worth mentioning. *Feel good* coaches only tell kids how good they are doing without acknowledging any problems or giving honest analysis. These types of coaches believe the goal of the positive coaching philosophy is to just keep everyone happy all the time. The problem arises when kids get false hope that never leads to in-game success. Coaches must be honest and willing to tell players where they stand in comparison to others and exactly where they need to improve to reach a higher level of play.

Then, there's the *hypocritical coach*, a model of the negative approach to coaching. These coaches say one thing and seem to mean it, but then often proceed to act the opposite. They tell players to play aggressively and without fear. But the minute players fail, they get angry. For example, a baseball coach may ask batters to be aggressive but then get upset if they swing at one bad pitch. These mixed messages can turn kids off to sports all together, or at the very least can result in losing trust in their coach. The hypocritical coach is one of the leading causes of players losing respect for coaches.

APPRECIATING THE DANGERS OF SPECIALIZATION

"Specialization issues are adult issues impressed upon youth."

– Coach Tim Corbin, Baseball

Preview – Research shows risks for youth exist with early sports specialization. Coaches must know this when developing young athletes.

"Just think how phenomenal he will be if he only focuses on this."

– A coach to a parent of a talented child

Sports specialization is dropping other sports to play only one, and usually involves year-round training. I've heard the reasoning many times over the years, and I'll admit it's convincing. The argument goes like this. *"He/She has real talent, with college and pro potential. If they concentrate on it more, they can reach that vast potential."* But the fact is, research doesn't show that early specialization leads to a better future in one sport.

The studies actually say the opposite. The consequences of early specialization are overuse injuries, less physical development, and burned-out athletes. Kids who play only one sport usually end up quitting sooner.

What Coaches Must Know About Specialization:
- ✓ Specialization dangers come into play for ages under 13-years-old. Kids who play only one sport at an early age risk their physical, mental, and emotional development.
- ✓ The perils arise with high-intensity programs, but not with recreational, seasonal programs.
- ✓ Intense concentration on one activity may stunt a child's social skills.

- ✓ Unrealistic expectations come with one-sport concentration. People and players expect more when their efforts are on one activity.
- ✓ Emotional exhaustion from continual pressure to perform may cause a personality change.
- ✓ In the end, talent wins, and playing other sports will not stunt growth in one sport over another. The facts suggest that other athletic activities help body enhancement and an athlete's best sport in the end. For instance, the agility and footwork kids gain playing soccer improves their balance and speed for other sports like baseball, tennis, and basketball.
- ✓ College recruiters look for and prefer multi-sport athletes.
- ✓ Mental and physical benefits exist for playing more than one sport.
- ✓ Overuse injuries often inhibit players' career possibilities.

What Coaches Can Do:
- ➤ Ask kids what other sports they play and explain the benefits they gain from playing them.
- ➤ Refer parents and players to studies that show the dangers of early specialization – parents can do a simple internet search and learn a lot.
- ➤ Note that just because a few elite athletes dedicated themselves at a young age to one activity does not make it right for most.
- ➤ Let parents know the odds of kids getting college scholarships and becoming professionals. The reality is that few college scholarships are available and the numbers of kids vying for them is enormous. Explain that specialization does not guarantee or even help those pursuits.
- ➤ Never ask, encourage, or insist players dedicate to one sport before the teenage years. The decision to stop any activity should be an athlete's decision with advice, but not pressure, from parents and coaches.
- ➤ Encourage kids to have non-sport hobbies, too.

➤ Don't treat the training regimen as if it's a college or professional organization.

➤ Give players time away from playing any one sport.

Suggestions for Time Spans of One Sport in A Year Are:

✓ 8 years of age and younger – *5 months of play at most*

✓ 9 - 12 years of age – no more than 6 months of play

✓ 13 and 14 years of age – *8 months at most*

✓ High school – 9 months tops

Other suggestions to keep things in perspective.

Coaches Should:

➤ Accept the notion that players may miss practice or games once in a while because they have other commitments.

➤ Suggest a sport in the off-season that may help players' physical development.

➤ Show curiosity or interest in other activities that kids do.

Final Thoughts

Coaches cannot make kids play other sports, but they can provide the scientific information so each family can make an educated decision.

Children playing other sports don't always make life easier. In the effort to avoid specialization, children often wear down because of overlapping seasons. Coaches become frustrated because players tire and miss games. Finding a happy medium may take collaboration between coaches, athletes, and parents. In the best case scenario, kids are playing only one sport at a time.

Coaches should also explain that college scholarships rarely cover the total costs of college. Parents and athletes should know that most monetary awards are partial ones that only cover a fraction of the overall fees.

It is imperative to keep in mind that every situation is different. When a child insists he or she only wants to play one sport, parents may have to allow it. Enrolling them in engaging non-sport activities is the perfect substitute for another sport, as long as they get some physical activity elsewhere. Adults must always help kids maintain perspective when they are obsessed with one sport. Parents are ultimately responsible for making sure their child takes time away from playing, but you can and should help with this, too.

COACHING YOUR OWN CHILD

"Shout praise and whisper criticism."

– Coach Don Meyer, Basketball

Preview – Coaching your own child can and should be one of the greatest experiences of raising them. Unfortunately, this is often not the case.

"Honey, why is Joey mad every time he comes home from games and practices?"

– A wife's question to her husband, the coach

My relationships with my kids were and remain today healthy ones. My philosophy on coaching my own children was simple. It took some acting on my part, but I completely forgot they were my own on the playing field.

All child-parent relationships are different. But, no matter how stable a relationship is, coaching your own child can create challenges. Many athletes have a difficult time having parents as coaches. They feel picked on, slighted, or want special treatment from mom and dad. Parents must be careful that bonds don't suffer from something that should be fun.

Often, I've seen a parent coach say something to their child only to get the *"why are you picking on me"* look. Yet, the player could receive the same message from another coach and he or she may respond by nodding in agreement and thanking them for the advice. The ironic thing is they can be the kindest-hearted kids who love their parents. Some young athletes just do not want to hear how-to-play instructions from mom or dad. Often times, a large part of the problem is that the parent coach says things in a different tone to their child. That voice usually adds stress.

The best way to coach your son or daughter is to act as if they are not your child, they're just another member of the team. Pulling this off is not always easy, and you must be decisive in the plan. Sometimes, a short explanation of your strategy may be necessary for younger athletes. *"I am so looking forward to coaching you, but I want you to understand that it's important that I treat you like one of the gang."* Hearing that message is often a relief to the player.

To Treat Your Own as Just Another Member of the Team, You Should:

➢ Have your son or daughter earn their positions, just like every other player has to. Nothing is worse than giving their child the prime spot when he or she did not earn it.

➢ Devote equal time to all players, no more or less to your own son or daughter.

➢ Keep the same demeanor, tone of voice, and emotion with every player on your team – this can be the biggest challenge.

➢ Not expect more from your child than you expect from other players. Managing expectations can be challenging, but you should allow children to be themselves.

➢ Go back to being mom or dad as soon as games and workouts end.

Final Thoughts

Some kids want their parent to coach because it provides them a sense of security. This is fine, but after a few years it may be good to have your child experience another coach at some point before high school.

Disciplining your own child is extremely hard, but it's necessary. Some coach's children have the *"coach is my parent, so I can do what I want"* attitude. As with any player, when you discipline your own child, you should do it away from the team in a one-on-one sit-down afterward.

Even with the same-as-any-player treatment, some kids may not accept their parent's input. In these cases, the next best plan may be to give the responsibility of coaching them to the other coaches. This hands-off policy may be best if your child never seems content. When tension remains no matter what, then you may want to consider taking a break from coaching your child's team the following season.

CHAPTER 4

---~---

Creating a Plan

The actions coaches make before the team gets together are critical for the season ahead. Any false moves or non-moves lead to problems at some point.

Following is a letter I received which points to the importance of having a plan before the season starts to avoid hassles later.

Jack,

My husband coaches a 7 - 9yr old tackle football team through Pop Warner (strong league, more commitment than a "rec or YMCA league"). He has a player who has made a travel hockey team and will now only make 1 out of the 3 practices each week and will miss (2) games. How do you think this situation should be handled? Should the 9-yr-old still be able to play in the games, how much, how often, etc.?

89

MIKE MATHENY

Mike Matheny, the well-regarded St. Louis Cardinals manager, is also famous in youth baseball. When he coached his son's youth baseball team, he wrote of his coaching strategies for youth. That document and now book is known as the *"Matheny Manifesto."* His philosophy gave details of his expectations of players, coaches, and parents. The report spells out the roles and guidelines for everyone involved. He wanted to establish a way of thinking and show the ambitions that he felt were relevant to the age and level of play. Most of all, he wanted everyone to know what to expect and the devotion that's involved. He understood the necessity of everyone being on the same page with his philosophy.

Another key to Mike's manifesto is that he felt parents sometimes put undue pressure on their kids. He emphasized the need for silent encouragement during games. He asked parents to trust the coaches with their decisions on many things because they had the best intentions for their players in mind and nothing more. His foremost objective was to create a season where each player wanted to keep playing the following year. This was the ultimate sign of success he desired, even more so than winning.

It helps that Mike has a major league baseball resume and reputation to get people to buy into his plan. But, that isn't necessarily needed as long as you have a well thought out strategy. You must provide as much pertinent information as possible from the beginning. Coaches should all share their desires and beliefs to give a sense of clarity which may limit future discord. When everyone knows their roles and potentials, in-season turmoil is less likely.

Mike Matheny's proposal to parents and players ends with this statement. *"Let me know as soon as possible whether this is an undertaking you and your son want to make."* Not all situations give people the chance to opt-in, but letting people know about your goals gives the group an initial direction.

A coaching philosophy is the initial step to becoming the best coach you can be. It's a key ingredient for having harmony with both your team and the parents. It may prove hard to live up to your desired goals, but a philosophy to follow gives you the blueprint to do so.

Lessons Learned from Coach Mike Matheny:

1. Explain your philosophy in as much detail as possible from the start.
2. Share your expectations with everyone involved.
3. Specify the roles of parents and ask for their trust.
4. The amount of commitment should reflect the ages of the team and level played. The number of games, practices, and length of season planned should differ for recreational and young players compared to older players and travel/club teams.
5. Help parents understand that an over-emphasis on spoken encouragement in games does more harm than benefit.

CHOOSING THE TEAM

"I don't recruit players who are nasty to their parents. I look for players who realize the world doesn't revolve around them."

— Coach Pete Carril, Basketball

Preview — Besides talent, other factors help when picking players.

"Let's add Joey's dad as a coach so we automatically get his son on our team."

— Conniving coach to his assistant

One day, I ran into one of my former students who was a better than average player.

91

"Why aren't you at the field today?" I asked.

"Oh, I didn't make the team."

"That surprises me. Did they tell you why?"

"I didn't help pick up the balls after batting practice."

Talent is the obvious thing that coaches are looking for when choosing their teams. However, to have the enjoyable experience everyone wants, coaches should also look for other intangibles. When players are of equal ability, looking for other factors helps get the right fit.

To make that point, some college coaches have even begun watching a recruit's parents' behavior at games. They want to have an idea of the tension parents create so they can get a feel for the kid's state of mind. Also, they try to find out the player's ability to mix with a team by asking questions of others who deal with them. That process is extreme and for the highest levels of sport, but the more you know about a player and their parents beforehand, the better equipped you'll be when it comes to choosing the team.

Experienced coaches who have a set coaching style may know what type of player they work with the best. When coaches can get a feel for a player's personality, they have a better idea if it's the type player they can coach. Following are the things that can help coaches choose their team. In tryouts, it may be difficult to discern some of these, but coaches can try.

Coaches Should Look for Players Who Appear to Be:
- ➢ **Hungry to Learn.** Nothing is more exciting for a coach than having players who are coachable, regardless of their ability in the beginning. Players who seem to know it all or who look bored may present a red flag. You can often determine the eagerness of a player from the look in his or her eyes and body language.
- ➢ **Savvy.** When kids seem to know the finer details and strategy of the sport, it helps a coach. You can ask players a question or two to ascertain their comprehension.

- ➢ **Instinctual**. Besides talent, it helps when players have a knack for playing. You should observe how players react to game situations.
- ➢ **Committed**. Players who don't seem to be trying hard, just go through the motions, or even fool around during tryouts may indicate little interest. A fine line exists between having fun and fooling around, and you have to be able to determine which is which because the same uninterested attitude may show up during the season. You may be able to find out how dedicated a player is by asking how much preparation they did.
- ➢ **Hustlers**. Having even one player who hustles on and off the field, who is not afraid to get his or her uniform dirty, is priceless. This team member can be an example to the rest of the players in regards to how to respect the game. You can watch how players get on and off the field. A player who's always the last player to arrive at a tryout station is a red flag.
- ➢ **Hard working**. This ingredient is a no-brainer, but it helps when you watch how players go about their business during tryouts.
- ➢ **Others-centered**. It's best to have kids who are willing to pull for each other. Notice the players who give high-fives and say well done to others – this indicates a team player.
- ➢ **Versatile**. It's beneficial to have kids who play or are willing to play various positions. You should ask your players what spots they've played, prefer to play, and are willing to play.
- ➢ **Athletic**. The more athletic kids appear, the higher their potential. Player speed, strength, and quickness is a solid indicator of athleticism.
- ➢ **Fun loving**. This player may be hard to see in a tryout, but it's nice to have at least one player who keeps things loose for teams with their wit and fun personality.

Final Thoughts

Before the tryouts begin, you should explain to the parents and athletes what the tryout process is and what you'll be looking for. You should reassure everyone that you will be fair in your assessments.

Getting information about a kid's past playing experience is helpful for choosing players, too.

Coaches don't have to go out of their way to find out about a tryout's parents' behavior, but they should think long and hard about choosing players with known overbearing ones. You must decide if a player is worth a bossy mom or dad.

A part of tryouts is preparing to tell players and their parents why he or she did not make the team. You should do so in an honest, but compassionate way. Just saying a player "*wasn't good enough*" isn't enough. Coaches should detail areas where players can improve. If a player is close to making the team, you should invite them to try out the following season. You can tell parents that rosters may change during the season and ask if they want you to stay in touch if that occurs.

Coaches should find a way of not making a cut when only one player needs letting go. Being the only player not picked is cruel to a kid, unless their ability is way below average for the level played. It's important to remember that putting a child in over their head is not fair either, and usually leads to a discouraged player.

GATHERING ADDITIONAL HELP

"Probably my best quality as a coach is that I ask a lot of challenging questions and let the person come up with the answer."

— **Coach Phil Dixon,** Basketball

Preview – Coaches must seek and accept help, so they can do the job they signed up for – teaching the game.

"Coach seems like a different person than at the beginning of the season."

– Player's comment to a teammate

When I began coaching, I wanted everything to be perfect. I believed the only way this would happen was if I did everything. Before long, I was completely overwhelmed, which made things *far* from perfect.

Even though it's "*only*" youth sports, managing all aspects takes energy and time. Coaches have to prepare for and manage games. Additionally, they organize practices, make schedules, and get fields ready. They have to communicate with the coaching staff, deal with player and parent issues, and handle their own child on the team. That can feel like a full-time job, but it's volunteer work added to your regular workload. As odd as it sounds, when coaches do too much, they actually have *less* time to devote to their athletes. Coaching responsibilities can take too much time away from other parts of life, too.

It's not uncommon for coaches with too many roles to lose perspective, have personality changes, and burn out from trying to do everything. You must delegate tasks to others.

Following are the things you can do to make your job as a coach easier and more enjoyable.

Coaches should:
  ➤ Find assistants who have the same general aspirations for the team as they do.
  ➤ Get other parents to help with travel, scheduling, field maintenance, and media communications.
  ➤ Ask someone to develop an inexpensive website to relay and keep all parties up to date on the team news.

➢ Devise a workable communication relay system among parents and players for any last minute schedule changes.

➢ Have parents keep score and do other in-game tasks. You should use parents who hang around a lot when needed. Involved parents feel useful and like they're a part of things.

➢ Get on players' calendars first. You should set practice and game schedules up as soon as the team is formed and for as much of the season as possible. Today's athletes have many other activities. Unless your workouts and games are on their schedule, player attendance may be sparse. Few things are more demoralizing than having few players attend practice.

➢ Make sure each assistant coach is aware of his or her responsibilities during each practice and game. Having unorganized coaches or having to explain things at the last minute takes up a lot of valuable training time.

➢ Encourage parents to pick up their child on time. You'll be busy enough without having to wait after team sessions because players are still there waiting for their parents. Recommend that parents have a backup plan when running late. However, parents must also be assured that one of the coaches will stay until all players have left.

➢ Have a cell phone rule for the times players can use or check their phones.

➢ Make players responsible for the post-game cleanup.

➢ Find a field preparation crew of parents to free coaches up for warm-ups and skill work before games.

➢ Use available online applications for compiling statistics.

Final Thoughts

Coaches should never immerse themselves so far into coaching that their family or work life suffers. When coaches come home irritable after team events, they may have too much on their plate. It's important that the coaches have fun, too.

CRAFTING THE COACHING STATEMENT

"Have a spiritual basis which guides you in life. Have a philosophy of life to live by."

– Coach Tom Osborne, Football

Preview – Coaches must never forget why they wanted to coach in the first place. They should have and follow a written philosophy.

"I can't believe I got kicked out of a game of nine-year-old players."

– Coach's lament after the match

It's important to remember that as a coach, you're never going to be perfect. I believe I have a healthy viewpoint and am as upbeat of a coach as anyone I know. But, even I would take back a few spoken words during games years ago if I could. I don't know how they slipped out, but they did.

Most adults believe they could never get upset with kids or be too harsh or unprofessional at a youth game. But, until you've actually coached, you really can't be so sure. Self-pressure, as well as pressure you get from the out-side can change you, even at the lower levels of competition. *"Losing it"* is easier than you may think. Even the most well-intentioned volunteers with common sense have trying moments. But even one negative utterance can lead to trouble and regrets.

Most coaches are between coaching styles. They are encouraging until apprehension and adversity arrive, and then the disgruntled side appears. An abundance of coaching demands, coupled with the emotions of competition can cause a weak moment in any of us. Annoying opposing coaches, game intensity, and nerves do funny things to people.

A coaching manifesto helps you maintain a healthy point of view and composure during those stressful moments. It serves as a season-long guide to appropriate behavior. Once devised, you can refer to it and add to it as the season or seasons progress. Collaborate with your whole coaching staff, so everyone has the same philosophy. A kindhearted coaching philosophy sets the stage for and expectations of everyone. The age of players and the level of play is a major consideration when developing your plan.

Your Coaching Platform Should Deal with 3 Areas:
1. Expectations of players
2. Expectations of parents
3. The coaching procedures to meet the expectations of players and parents

Every Coaching Philosophy Statement Should Include:
- ✓ Details on how the coaches plan to develop players. You should outline the team and individual goals.
- ✓ A vow that each coach will help all players to the best of their ability.
- ✓ The amount of emphasis that will be on winning. Parents deserve to know your viewpoint and expectation of winning. Coaches have various positions on the importance of playing to win. It is best to be upfront with that stance.
- ✓ The proclamation that having fun is a top priority.
- ✓ The expectation that players commit to working hard and giving their best.
- ✓ An outline of parent and player behavior towards the coaching staff, opposition teams, and officials.

Coaches Should Include Views On These Issues:
- ➢ Policy for missing practice for non-health reasons.
- ➢ Stance on personal coaches. Many of today's athletes have personal trainers and it's best when you're upfront with parents about your

view on the use of them.

➤ Fan (parents and other team-supporters) conduct during games.

➤ Corrective measures for out of control players and parents.

Final Thoughts

The scheduled number of games and practices should reflect the degree of concentration stated in the coach's philosophy.

Recreational league coaches don't need to be as in-depth with their plans as competitive team coaches do.

CONVINCING WITH THE CRUCIAL PRESEASON MEETING

"A person really doesn't become whole, until he becomes a part of something that's bigger than himself."

– Coach Jim Valvano, Basketball

Preview – The best chance of stopping overbearing parents is at the preseason meeting.

"We didn't know those were the rules; if we had known, we would have planned differently."

– Parent cry half way through the season

The above statement is a reasonable complaint from parents. Without knowledge of team policies from the beginning, people may be in awkward positions during the season. When coaches come up with unmentioned regulations during the year, trouble may follow.

Years ago, kids had fewer options – they could play in the local league for non-school sports or they could play on their school teams. Now, athletes have many more options on where, as well as what level, to play. Travel and club teams have added possibilities, and more issues need addressing now.

You can get ahead of potential problems with a preseason parent meeting. This opening adult session should include discussion of any foreseeable situations and troubling issues. The get together should be mandatory for at least 1 parent of each player. The opening parent and coach meeting is also the time you can make allies with parents by letting them know you have their children's best interest in mind. The get together lets everyone get to know the coaches and each other.

At the **Preseason Assembly Coaches Should:**

➢ Introduce the coaching staff and give sports' backgrounds and reasons for wanting to coach.

➢ Describe each coach's role if a delineation is necessary.

➢ Express the sentiment of how honored the coaches are to be coaching the team.

➢ Make the point that the coaches are volunteers, not experts, but they plan to continue to learn as they go. Even paid coaches and those with previous coaching experience should state this message.

➢ Hand out, read, or give the coaching manifesto that describes the staff's philosophy.

➢ Open up a dialog about philosophy, goals, and team regulations. Parents have a right to know the coach's perspectives and coaches must know that parents are in agreement with them on most things. You must be willing to adapt your plans to accommodate the desires of the majority of parents.

➢ Discuss how coaches plan to choose the positions kids play.

➢ Talk about how missed practices will be dealt with. Players should not be penalized for missing practice for health or family emergency reasons, but deciding on and making known any penalties that will be enforced for other reasons for absenteeism is necessary. The penalty may include not starting the next game or a demotion in the lineup. It should never include taking away all playing time. Fairness is important and everyone must decide on what fair is, as it can change from team to team based on the level of play.

➢ Explain and discuss the coaches' philosophy of equal playing time and explain that may mean kids might not start every game.

➢ Inform parents the coaches will be honest but compassionate with players and reinforce the recognition that honesty is never intended to hurt feelings.

➢ Let parents know that coaches are willing to listen to players' concerns and you appreciate it when kids learn to speak for themselves about minor issues. Many of today's youth expect mom and dad to handle all their problems.

➢ Ask parents to talk with the coaching staff about any players with behavior issues. Coaches have a better chance of relating to kids when they are aware of any conduct issues.

➢ Explain the dangers of *social media*. Once something is online, information travels fast and has a way of getting back to others. Offensive comments can ruin relationships and disrupt the whole team. Coaches should also ask parents to give the same message to their kids.

➢ Set up procedures for discussing any in-season parent or player concerns. Everyone should understand that right after games, as well as in front of others, is not the time to confront the coaches. Head coaches should insist that parents come to them first on critical matters. Many problems blow up when things fester among parents. For prominent issues, coaches should insist on in-person talks. Text and emails lead to a lot of time-consuming back and forth. Regrettable things have a better chance of coming out in this manner, too. Also, having a paper trail may result in future problems. Any parent-coach meetings are best with more than one coach when dealing with a tense situation.

➤ Have a vote to solve policy disagreements. It helps to have majority rule, instead of coaching declarations, on some decisions.

➤ Explain game day etiquette. You should voice the fan behavior you feel is inappropriate. Actions like excessive yelling, hurtful words towards anyone, or showing disgust are unacceptable. Low key encouragement is best. Everyone should leave the meeting with this understanding – the coaches will coach, the parents will cheer, and the officials will officiate.

➤ Prepare everyone for opposing team coaches and fans who may not behave in ethical ways. You should explain that there will sometimes be hostile people who yell inappropriate things. But, that behavior does not give your team's players and parents the right to act the same way. Make it clear that the coaching staff will deal with things the best they can and that you expect everyone to take the *"high road."*

➤ Have and explain the benching rule. This rule should be enforced only as a last resort, but the current state of youth sports makes it mandatory. The regulation says that any in-game, rude parent behavior results in their child being benched for the rest of that game. While this rule may seem harsh because it penalizes the kids, when warnings do not keep parents in line, it's often the only alternative. You can ask parents to consider finding a new team for their son or daughter if they do not agree with this rule.

➤ Agree to discuss with parents any future need for policy changes. Changing any approved rules mid-season without discussion is not fair and is a sure way to lose authority.

➤ Make it known that coaches are willing to discuss with parents how players can improve, player-treatment by others, or their child's behavior in a one-on-one situation.

➤ Explain that the only time parents should approach the bench in games is when they feel a player is in danger of some sort or if a player has been severely injured.

➤ Remind parents that they may have different goals for their kids than others do, but everyone must make the effort to understand each other's viewpoints without judgment.

Also, at this meeting, coaches should ask for the parents' agreement with the following. **By volunteering, the coach has the right to:**
1. Make the in-game decisions, and that second-guessing is unfair.
2. Deal with umpires.
3. Deal with opposing coaches.
4. Be the deciding vote when opinions are equal.

Final Thoughts

Having everyone understand the above points is crucial for avoiding discontent later.

The Positive Coaching Alliance has a social media agreement for coaches to use with teams to make sure everyone understands the dangers of and rules for posting things online. You may want to consider employing it with your team.

With the fees involved in today's games, the parents' willingness to speak up has increased, too. Coaches must prepare to answer and discuss all concerns.

As implied, one goal of the gathering is to get the parents' oath that they'll accept and support the coach's in-game decisions. You must explain you will always try to do what you feel is best for their children. You can express that you value helpful input at the appropriate time, but you won't tolerate second-guessing. Failing to get the parents' buy in to the coach's authority at the beginning usually leads to trouble down the road. Coaches can consider having parents sign a code of ethics agreement also. Those agreements are becoming more popular and necessary and can be found online.

Having time for socialization before or after the meeting to develop relationships is valuable. Simple things like getting to know everyone's names and occupations go a long way. The better the relationships, the less likely parents will become disgruntled later.

Coaches should have a note-taker for things discussed, promises made, and parent concerns. Documentation may come in handy at a later time.

Some leagues have a written code of conduct for parents to sign. You can consider implementing this on your own if your league doesn't have it. This way, if needed, you can show parents they agreed to things at the beginning.

Coaches must explain finances at this meeting, too.

COMPREHENDING MONEY BALL

"Now all these athletic departments are bigger than the Pentagon."

– Former Coach Jay Bilas, Basketball

Preview – The higher the costs parents pay to have their kids play, the higher the expectations they have of the coaches.

"I am paying big money; I can say whatever I want."

– A parent statement

I would hate to think that I had something to do with a significant problem in youth sports today. Unfortunately, I am not guilt free. Almost 30 years ago I charged people for my baseball expertise. Once parents began to pay more for play, they had higher ambitions for their kids.

The fees parents were willing to pay put strains on athletes and coaches, demands they did not have before. Expectations of victory and stardom came with the higher prices. The problem is that success is not that easy. No guarantee of better play comes just because of better coaching or increased costs. When performance does not meet aspirations, parents want to blame someone. That someone is the player, the coach, or both.

Money may not be the root of all evil in youth sports, but it has enhanced many of the problems. Higher playing costs have led to increased incidents of unacceptable, hostile behavior. Because of the money shelled out, many people now treat youth sports as professional ones. The demands for exceptional play, winning, and stardom at the amateur levels have grown to heights like never before.

Youth sports are now a money business. Club teams, expensive tournaments, hired coaches, all add to the costs. It's now typical for parents to pay thousands of dollars for one child to play each year. Add in other sports and more kids in the family, and it's easy to see how much the cost to play can become. This financial commitment can put stress on many households, further increasing tension levels. These anxieties can cause people to act in questionable ways.

An even bigger problem with the high cost of play is the exclusionary effects. Many kids from low-income areas cannot play some sports simply because of a lack of funds. Depriving any child of an equal chance to play any activity is harmful to both kids *and* society. The way youth sports are heading, no easy solutions exist, and the situation seems to worsen each year. Hopefully, we will find balance with the increasing costs to play, so all kids have equal access to play.

In this new era, you must address the money situation right from the start. Here are the things you can do, so parents feel their fees are worth it.

Coaches Should:
> ➤ Find the right money fit for the families. Knowing the incomes in the area before committing to a particular level of play is crucial. Joining

an expensive travel system is not going to work in some communities without sponsors and creative ways of fundraising.

➢ Not blame parents for expecting to receive value for their investment, which is how they look at the price of playing. You should never forget that hard earned dollars and sacrifice go into athletes being able to play. A larger percentage of family incomes goes to youth sports than ever before, so it's understandable that parents want coaching passion and dedication.

➢ Let people know what they get for any fees associated with the season. The assurance of an honest effort to deliver on the coaching promises is critical.

➢ Inform parents on whether coaches will receive pay, why, and how much.

➢ Show parents projected expenses so each family can decide if it's in their budget or not. Put the fees for playing in writing and try to give exact dollar amounts for every cost.

➢ Explain possible future charges if certain circumstances arise. For example, teams advancing in tournaments further than expected may result in more expenditures.

➢ Include parents in variable spending decisions. Deciding on what uniforms and equipment are needed should be a group decision. Optional items like team websites, team clothing, and equipment should be open for discussion.

➢ Be transparent with everything money. You must decide who's in charge of the money. It's best when more than one person handles the receiving and dispersing. For high expense teams, it's best when that person is not the head coach.

➢ Have the individuals who are in charge of the money draw up monthly finance reports. Findings of theft of league and team funds are a regular news occurrence these days, so teams cannot be too careful.

➢ Explain any fundraising plans and decide who's in charge of them. You should make sure people are on board with money-raising methods and that they are willing to help. Season costs should be detailed in both scenarios: if fundraising works and if it doesn't – keep in mind that not all fundraising efforts are effective every time. Teams can find many ideas for raising money online, and some are more sophisticated than others.

➢ Have deadlines for when fees are due and express importance of meeting them.

Final Thoughts

Coaches should reinforce the idea that just because parents pay a substantial amount to pay, they are not assistant coaches and only the coaches have the right to make game decisions.

Also, coaches should make it clear that playing on elite teams does not guarantee the attainment of scholarships. It is unfortunate that many parents begin to think of a college scholarship for their child at very young ages, now. That thought process adds pressures on players and coaches.

After more instruction and commitment, players often have higher expectations of triumph too. When that fails to come, their disappointment is evident, too. Coaches may lose the player's appreciation because of that, one of the pitfalls of coaching.

DEVELOPING STAFF CHEMISTRY

"Empower the people around you, from the janitor to the athletic director. You do that by being sincere, caring about others, and then putting it into practice."

– Coach Sue Gunter, Basketball

Preview – Coaching disagreements create disharmony on teams like few other things. Nothing gives youth a worse impression than having the coaches at odds with one another.

"Disregard what Coach Joe told you, do what I say."

– Head coach to player

I remember once when nearby spectators had to pull my son's two coaches apart from a fight on the sidelines. That was embarrassing for the players *and* parents to observe.

It's hard to have team harmony without first having positive vibes among your coaching staff. The chemistry among the coaches begins with choosing the right individuals to assist. The head coach should look for aides with similar philosophies. Next, he or she should make sure each coach knows their role and feels comfortable with it. Then, coaches should work to develop an excellent working relationship with the staff.

Coaches Should:

➤ Have a coaches' meeting before the season. You should discuss the team and coaching objectives, along with the coaching roles. Finding out about other's lives is always an excellent first step with new acquaintances.

➤ Talk about coaches having a "kid-first" mindset and what that means.

➤ Send all coaches each session's agenda beforehand and ask for feedback on it.

➤ Request input from the other coaches as often as possible in front of the team. Head coaches should make a point of letting assistants show their knowledge.

➤ Allow other coaches to teach without looking over their shoulders.

➤ Have a short analysis of each day's procedures with coaches after practices and games.

➤ Never have coaching disagreements in front of the players. Clear up any differences and make any adjustments later.

➤ Always have the stance that everyone works *with* the head coach, not for them.

➤ Discuss any sensitive issues with the whole staff, so a consensus can be made for how to deal with them.

➤ Help each other maintain the correct outlook in the heat of the season. It may be best to talk things over away from the fields when emotions have had time to settle down.

Final Thoughts

Head coaches must be careful about taking on an assistant just because their son or daughter is a superb player. They should discuss coaching philosophies with prospective people before taking them as assistants.

It doesn't take long for players and parents to sense divisiveness among coaches. Team divisions can form soon after.

Head coaches may have to remind the other coaches that *they* have the final call on things. It's best when that call comes after consultation with the others, though.

CHAPTER 5

~

Creating a Practice Agenda

The season's preparation begins with well-run practices. Organized coaches, who center on skill enhancement and game strategy, give players the best chance to improve. Add in the fun factor and kids may fall in love with the sport, too.

Following is a letter I received from a former student. It attests to the effect quality teaching has on players.

Jack,

What I truly appreciate even more is what a super teacher you are. I employ many of your drills and demonstrations with my sons and with the Little Leaguers I coach. With reps and the proper encouragement, I see the smiles and they all improve. Those small successes, week by week and year by year, build confidence and make the baseball field a place kids can go and are happy to be. To me, that's the most important thing in sports.

THANK YOU for all of your insight and expertise and thank you twice as much for being such a great teacher. It's still a great game!

PETE CARROLL

Another coaching icon is football's Pete Carroll, currently of the Seattle Seahawks. The title of Pete's book is *Win Forever*. One's original impression may be that the book is all about showing teams how to win. But, the word *forever* gives it added meaning because athletes do not play forever.

Sports journalist Ben Malcolmson writes on petecarroll.com about how Carroll believes that accomplishments on the field are only a small segment of the overall goal. Winning forever is about much more than the next game or season, according to Coach Carrol. *"It's about competing, maximizing your abilities, and making the most of the opportunities in front of you,"* Pete says. *"…so that each player can become the best he can be and each team can achieve its fullest potential. Realizing that is a tremendous accomplishment, whether it's in football or life."*

He goes on to talk about the idea that a sense of achievement comes from doing the small things. He emphasizes that practice means so much, as one cannot win forever without dealing with the now. Like many of the great leaders, he recognized the value in communication, and encourages it from team members. Coach Carroll's philosophy helps players reach their potential as both athletes *and* people. Pete knows that getting the most out of players at every session will lead to success and satisfaction down the road, win or lose. Just as noteworthy, winning forever leads to few, if any, regrets, knowing one gave their best.

Lessons Learned from Coach Pete Carroll:

1. It is OK to play to win, as long as the emphasis is on players learning how to compete and reaching their potential.
2. Practicing the day-to-day things is the beginning of winning forever.
3. Doing the little things will build a sports career and life after sports.

4. Competition is about maximizing one's talent, taking advantage of opportunities, and having no regrets.

VALUING SAFETY MEASURES AND INJURY AVOIDANCE

"Remember this, the choices you make in life, make you."

— Coach John Wooden, Basketball

Preview – Safety over sorry.

"I can't believe they are taking me to court."

— Anguished coach

I cringe watching some youth baseball teams' workouts. I see balls and bats flying all over the place and know it's just a matter of time before a serious injury comes. Many dangers exist for all sports. When coaches do not know or follow the best safety procedures, preventable injuries will follow.

Accidents and injuries happen in sports. But that fact does not excuse coaches from possible negligence. Lawsuits were once rare occurrences, but are much more common in today's world. Many injuries are avoidable when knowledgeable coaches insist on cautious proceedings. For the most part, knowing and using safety procedures will absolve coaches of negligence charges.

Of course, no one wants to see athletes injured at all. You must make everyone's well-being priority number one and be aware of any of the possible dangerous aspects of play. Running safe training and games takes planning and observant coaches.

Here are the safe measures to apply.

Coaches Should:
- Know the most common injuries associated with the sport. Inform parents and players of these, along with any preventative measures and possible post-injury treatments. You can give basic advice for treatment of the most common minor injuries, but be sure to advise parents to seek medical advice for any possible serious injuries.
- Go over protection issues with all your coaches, so everyone can act as guardians of safety.
- Explain the overuse injuries that come from excessive practice and play. Overuse injuries lead to missed time and, in worst case scenarios, possible surgery or the end of a career.
- Recommend some age appropriate strengthening exercises that can help avoid injury.
- Use appropriate conditioning exercises to build up player strength, agility, and stamina.
- Know the value in warm-up and cool down periods. Many injuries occur because players are not ready for the fast-paced action. A warm-up period of stretching and easy running before beginning workouts is essential. Ending workouts with easy stretching and cooldown time can help muscles recover and prepare for the next day.
- Establish safe warm-up areas and routines – this is a must.
- Keep nearby people in safe spots, especially when many things go on at the same time. You have to be on the lookout for fans and people walking by too, so they don't wander into dangerous areas.
- Be careful when instructing. Alerting players during the action can be hazardous because they may stop to listen. Listening is a marvelous thing, but pausing to hear may put them in vulnerable positions.
- Be aware of field conditions and surrounding areas. You should look for areas of possible danger before and during play.

➢ Adhere to weather warnings of any type. Getting players out of harm's way early is essential as Mother Nature works fast. You should check weather forecasts and have plans in place for shelter and quick evacuation.

➢ Make sure players wear the appropriate gear and that all equipment is up to standards. Sometimes coaches get lax with having players wear protective gear in practice and that should not be the case.

➢ Show players ways to avoid collisions with others and the object used for play.

➢ Teach player-to-player communication procedures. In-game talk among players is essential to prevent accidents.

➢ Help players recognize the difference between hard and dirty play. The latter involves the intent to injure and goes beyond aggressive actions.

➢ Ask players to inform the coaching staff of injuries, no matter how minor.

➢ Only play players in positions they have rehearsed.

➢ Explain to players the possible dangers of playing certain positions. Players often think they want to play a spot without realizing the risks involved.

➢ Never get lax with safety measures as the season progresses. Reviewing practice and game well-being procedures with all coaches, parents, and players from time to time is necessary.

➢ Have and maintain documentation of any severe injuries for future referral.

➢ Have ice and a first-aid kit present. All coaches should have basic medical care on hand. That preparation may avoid a negligence charge.

➢ Follow up after an injury with a player's parents.

Final Thoughts

Coaches must be honest when a player's skill level isn't ready for spots they wish to play.

Gone are the days when "*shake it off*" can be a coach's mentality like it once was. You must listen, take injury concerns seriously, and deal with them accordingly.

The advancement in concussion research makes any head injury an utmost priority. Extreme care and follow-up procedures are essential, no matter how minor a head blow is. When there is any doubt, players must leave play and see a physician immediately. In sports where concussions are most likely, coaches should know the signs and initial treatment, too.

IMPROVING SKILL DEVELOPMENT – HOW KIDS LEARN

"If you have something critical to say to a player, preface it by saying something positive. That way when you get to the criticism, at least you know he'll be listening."

– *Coach* Bud Grant, Football

Preview – Instructing with words alone are not enough and a sure sign of an inexperienced coach.

"I can't believe they keep messing that play up; I have told them how to do it a million times."

– Bewildered coach

One of the most important teaching tools I use are pictures and the showing of video of experienced players' methods of accomplishment. Until players have the right imagery and knowledge of how, learning is evasive.

Coach John Wooden wrote about *"The Laws of Learning"* in his book, *Wooden*. They just as well could have been *"The Laws of Coaching."* His principles refer to the best training methods for player evolvement.

Voice instructions guarantee little. Learning comes from many ways of providing information. John Wooden describes the keys to knowledge as: explanation, demonstration, imitation, and repetition. He goes on to emphasize the last one by repeating the word, repetition, over and again. Correct repetition is the key to athletic achievement. Game execution comes once things become second nature. It takes doing it right once, though before the correct repetition is possible.

Following are the keys that you must use to develop the skills and game strategy.

Clear Explanations
You should detail movements and plans in understandable terms. Having the ability to say the same things in various ways is helpful. You never know what words might trigger a player's insight.

Accurate Descriptions Can Help Athletes:
✓ Learn the right way to perform the moves and plays.
✓ Improve quicker.
✓ Make adjustments.
✓ Have confidence.
✓ Assist other players.

Demonstrations which Give the Visual to the Explanations
Being able to visualize plays is vital for education. You should show the correct techniques that provide the proper images. That display helps players make sense of the explanations you're giving them for the how and why of things. Players learn as much or more by seeing as they do from hearing. The

earlier in the season (and in life) that an athlete sees well-performed actions, the better their chances become of doing them well. Pictures, videos, and demonstrations are valuable teaching tools.

Imitation of the Things Players Observe

Players combine verbal explanations and mental images before trying to imitate them. Reproduction of actions and strategies is a career-long trial and error process. Players improve, plateau, and regress in search of the right way. The difficulty of most sports moves do not allow perfection, but coaches who can show, see, and point out the right from wrong moves are invaluable for player maturation.

Repetition Is the Final Step of Learning

Players must put the above things together correctly many times for better play. One correct move and one false one get them nowhere. Efficient muscle memory repetition leads to certainty. With hard work and guidance from a patient coach, skill sets improve. Performing things the right way, time and again, paves the way for the recurrence in games, which is the ultimate goal.

Final Thoughts

Without enough practice time, players won't get enough repetition to result in improvement and possible long-term excellence.

Even at the advanced levels, the coaches who can educate in the simplest of terms are best.

Coaching analysis is a necessity each step of the way. When coaches neglect any of the above, players have a difficult time progressing. However, experienced coaches recognize there are moments when it is best for coaches to back off and allow players time to figure things out for themselves.

HAVING A MEANINGFUL DEFINITION OF SUCCESS

"Success is peace of mind which is a direct result of self-satisfaction in knowing you did your best to become the best you are capable of becoming."

– Coach John Wooden, Basketball

Preview – Failing to have a realistic definition of success sets most up for disappointment.

"We may have lost; that doesn't make you losers."

– Coach to the team after a game

"I didn't get any hits last game," were one of my player's words to me. *"Did you swing at good pitches and take aggressive swings?"* I asked. *"Yes,"* he answered. *"Then you did all you could control, and that's a successful night."*

When I look back, it was a dream come true to make the major leagues. In all honesty though, the striving for the goal was what was most satisfying. Overcoming the challenges, preparing year after year, and giving close to 100% in games were the things that made it all worthwhile. The thing that made it even more gratifying was the support of family, coaches, and friends along the way.

The standard definition of *success* is *victory* and *being the best player*. Those apply to some degree, but this is short sighted and only includes a small group of athletes. When kids get the message that they have to win and be the best to be a success, their chances of satisfaction are slim. Most of all, no player, regardless of his or her ability, should be made to feel like a loser.

A lack of a proper definition of success disheartens many athletes. An unhealthy image of accomplishment damages self-worth and leads to lost

hope. Coaches should define and recognize achievement in ways that are under players' control. You can convey this definition to build motivation and
self-esteem.

Players can be taught what entails success. **First,** it is preparing to a satisfactory level, which is different for each player. **Second,** it is overcoming
the trials along the journey, and **third,** it is giving one's best in games. **Making it about winning, being the highest scorer and the best player is
unfair to athletes.**

Here are some suggestions coaches can try so kids feel satisfied.

Coaches Should:

➢ Recognize that each player is different. You must help each player
   feel they're as prepared as possible based on individual abilities and
   their own desires.

➢ Associate success with effort. Asking *"Did you put enough effort into
   preparations? Are you comfortable with how prepared you feel?"* When players
   answer *"Yes,"* that is a victory, and coaches should point it out.

➢ Ask the follow-up question, *"Did you give your best effort in the game?"* If
   a player can honestly answer *"Yes,"* then coaches and players should
   both feel pleased.

➢ Make it clear that any improvement, no matter how small, is a sign of
   personal progress. You should make players feel good about their ad-
   vancements.

➢ Explain that long-term expertise comes from performing the tedious
   steps along the way and that shortcuts do not exist.

➢ Never fail to express that hard work is the goal that signals success.
   Coaches should always applaud those who work hard, especially
   those who do it without prodding.

➢ Explain the word *"potential"* and why it's important that players strive
   to reach it.

> ➤ Convey the idea that triumph is only one measure of achievement. Kids should learn that a mindset of determination and love of playing are more important than victories.
> ➤ Thank kids for their effort, win or lose.
> ➤ Never stop encouraging players to work hard, without forcing them to do more.
> ➤ Relate that having coachable and optimistic attitudes are signs of achievement.
> ➤ Explain that complacency brings regrets.

Final Thoughts

My definition of success: *Steady, Unyielding, Consistent, Character, Every Single Step.*

It's normal and OK to congratulate the winner and player with the best statistics. Coaches should never diminish the better players' achievements.

Even when athletes are contented with their performance, you should offer areas of concentration for continual development and improvement.

Some achievement is vital for the continued desire to play. A lack of progress weakens desire as quick as anything. Even kids with the best outlooks need to see some personal skill advancement and coaches must point those out at every opportunity.

Accomplishment usually breeds a desire to do more. When players are not pushed to do more and have some personal advancement, most learn to give the increased effort in time.

It can be hard to convince everyone that success is not just coming out on top and being the best player. Adults who are pushy and never content make this even more challenging. Coaches who stay enthusiastic and optimistic throughout can change people's attitudes.

PINPOINTING THE "ONE" GOAL

"Excellence is the gradual result of always striving to do better."

— Coach Pat Riley, Basketball

Preview – If the top athletes have this goal, it must work.

"I guarantee if you train as hard as you play in games, it will pay off."

— Coach to the team

All motivational experts seem to agree that goal-setting is critical to achievement. The ambition of being the best one can be gives athletes focus and determination. However, having the wrong objectives, those based on statistics, rewards, and recognition can lead to unfulfilled feelings. Statistics work to drive players for a period, but those often fizzle out.

Everyone wants to see progress, feel competent, and ultimately win, but all of this may not be possible for every athlete. I remember the many times I set goals, only never to look at them again or to soon figure out they were unattainable. I learned to set the same goal every year, and every year I came closer to meeting it. This one goal is within every player's reach, and the one you should impart.

Of all the goals a player could have, you should stress this *one*:

"Working hard to improve daily is the goal."

A day-to-day work ethic is an aim that keeps athletes hungry and allows them to eventually reach their potential. A gritty and consistent philosophy is possible for all. Whether the improvement comes or not, developing a robust work plan is an excellent life lesson.

You can create a solid work ethic in athletes a number of ways.

121

Coaches Should:

➢ Work hard – most students will recognize what working hard means by the presentation you give. If coaches slack off with their instruction as time goes on, players will often do the same.

➢ Recognize and reward exertion and determination at every occasion.

➢ Help athletes understand they don't have to be elite, but that striving to reach their potential makes them unique in your eyes. Many athletes feel like they have to prove themselves with statistics. Posting of individual stats embarrasses some athletes and parents, and is inadvisable.

➢ Remind athletes that the journey is what's important, and the enjoyment of the game itself will motivate players.

➢ Never fail to express that hard work pays off in the end. Many kids lose faith quickly when they don't see instant results.

➢ Communicate the importance of an impeccable work ethic in non-sport activities, too.

➢ Give examples of athletes in the sports world who are hard workers.

➢ Praise kids who work on their craft at home.

➢ Stress the importance of practicing the basic plays. Doing the routine actions over and over pays off more than performing the occasional fantastic play.

➢ Help youth feel that working hard makes one a winner no matter the score or the statistics.

➢ Explain that those who *"stick with it,"* often outperform the most talented players in the long-term.

Final Thoughts

Coaches should not fall into the trap of setting performance targets for kids or teams. They are satisfying when reached, but more often lead to discouragement. Goals that focus solely on statistics and victories may harm players' self-assurance and self-worth. Unmet goals can make them feel like losers. If athletes want to set personal marks to reach, that's fine, but it shouldn't be your concern.

No child deserves the label "*underachiever.*" Also, that casting may affect a coach's attitude towards those athletes, which is unfair.

The opposite occurs for some players who set goals, too. Once reaching them, they become satisfied with their progress, and may become complacent. When coaches notice players easing up, they must remind them of that one goal of working hard to improve daily.

If kids learn nothing else from sports, recognizing that hard work is the one thing under their control makes playing worth it.

A team stance of daily execution is a coach's dream come true and often leads to winning.

DEVELOPING FOCUS

"Focus on the play like it has a history and a life of its own."

- Coach Nick Saban, Football

Preview – Without concentration, all the talent in the world is of little value.

"*Don't think, just do it.*"

– Coaching tip to athlete

I hate to admit it, but there were times early in my major league career that I played scared on the baseball field. I was so afraid I would screw up that my concentration level was not where it should have been. When I felt like that, the result was exactly that – I screwed up.

When our team takes the field, I often yell *"Don't take the bat out to the field with you."* Sometimes I see a quizzical look on my players' faces, and inevitably one will ask, *"Coach, why would anyone do that?"* I explain *"Your last at-bat is over, forget it and concentrate on saving us a run on defense. If your mind is on your batting, you will not be ready to make the play."*

When athletes worry about the past or the future, concentration is difficult. Playing with fear from the weight of parents' and coaches' demands increases tension for players, too. The best athletes are those who are able to clear their mind and prepare for the next play and nothing beyond that. This ability is a learned skill for most. As a coach, you have a significant role in the mental preparedness of your players.

Most coaches think yelling, *"Concentrate!"* all the time helps players' readiness. This rarely does the trick, and in reality may do more harm than help. Overwhelming athletes with instructions right before or during the action makes awareness difficult. Athletes must make spontaneous decisions. That decision making is hard when a coach is yelling at them about concentrating or what they should do.

Here are the techniques you can try to help your players stay in the moment and develop concentration.

Coaches Should:

➢ Remain quiet during plays and limit pre-play instructions.

➢ Give simple preparation tips like, *"Who wants the action (ball) coming to them?"* or *"Ready positions, everybody."* These are OK because they are helpful for keeping players' minds in the present, without diverting attention.

➢ Never threaten or intimidate. Focus is easier when people enjoy what they do. Enjoyment is hard when players cannot relax due to intimidation and fear of messing up.

➢ Encourage players to talk about the game between plays and when on the bench.

➤ Ask questions at practice and before and after games about different game scenarios. That mental challenge will help players understand their responsibilities, think for themselves and develop solid instincts.

➤ Help players develop a plan and a process to achieve it.

➤ Insist that players *trust* their abilities and their preparation without thinking of any possible negative outcomes of their actions.

➤ Assist players in learning to anticipate various situations. Correct in-game decision making is more likely after thinking of all possible scenarios before the next play.

➤ Keep players strong. You must help kids and parents realize the importance of being rested. Tired athletes have mind distractions, which can lead to mistakes.

➤ Help players keep their mind in the present, without thought of what has happened or could happen. The phrases *"It's over"* and *"Forget about it"* should be at the tip of the coach's tongue.

➤ Ask players to repeat what you just said. Knowing they may be called to repeat any tips helps players remain accountable and in the present.

➤ Have players speak to themselves of what they plan to have happen before the play. This voice helps players' visualization skills.

➤ Explain that their mental game improves with practice just as the physical skills can. Asking players to try to increase their concentration an extra minute at a time is a good start.

➤ Help players learn to use positive self-talk after plays, so they do not beat themselves up after mistakes.

Final Thoughts

Well-run and engaging workouts maintain player curiosity and focus.

Sometimes, players "get in the zone" – a mental state in which players see the action in a slower state. It is a mentality which allows their experience and instincts to take over without having to think of what to do. When this happens, players just react and the results are positive ones. Some players get into the zone more often, while others never find that experience.

The best coaches remain calm under intense game conditions and after mistakes. Playing is easier for youth when they don't have a fear of letting you down. Grilling and condemning players after gaffes hurts their concentration the next time.

REALIZING A COACH'S PURPOSE

"I've never felt my job was to win basketball games – rather that the essence of my job as a coach was to do everything I could to give my players the background necessary to succeed in life."

– Coach Bobby Knight, Basketball

Preview – Although having fun is a child's primary goal of playing, coaches have a nobler purpose.

"Team, it's OK to feel down, that was a tough loss, but we will learn from it and move on."

– Coach after a loss

Looking back, I feel that playing sports prepared me for many of life's situations. Some of the education came from playing actual games, but most of it came from dealing with people. Often, my coaches were instrumental in helping me through both the easy and the taxing times.

Coaches have a platform to prepare youth for more than just their on-the-field adventures. Healthy life lessons serve kids long after their youth sports days are over.

Following Are Some of the Sports Experiences That Coaches Help Players with:

- ✓ **Adversity.** Helping youth deal with failure is a vital coaching responsibility. Everyone deals with hard times sooner or later, and guidance can help them through the tests. Some athletes are more resilient than others, but bad performances can be upsetting for anyone. You should set an example with how you handle mistakes and losing.

- ✓ **Success.** Equally prominent is that athletes learn to deal with personal and team achievement. Some players become cocky after a while and you must not allow that attitude to form.

- ✓ **Relationships.** Helping players' capacities to relate to others is a worthwhile task. Players discovering ways of working with others is invaluable. You should help kids, especially those who do not seem to fit in, assimilate and gain acceptance from others.

- ✓ **Competition.** Helping players grasp how to give their best is another noble goal.

- ✓ **Sweat.** Realizing that a satisfying performance only comes from hard work is a valuable lesson. You must help players understand that often, a satisfying outcome directly relates to the amount of effort they've put in.

- ✓ **Pressure.** Developing a player's self-assurance when things get tense is another priceless lesson. Helping athletes feel comfortable in games is a never-ending coaching task.

- ✓ **Teamwork.** Recognizing the value of relying on others is meaningful for kids' futures. You have a role in helping youth value friendships and groups.

- ✓ **Appreciation for adults.** Showing respect for authority figures is an instrumental moral. You must help team members treat adults, including their parents, with kindness.

- ✓ **Goals.** Coaches must impart the importance of players striving to reach their desires.

- ✓ **Roles on the team.** Helping players remain aware of, accept, and value their role on the team is part of the maturation process.
- ✓ **Accountability.** Coaches help players learn that making excuses and assessing blame is wrong. You will teach players about their responsibilities as athletes and ensure they understand they are representing a group.
- ✓ **Self-control.** Helping kids learn to play with composure and fairness is another important message.
- ✓ **Attention to Detail.** Helping kids understand that no shortcuts to success exist and it only comes by doing the little things.

Final Thoughts

Often, coaches have more influence on athletes than even their school teachers do. Coaches should be role models and use their platform to guide kids. You may not know right away if your life lessons take hold, but you must believe they will someday.

USING THE PSYCHOLOGY OF COACHING

"Prepare for every game like you just lost your last game."

– Lon Kruger, Basketball

Preview – The best coaches know when to push a little, when to relax the team, and how to act a little.

"I can't figure Coach out; he rants and raves in practice, but at games is all smiles and encouraging."

– One player to another

Some of the best coaches I had confused our team. We would play well and win, and our coach would rant and rave as if we were the worst team on earth. Other games, we would play poorly and lose. Our coach laughed it off, told us to hang in there and hold our heads up high. I now realize that when coaches do this, they're using sound psychology. Underneath the outward behavior, of course they didn't enjoy losing and they wanted to win, but they had the big picture in mind. They didn't show their true feelings because their aim was on long-term improvement. They wanted to keep players motivated and concentrated, win or lose.

Coaches don't want teams to be complacent after wins or discouraged after losses. Coaches act in ways that don't always reflect their inward contentment or disappointment. They see that satisfied players often don't put in as much effort, and disheartened ones do the same with a *"what's the use"* mindset. The best coaches are familiar with human nature and use psychology to overcome that.

The Psychology of Coaching Includes:
- ✓ Acting calm and in control, even when the heart is pumping fast in games.
- ✓ Showing confidence in game decisions, whether you're sure or not.
- ✓ Having a sense of humor even when things do not seem funny.
- ✓ Recognizing the mood of teams and players to know when they need relaxation or a *"pick-me-up"* pep talk.
- ✓ Maintaining enthusiasm when things do not go as planned. It motivates others to know you're just as engaged as ever and have not given up on them.
- ✓ Losing with a gracious look, even though upset inside. Your manner after games sets the tone for how players deal with losing.
- ✓ Being happy with a win but still addressing opportunities for improvement. You want your team to remain hungry to grow. You do not want them to lose the edge after the victory. You should show

pride in your team, but never let them feel too satisfied. The season's end is your time to celebrate and let your guard down.

Final Thoughts

The best coaches display two different personalities, one for training and one for games. Their practice presence is a guiding one with an insistence on detail. During drills, keep kids captivated on learning.

Your game character should be different, with a resolve of just letting kids play with much less coaching input. Game coaches encourage, remain upbeat, display patience, and never humiliate athletes. Seen but less heard is the best game day demeanor.

Unfortunately, many coaches do the opposite. They are nonchalant in workouts and too intense during games.

Coaches must learn when to take charge and when to get out of the way. The best coaches have a knack for that. If it takes some yelling to get the players' attention, it should occur during workouts, not games. Players have enough worries on game day already. When you need to motivate in games, it should be done in a reasonable, encouraging way.

CHAPTER 6

---~---

Creating the Practice Environment

Practice is a coach's time to shine. They should not miss that opportunity.

Here is a letter I received from a coach who understands what youth sports are about.

Jack,

I'm fortunate to coach a Local High School Baseball Team, as well as coach a 6-year-old softball team and 4 - 5-year T-Ball Team (my kids' teams). There is one consistent message regardless if I'm talking to my 16-year-old ace who throws 85 mph, or to the little girl who wants to play just to be around her friends. "Rule #1 is to have fun." Say it out loud. It rhymes. I have all of my teams say it before each practice and game. Even, the "cool" high schoolers get the message.

BILL WALSH

Another legendary coach of the past 50 years is football's Bill Walsh. The title of Bill's coaching leadership book, ***The Score Takes Care of Itself,*** is a lesson itself. If youth coaches coach with this premise in mind, youth sports will have a bright future.

Bill Walsh believed in creating a culture of high standards. He expected hard work and a pledge to being first-class in *everything* his teams did. He wanted players to know that sports and life are about core values, principles, and ideals.

Bill Walsh Created This Culture by Educating Athletes to:

- ✓ Train the right way before the season.
- ✓ Work to a comfortable level.
- ✓ Compete to one's best.
- ✓ Lead by example.
- ✓ Conduct themselves with class on and off the field.

He also believed that all those things began with the coaches, as pointed out in his book. *"If you want your athletes to model the passion, commitment, and work ethic to be successful, you must demonstrate it yourself in everything you do."* Bill Walsh felt that if he made people winners off the field, the victories would follow.

Lessons Learned from Coach Bill Walsh:

1. Attitude begins with the coaches.
2. Before they can expect them to play well, coaches are responsible for teaching athletes.
3. Emphasis should be on the process, not the scoreboard.
4. When the intent is on fun and education, everybody is a winner in the end.

CHOOSING PLAYING POSITIONS

"He's going to play several positions. He's all for it. We're going to give him primary work at third base, but he's also going to get work at first base and in right field."

– Coach Joe Maddon, Baseball

Preview – When coaches aren't fair with the positions kids play, contentious situations usually arise.

"I know she wants to play another position, but she doesn't have the skills to play that position."– an honest Coach to parent

One of my regrets from my playing days is that I did not learn to play other positions on the ball field. That strategy would have helped me in my career.

Keeping everyone happy is not always possible. Nowhere is that more clear than when it comes to player positions. Coaches must prepare to hear the *"I don't want to play there,"* talk from players. Coaches face many problems when it comes to where kids play.

First, only one player can play a position at a time.
Second, parents often overestimate their child's skill.
Third, a player's strengths may not fit a particular area.
Fourth, some athletes are better than others.
Fifth, coaches must consider what's best for the team, not just individual desires.
Sixth, kids do not or will not play the spot you want them to play.

All sports have their most sought after positions – pitcher, shortstop, quarterback, point guard, etc. Many parents want their children in these glory spots. When the coach's child gets one of those, complaints may follow. The process for choosing places must be as fair as possible. Coaches must take into account all scenarios and have a process for deciding who plays where. The spot that players *want* to play and maybe even are best at, does not always match up with what makes the team better.

Convincing players and parents that you have everyone's best interest at heart is the initial challenge. You should discuss this with parents in the beginning. Then, people may better understand your coaching moves during the season. Each team is different, and position movements depend on the team's objectives and philosophy. Elite teams may have a different approach than lower level teams. You must adjust to the level played.

No matter the level of play, with players under 12-years of age, you should rotate all players to more than one spot. You shouldn't set in stone a players' ultimate place on the playing field at a young age. That movement helps players find out where they like to play and where their natural talent is. Once players reach an advanced level, more specialization of positions is OK. Whatever the situation, you must be fair when assigning positions.

Following are the suggestions to keep things fair.

Coaches Should:

➤ Make it known that they have earned the right to decide which positions kids play. You should remind players and parents that you intend to be fair with your decisions.

➤ Make it clear that positions aren't granted based on a player's past, although it may be taken into consideration.

➤ Talk to players and parents at the season's start to find out any position preferences. This shows that you care about their desires, too. However, be careful to never make a promise of a specific spot to a player or their parent before the season begins.

➤ Not be naïve to the fact that many parents have preconceived ideas of where their child should play. With that knowledge, you should be compassionate but honest when talking to players and parents. Many players get their heart set on playing certain spots, and it's disappointing when they don't get them.

➢ Ask that no one takes any decisions as a personal affront. Explain that you have to do what is best for the whole team.

➢ Have a skills day or two, in the beginning, to allow players to show what they can do. This session is a tremendous opening step for making things as fair and accurate as possible. Players should have the chance to work out at their favorite spots and a few others.

➢ Discuss with other coaches what they saw in practice before announcing any decisions. The head coach should be the one explaining decisions if there is any sense of disagreement.

➢ Pull disappointed players aside and discuss the decision, encourage them to keep working hard, and explain that things may change down the line.

➢ Coaches can set up a depth chart to present to players and parents. That posting shows players where they stand. It can help spur players to work harder to earn their favorite spot back.

➢ Remind players that a place won, at season's start, doesn't mean it won't change later. Explain that the coaches are open to giving players future opportunities.

➢ Encourage players to work at their favorite positions on their own. Their current role may be different later or the next season.

➢ Reinforce the idea that the more places kids learn at young ages, the better for them in the future. Ask players to stay upbeat and help the team when not at their favorite spots.

➢ Make sure players get some practice time in any positions they may play in games.

➢ Have occasional practices when players get to play a position other than their regular game spot. Athletes often welcome the movement, and it provides an opportunity for coaching observation.

➢ Give players opportunities in their favorite spots in non-pivotal games or when the score suggests it is out of hand.

Final Thoughts

Coaches should always be ready to explain their reasons as to why kids play where they do.

Getting players and parents to believe that versatility is valuable is not always easy, but it's necessary.

Coaches have the option of inviting disgruntled parents to practices. When they see their child compared to other players at certain positions, they may see that the right decision has been made.

EXPLAINING THE RESPECT RULE

"It's not what you tell your players that counts, it's what they hear."

– Coach Red Auerbach, Basketball

Preview – Youth coaches do not have to have many rules, but this one is mandatory.

"Did I say something funny?"

– Coach to players

It doesn't bother me when players don't look at me when I talk. I have come to know that looking at the speaker is not always a sign of listening. However, I do care when people are disruptive and not paying attention.

A valuable message from day one is what I call the respect rule. Anything that distracts the speaker and diverts other people's attention breaks the rule. When players, coaches, or parents whisper or giggle among themselves during a presentation, they break the rule. Talking on cell phones and laughing in the background are other instances of the regulation breakers. When you notice a rule breaker, you should call for a quick lap around the field or a few pushups for the whole team. Players pay with a little extra exercise no matter who the disrespectful culprits are.

This physical exercise makes the point that *everyone* should show the presenter their attention. Players will not want the penalty, and that is the point of the rule. They learn to listen to the person talking after a while, and after a few additional laps or exercises. The word of this law passes to everyone in time, including to parents. Before long, the result is silence when others, especially you as the coach, have the floor.

You could stop and wait until everyone is quiet or ask the offenders if they have something to share. But these methods may embarrass others and create bad feelings with some.

This lesson is imperative for athletes in other areas of life, too. High school teachers and coaches do not stand for fooling around or inattentiveness and the consequences can be harsh. Tryout players may not make the team because of their inappropriate behavior. This is also a worthwhile lesson for adults, who are often as guilty as the kids are.

Final Thoughts
Coaches should ask parents to answer phones and talk to others out of earshot from the team.

Coaches can ask questions to find out which players were listening when they may not be looking at the speaker.

Running and other physical exercises as punishment for poor play are not right, but using them to make a point about a life lesson is OK.

IMPRESSING WITH THE FIRST TEAM GET TOGETHER

"There are only two options regarding commitment. You're either in, or you're out. There is no such thing as life in-between."

– Coach Pat Riley, Basketball

Preview – Only one chance exists to make a good first impression. The opening talk is your opportunity to "*wow*" them.

"Guys, girls, we are here for you."

– Coach message to the team

When I begin camps and clinics, I know I have to get everyone's buy in on what's to follow. I spend a lot of time making the opening speech one that convinces everyone of my enthusiasm and dedication. I also use this time to explain the benefits to players if they believe in the program. Those benefits include noticeable personal and team improvement, along with the confidence and satisfaction that comes with those. The opening talk should give everyone the feeling that the coaches are out for the well-being and advancement of their athletes.

The opening address gives coaches the chance to inspire and win everyone's trust. You should invite and encourage parents to attend the opening talk. Also, the first speech speaks of player and parent commitment to a mutual cause. You can enthuse everyone with the stance, "*Together we can do this.*"

The Opening Speech Covers These Points:

- ✓ **Coaching promise.** "*The coaching staff is here for you, as individuals and as a whole. We will listen to your concerns, so don't be afraid to voice them at the appropriate time. We will always try to make decisions based on what's best for the team.*"

- ✓ **Goals.** "*Everyone should think long-term. I don't need the players who are the best at the beginning as much as I need the players who improve the most by the end. The hard workers have the best chance of playing the game for a long time. Remember, it's not how good you are now; it is how remarkable you can be. We are here to help set you in that direction.*"

✓ **Importance of the fundamentals.** *"There is no substitute for the basics. Doing things the right way is the only avenue for long-term growth. The coaching staff will keep attention on the mechanics day in and day out."*

✓ **Player pledge.** *"Improvement only happens when you commit to working hard. Those who remain dedicated, and who work here and at home, can pass up even the more talented players who do not put in the time."*

✓ **Keys to progress.** *"We explain things for reasons, not just to hear ourselves talk. Please pay attention. You should be willing to try our suggestions and practice when you leave here."*

✓ **Versatility.** *"Learning more positions at a young age will only help you in the future. Don't worry if you're asked to play different positions than the ones you like."*

✓ **Feeling comfortable.** *"Don't be afraid to fail, because whether you are afraid or not, you will fail at one time or another. Mistakes happen, and we will help you learn from them."*

✓ **Team contract agreement.** *"We want you to pull for each other. When one player struggles, the next one picks them up."*

✓ **Parent responsibility.** *"Parents, we want you to support the coaching staff and the players. Reinforcing the things we teach in encouraging ways is vital."*

✓ **Final pledge.** *"The coaches will do our best to keep the fun in the game, but part of that is the attitude you bring each day."*

Final Thoughts

The initial team address is a reiteration of the coaching staff's philosophy. The opening talk is most valuable with older athletes, as they can be a *"tough sell."*

When coaches fail to enthuse everyone the first day, it makes it harder to develop the passion later.

There's no need to mention winning in the lead-off speech – it should be about players' improvement and the excitement of playing.

CONVINCING THEM ON DAY 2 - THE "FUNDAMENTALS HOOK"

"The key is not the will to win. Everybody has that. It is the will to prepare to win that is important."

– Coach Bobby Knight, Basketball

Preview – Coaches must convince people of the importance of doing things the right way.

"There is a reason you can do it in practice but not in games."

– Coach explaining the importance of the fundamentals

Of all the unease I hear from parents, at the top of the list is the notion that players can do so well in training, but then not perform as well in games. With the second talk of the season, I try to establish the importance of the fundamentals. My goal is to convince players and parents of the necessity of doing things the right way. I want them to trust that the coaching staff knows ways for players to be successful when it counts most - in games. I further want everyone to know that previous ways of doing things may need to be adjusted, and that usually the change pays off in the end.

The above message may seem a bit excessive, but I assure you it's not. I see this all the time with youth athletes. After a coach tells a player what to do, the player looks to dad for affirmation or further instruction. Coaches find out soon how many experts are out there – parents that is. Many parents have a background in the sport, so they believe they know the best ways to do things. Coaching frustration sets in when players look elsewhere for instruction and disregard what the coaches are trying to teach them.

140

At some point in your coaching career, you will likely have one of these hesitant-to-change players. Many athletes, at all levels, are unwilling to make the changes that the coaches advise. They believe their parent, friends, or another coach's suggestions are the right ones. And sometimes they're right, but you must convince everyone that you know a thing or two about the game, too. Without getting the parents on your side, players may be hesitant to try your suggestions. When this happens, player development becomes difficult and slows down. Most of all, you may get the sense that your time and expertise is going to waste.

Your second speech of the season should also include parents. It should stress the importance of doing the basics.

The fundamentals talk, mentioned some in the introductory message, consists of these points:

- ✓ **An optimistic thought.** *"There is a good chance you already know how to do some things. I am sure your parents taught you well. That is super, and we will continue to reinforce those habits."*

- ✓ **The reality.** *"But, you must see that success now is not always an indicator of correctness. Superb athletes, which I know you are, overcome bad mechanics for a while. However, doing things incorrectly catches up to everybody. Remember, there is always room for improvement, and that is one reason you are here."*

- ✓ **The hook.** *"For those of you who have hopes of playing in high school or beyond, doing things the right way is a must. That correct way has to start now. The longer you wait to change, the harder it will be later."*

- ✓ **The reward.** *"Players who commit to the fundamentals have the best chance of having fun and playing down the line."*

- ✓ **Your options.** *"You have a choice. You can continue to do it your way and be competent for a short while, or you can learn to do it the right way and have an excellent chance of reaching your potential. Doing something 'right' vs. doing it 'almost right' is the difference between a long career and short one. Ask your parents about that if you have doubts."*

✓ **The final hook.** *"Now, for those willing to make the changes, no guarantee of immediate success exists. But, I promise it will come. The correct way of doing things can open the door to betterment. Most of all, doing things the right way leads to more joy, trust me."*

✓ **Ending statement.** *"As coaches, we would appreciate you following our instruction. Any parents who want to discuss this with us after are welcome to."*

Final Thoughts

Over the course of the season, I am constantly reinforcing the above ideas. Some of my often-used comments attest to the importance of great fundamentals.

✓ *"Give me the fundamentals and I will take my chances with the mental part of the game."*

✓ *"Fundamentals are fundamentals for a reason; they work."*

✓ *"Fundamentals are the same for the Little League player and the major league player."*

✓ *"If you stay focused on the fundamentals day in and day out, you will surprise yourself with how fast you improve."*

✓ *"When things are not working, get back to the basics."*

✓ *"Talent only takes one so far, the mechanics are necessary to take you the rest of the way."*

You should never be disingenuous and promise things you cannot deliver. Sometimes, you must admit your knowledge level is insufficient to help players overcome their faults. People admire that honesty.

With older athletes, I add this: *"Not only do you have to be able to do the mechanics the right way, but you must learn to do them faster. There is always work to do, no matter how capable you are now. Those unwilling to make changes and put in the time are sorry later."*

EMPLOYING THE KEYS TO QUALITY TRAINING

"Most people get excited about games, but I've got to be excited about practice, because that's my classroom."

– Coach Pat Summitt, Basketball

Preview – Thriving workouts are the key to fun, player and team growth. When players look forward to their training as much as they want to play the games, the coaches have won.

"To find out how effective a coach is, attend a team practice."

– Suggestion to parents when looking for a new team.

I have done thousands of clinics, camps, and group classes over the years. Even after all that experience, whenever I just wing it, I feel unsatisfied afterward. I always seem to feel that not as much progress occurred as should have.

Teams with talent usually win, but coming out on top is not always an accurate measure of a quality coach. The best leaders have teams that show season-long improvement and obvious athlete enjoyment while playing. That result begins with having well-run practices. Boring, unorganized practices are the reason many kids lose enthusiasm for an activity. They are also the basis for players showing little improvement throughout the season.

A primary step in the process is to actually define practice.

Practice Is:
1. A time for teams to learn and work hard.
2. A time for experimentation, preparation, and progression.

143

3. Not a guaranteed success maker, but it makes achievement and improvement possible.

4. A commendable goal itself, regardless of the end results.

5. A way of keeping regret away because it helps players know they prepared.

6. An avenue to knowledge of the sport and conditioning of the body.

7. A time for team socialization and bonding.

After Giving Teams a Definition of Practice, Coaches Can

➢ **Explain the nature of practice.** Impressive practice does not always lead to the desired game outcomes, and bad practices do not predict setbacks. You should remind players to not get discouraged *or* over confident from practice. *"Hey, it's only practice; don't beat yourself up over it,"* and *"Do not take it for granted, games are a whole other thing"* are some of my typical statements.

➢ **Plan workouts in advance and tweak as necessary.** Omissions occur with last minute planning.

➢ **Prepare captivating talks, drills, and exciting things, especially during the opening weeks of training.** Hooking kids on the sport from the start is the key to their season-long interest.

➢ **Use video in early sessions.** Kids love seeing themselves, and it helps them understand what they are doing and what they need to do.

➢ **Follow a written agenda.** Having something in writing designates what to do and the time limits for each segment. Supervised stations with reasonable time limits work well.

➢ **Set objectives.** Give coaches and players objectives to meet at the start of every practice.

➢ **Challenge players according to their ability.** Often, the better players are bored or leave for another sport because they are not challenged appropriately.

➤ **Have some free play sessions.** Let players pick their teams and play with little or no coaching. This time relaxes teams and gives coaches an opportunity to observe who the team leaders may be.

➤ **Avoid long lectures.** Talking too long can become ineffective, as attention spans are short in younger athletes.

➤ **Use game-like action and skill work for conditioning purposes.** Instead of wasting time with non-sport specific activity during practice, coaches should use normal training in ways that enhance conditioning.

➤ **Use pictures and demonstrations.** An image can say more than a lengthy explanation.

➤ **Give players strength gaining, sport-specific exercises from the first day onward to do at home.** Continuing to work at home will help players advance more quickly.

➤ **Have breaks.** Giving players time to rest and develop friendships is important.

➤ **Use competitive contests, especially when kids appear sluggish.** Contests spur interest and effort as much as anything.

➤ **Begin with something exciting, but save the things that players enjoy most for later in practice.** Athletes maintain some enthusiasm when they have something to look forward to.

➤ **Incorporate variety into every get-together.** Players grow weary from doing the same things. Find different ways and methods to keep them engaged.

➤ **Make note of what worked.** That analysis leads to adjustments for the next time.

➤ **Have players self-analyze and explain their actions.** Doing so helps them absorb the correct concepts.

➤ **Find the drills that counteract bad habits.** These methods are often different from player to player.

➤ **Encourage questions.** End practice with, *"Any questions?"* and *"Are you sure no one has any questions?"* Coaches need players to have a clear idea of the things that need work, so it's important to make sure they have that clarity and know kids feel comfortable to ask.

Final Thoughts

Coaches will see that for many athletes, the learning window is only open for a short time. Once games begin, things change as production concerns and parental coercion come into play. The best time to reach players is the first few weeks of the season. The early-season practices are when players are most receptive to coaching instructions because:

- ✓ Enthusiasm is high after a break away from the game.
- ✓ Players are not as comfortable around the coaches in the beginning, so they are on good behavior.
- ✓ Attention spans are longer when the material is new.
- ✓ Players are not overwhelmed yet with "*do this, do that*" instruction from many sources.
- ✓ Players have less duress on them in the preseason.
- ✓ Habits have not formed yet. Mechanical changes come easier in the beginning than they will after many weeks of incorrect skill repetitions.

With that in mind, you should use your best material from day one to hook players on learning and the love of the sport.

You should end sessions with all players in mind, those who were productive, and those who were weak. "*Hard work pays off, no matter how things went today,*" is the coaching message to pass on.

Some of the best athletes are not effective practice players, but they raise their level of play in games. This type of player is few and far between, and not the ones you should use as examples to other athletes.

COACHING THE WHY

"I think the most important thing about coaching is that you have to have a sense of confidence about what you're doing. You have to be a salesman."

— Coach Phil Jackson, Basketball

Preview – Knowing *"why"* is critical for change, advancement, and coaching credibility.

"There's a reason why I want you to do it this way."

— Diplomatic coaching argument

I learned early on in my coaching career the many reasons why it's important to give clear explanations of why and how.

First, athletes are often resistant to change and need a reason to understand why your way may work better than their current way.

Second, coaches are competing for players' ears with parents and other coaches.

Third, players learn faster when they understand the strategies and fundamentals.

Fourth, knowing the why helps players adjust in the heat of the moment. Adjustments are a crucial element of sports and knowledge helps players make them.

Fifth, if you're able to give convincing reasons, you'll gain credibility with your players.

Here are typical situations where knowledge of why pays off.

Scene 1 - Two players of the same ability and fundamentals encounter a powerful opponent. One of them has a real understanding of the mechanics and strategy while the other does not. The player with better knowledge has a chance of figuring out how to adjust and often does so.

Scene 2 – A player goes into a slump. Without knowledge of the basics, he or she has little clue of how to get out of it. An understanding of the basics creates a better chance of making the necessary adjustments.

Here are teaching suggestions that can work.

Coaches Should:
- ➢ Give the how and why of actions and strategies. Even the youngest players should be told *why*, though concepts may go over their heads.
- ➢ Point out the incorrect ways of doing things, too, so players know what not to do.
- ➢ Ask players, "*Why do we do it this way?*" Their answers can demonstrate what and how much they already comprehend.
- ➢ Review the whys before and after workouts and games.
- ➢ Give written or emailed copies of game plans and skill work with explanations of how and why to do them.
- ➢ Make sure other coaches know the reasons for moves and are giving players the same consistent answers.

Final Thoughts
Performing is easier in a controlled practice environment. But, in a more uncontrolled environment, like during pressure-packed games, adjustments are more difficult. Players with a deeper understanding of the game have a better chance of playing well.

Knowledge builds conviction.

You should instruct as if all players will coach someday.

BEATING BOREDOM

"To be as good as it can be, a team has to buy into what you as the coach are doing. They have to feel you're a part of them, and they're a part of you."

– Coach Bobby Knight, Basketball

Preview – Preventing boredom is a consistent challenge for coaches.

"Do we have to do this?"

– Everyday athlete statement

Having run thousands of sports camps and clinics over the years, I know about bored athletes. I've learned what kids like. But, that doesn't mean I keep all players engaged and happy *all* the time. Some players lose interest right away, no matter how exciting the drills. Maybe they lack real caring for the sport from the beginning. Coaches aren't miracle workers. I feel successful if I can keep most players engaged and I accept the challenge of getting them all interested as time goes by.

At one time or another, all coaches have heard the *"This is boring"* statement, or they've seen that look on a player's face. Multiply that sentiment by a whole team, and coaches have their work cut out for them. All sports have dull moments when coaches must work on tedious aspects. Players tire, a loss of interest sets in, and little progress comes. Coaches might notice players looking around a lot or rolling their eyes at suggestions. The bold kids whine about what they're doing and ask what time it is or when they're going to do something else. Young athletes ask to go to the restroom every couple of minutes.

Keeping boredom away is challenging enough with dedicated players. Maintaining energy with those who have little interest is even more difficult. All athletes need inspiration at times, or developmental stagnation comes. Coaches must know the things that tend to produce monotony, and it's important to find ways to keep things exciting and fresh.

These Will Often Result in Team or Player Boredom:
- ✓ Too many players standing around with nothing to do.
- ✓ Coaches talking too long.
- ✓ Spending too much time on one thing.
- ✓ Repeating what players are doing wrong to the point that they tire of hearing it.
- ✓ Failing to challenge players.
- ✓ Coaching only a select few players, leaving some players feeling uninterested and underappreciated.
- ✓ Too little competition.
- ✓ Having the same practice agenda time after time.

Coaches should use the following ways to keep things vital while maintaining the goal of player development.

Coaches Should:
- ➢ Figure out ways to have as many players as possible active at all times. Small group stations are a great way to accomplish this in practice.
- ➢ Use different ways of instructing the same things.
- ➢ Give short instructions throughout. This is better than giving one long speech or many details in the beginning. For instance, coaches provide brief instructions for plays and have players go out and practice. After doing that, coaches call players back in for another explanation of the next drill. This process of short *explanation, then practice* is more effective. These quick meeting sessions are a great way to en-

sure players focus on one thing at a time, rather than working on many things at once.

➤ Actually *show* athletes how to do something and rely less on verbal instructions. There are more visual learners than there are auditory ones.

➤ Challenge athletes and teams with daily targets to meet. Regularly testing each player on what they are capable of doing helps maintain interest and progress.

➤ Use competition often. Nothing spices up a practice like a little competition can. Games and contests enthuse kids. You can add a little rivalry into almost any sports situation with some imagination. Working on monotonous things by making them competitive in some way helps maintain athletes' attention.

Final Thoughts

When I sense players are losing interest, I pose this question - *"Who wants a challenge?"* That query gets kids excited, and they begin to anticipate something more stimulating. This go to plan should be something that's more challenging than usual. It's an excellent way to pick up the energy levels. It also works because it's almost impossible to ask, *"Who wants a challenge?"* without changing your tone of voice and energy level. Kids and coaches recognize that spirit and become excited. Most athletes love challenges.

Individual or small group contests should be in a way that everyone has a chance of being victorious. Coaches may have to handicap some of the competitions. All team members should win from time to time, so discouragement and a lack of effort do not set in.

Players must take some initiative to prevent boredom from setting in, too. Coaches should help players with self-motivating actions. I find myself saying this a lot, *"I know it may seem boring, focus more on doing it right, then we won't have to keep doing it."*

UTILIZING OTHER EXCITING PRACTICE IDEAS

"Get the buy in, coach the mind, the rest then follows."

– Coach Robin Clarkson, Field Hockey

Preview – Besides the normal skill and game strategy practice, other ways exist to excite athletes.

"Practice was awesome today."

– Player to parent

Many kids just want to play the games, but going to practice is another story. Kids not wanting to go to practice is at the top of the list of parent concerns that I hear. My response to that is always, *"What is the coach like?"* Coaches who know how to spice things up keep up player enthusiasm. Adding something unique to every workout helps players look forward to them.

Following are samples of ways you can add some energy and excitement.

Coaches Can:
- ➤ Tell or ask players for an appropriate sports-related joke during break times.
- ➤ Begin or end sessions with an inspirational short story about a famous athlete.
- ➤ Open with high energy and competitive things. Sandwich the tedious parts of training in the middle with a rousing end.
- ➤ End sessions with gameplay and less instruction.
- ➤ Have an exciting go-to exercise or competition for times when kids need a pick-me-up.

➤ Sport-specific relay races are always something to fall back on. They condition players, too.

There are other creative ways you can add some liveliness and unpredictability.

Coaches Can:

➤ Have an autograph day with kids exchanging pictures and autographs.

➤ Film interviews with players to view at a team party.

➤ Devise a parents' vs. kids' game and handicap the adults in some way to keep it fair and safe.

➤ Come up with a safe player vs. coach challenge of skills.

➤ Have a team parent make a scrapbook online for players to download during or after the season.

➤ Take the team to a local college or high school game and point out how the players execute plays.

➤ Bring a guest player to meet the players. Even a local high school player is memorable to young athletes.

➤ Set up a movie night. Getting the team together to watch an inspirational sports movie, especially before big games, is a bonding and motivating move.

➤ Encourage the team to develop a unique team congratulatory gesture for use by them only.

➤ Use sports trivia contests to encourage players to watch or follow the college or professional games at home.

➤ Set up a simple fantasy league of the professional sport.

➤ Give out handouts related to the sport at the end of practices. Kids love getting things even if they are practice tips or sport specific pictures.

Final Thoughts

Having little prizes like trading cards to spur a little more effort is OK.

Having alternating, designated parents bring a little healthy treat occasionally is good for exciting young athletes to look forward to practices.

Memorable occasions build enthusiasm and may hook players on the sport forever.

High school and college-age athletes are helpful assistant coaches, too. Many kids are less intimidated by younger adults.

APPLYING THE FUN PRODUCERS

"Do you know what my favorite part of the game is? The opportunity to play."

– Coach Mike Singletary, Football

Preview – Quality coaches know that having fun is more than appearance and suggestion.

"What do you mean did I have fun? I sat on the bench most of the game."

– Annoyed player

The one thing I hear coaches say all the time is, *"Have fun."* The *"Just have fun"* message is useful advice, as it should be. However, simply saying or insisting that enjoyment is a priority does little to actually make it so. The problem is that many coaches don't make things enjoyable because they don't know what that involves. They intend playing to be pleasing, but what makes up fun is vague to a lot of volunteer coaches.

A top coaching goal, along with player development, should be giving kids what they want – fun. It must be a priority at all levels, from the non-competitive level to the most competitive teams. This is only possible when coaches know and apply the things that make playing pleasurable.

Enjoyment Comes from these:
- ✓ **Opportunity.** Satisfaction rarely exists without sufficient testing of skills. That alone is the reason why equal playing time is crucial for youth sports. The more you believe triumph is the primary goal, the less opportunity you'll give to players. Playing less than others wears on athletes, and the enjoyment will eventually fade. Just because kids may not flourish as much as others doesn't mean they will be OK with not playing as much.
- ✓ **Contests.** Competition is exciting for athletes. They enjoy a test of their abilities against others.
- ✓ **A measure of proficiency.** Experiencing joy relies on achievement, no matter how minor it may be. Constant setbacks can take the desire away faster than anything else. Player skill enhancement is crucial before frustration gets a hold of them. Even minor improvement is enough to keep most going. Of course, players have a responsibility too because minimal effort produces few favorable outcomes.
- ✓ **Education.** Learning excites people.
- ✓ **Personal challenge.** Athletes not only enjoy competing against others, they like to outdo their previous efforts.
- ✓ **Pride.** Athletes love the feeling of doing something well. Also, they gain great pleasure from making their biggest fans – their parents – happy.
- ✓ **Attention.** All kids deserve the coach's time and tips.
- ✓ **Enthusiasm.** Players take on the expression of their coaches. When the leaders have little passion, players tend to follow suit with less energy and zeal for play.
- ✓ **Approval.** Little in sport is more fun than receiving recognition for advancement and achievement.

✓ **Being part of a team**. Belonging to a group of people who are out for the same goal helps players have an identity beyond themselves.

✓ **Physical activity**. Running around to release energy and tension is stimulating for most kids.

✓ **Variety of practice methods**. Same old, same old is never exciting for young players.

✓ **Camaraderie**. Developing friendships can make the hard work bearable.

✓ **Maximizing effort**. Giving one's best brings a euphoric feeling.

✓ **Contributing**. Bringing one's unique gifts besides their sport skills is stimulating and fun for kids.

Final Thoughts

Failing to captivate kids is not always a coach's fault, even though they may be the ones blamed for it. With some players, it's not the coach, but a lack of competence or love of the sport that causes a lack of enjoyment. Players rarely persevere for long without liking to play at least a little from the beginning.

Often, parents' expectations of volunteer coaches are too high. When it's evident players are not enjoying it, you should ask the athlete what's going on. Their answers may help you figure out ways of making things more exciting. The season drags for everyone when players aren't having fun.

Winning helps attitudes, but coaches must never forget that players do not have to win to have fun.

When the coaching philosophy revolves around player growth, amusement usually follows for all interested athletes.

CHAPTER 7

———⁓———

Creating Positive Communication

Knowing the little things that get the best out of players and teams is pivotal. That knowledge and ability separates the merely competent from the outstanding coaches. Giving players a voice is crucial for their and the team development.

This story is an exchange I had with an athlete, which attests to the importance of having open communication with everyone involved.

One of my ballplayers was ripping the cover off the ball with a great swing. I was so proud to see it, because I had observed how far she had progressed over time. She returned the next practice and fell back into her old inconsistent, incorrect habits. It hurt me to ask but I did, "*What happened?*" She replied, "*I don't know, I worked so hard this week.*" I countered with, "*Next time we get it figured out, don't work so hard.*" She came back with, "*I didn't know you could work too hard?*"

She had me, because if I said *"You can,"* I would destroy everything her parents and coaches had preached to her. I was grateful her dad chimed in with *"If it ain't broke, there's nothing to fix."* I came back with, *"When it all seems to click, ease up on the work load on that particular skill and devote more time to other aspects of the game."*

MIKE KRZYZEWSKI

Another of the coaching superstars is Duke University's men's basketball coach, Mike Krzyzewski. *"Coach K"* creates a champion's environment without putting all the emphasis on winning.

Mike Krzyzewski is one of the finest recruiters of athletes. He is up front with players about what they can expect when they join his team. Coach K does not talk about national championships. He does talk about developing relationships and being a family. He not only talks of this, but he also creates a family atmosphere with his players that demonstrate it.

Mike helps players feel togetherness in 3 ways.

First, he has his team set goals on what they want to achieve and how they will present themselves in that process.

Second, Coach K makes sure players understand that their role and everyone is a crucial part of the team, no matter how much they play.

Third, he allows players to express their opinions and have a part in team decisions. All these things connect players with a closeness that makes them feel like a family.

Coach K helps his players learn how to be there for each other through the extraordinary and harsh times. He creates relationships that work beyond the courts and forever. Mike is a believer in observing players' demeanor, and when he senses change, he asks players about it. He is cognizant that there is a person behind the athlete, and when a player is hurting off the court, it affects them on it. He wants players to speak their mind and to have someone who'll listen to them when they need to get things off their chest.

Lessons Learned from Coach Mike Krzyzewski:

1. Coaches can teach players how to be there for each other in all situations.
2. Relationships are what sports are all about. That awareness means things pass both ways – from player to coach as well as from coach to player.
3. Players, who have a vision, feel valued, and have input, show it with a determined approach.
4. Teams can be like families where the bond goes deeper than just playing together.

ERADICATING BULLYING

"Coaches have to watch for what they don't want to see and listen to what they don't want to hear."

– Coach John Madden, Football

Preview – Coaches must know the signs of harassment and act on it immediately.

"I can't believe Mikey slugged Bobby; it was just some good natured trash talking going on."

– Coach to an assistant

Early in my coaching career, I let little things slide with players. I quickly learned this was wrong. Failing to act led to a bigger headache, as parent involvement came and I had to explain my hesitancy.

A fine line exists between good-natured ribbing and intimidating tactics. At the youth sports level, small intimidating acts often start as a fun thing. People believe it's just *"kids being kids."* Harmless actions may begin with knocking off players' hats or snickering. But it can get uglier with someone pulling another player's shorts down and making fun of others. Players laugh and seem to think it's amusing, so coaches believe everything is OK. What you may not know is that the player being taunted may not be laughing inside. The seemingly fun acts turn into bullying – aggressive behavior that means to intimidate. The bully wants to exert control over another.

Just as serious an issue in sports is hazing – rituals that initiate players to the team in some way. The consequences of bullying and hazing are psychological and emotional confusion. Those offensive actions can depress the victims for a long time.

Hazing, bullying, and harassment of any sort has no place in sports, at any level. You need to be able to recognize that what might seem like fun to some is offensive and hurtful to others. When coaches do nothing, things can escalate quickly. You must stop harassment at the initial sign of it no matter how innocuous it seems. If you're not sure about questionable interactions, you should act on the side of caution and end them. When parents get wind of an issue, lawyers and a coaching nightmare may follow.

Following are suggestions to stop harassment in its tracks.

Coaches Should:

➤ Never bully players, either. Players will follow a coach's lead, and if they see adults do it, they will act the same.

➤ Tell parents they should be careful of what they tell their children. With or without realizing it, some parents encourage behavior that leads to harassment. When parents give their child instructions like *"Take no bull from anyone"* and "Show *them how tough you are*," it may result in alarming incidents.

➤ Institute a no-harassment rule to everyone at the opening parent gathering. Inform parents that any sign of threatening player-to-player behavior is unacceptable. You should advise parents to relay this message to their kids.

➤ Encourage team members to come to the coaches if another person bothers them in any way. A subtle sign of harassment is small talk when players are out of the coach's hearing range. Any report of players picking on others is worth investigating.

➤ Have a policy of keeping words to self, no swearing, and no offensive talk about body parts.

➤ Institute these guidelines:

- Hands-off others.
- No cutting in lines.
- No laughing at other players' play or skill level.
- No trash talking.

➤ Watch for and discourage cliques. Small groups may exclude others and be another subtle sign of player mistreatment.

➤ Watch for and disallow any signs of an initiation ritual, even when it seems like harmless behavior. Once players believe it's OK, initiations can lead to distasteful acts the next time.

➤ Talk to athletes whose demeanor changes to find out if anything is bothering them. Individual conversations are always necessary if you notice behavior changes.

➤ Show appreciation for all and talk to teams with consideration, too.

➤ Talk to the team often about the importance of valuing teammates and opposing teams.

Final Thoughts

It bears repeating; coaches must never dismiss offensive actions as *kids just being kids*.

Coaches must follow up on any accusations, even in cases where the accused is the child of a close friend, one of the best players, or a coach's child.

Stopping bullies and hazing at the lower levels will limit them at the upper levels.

RELATING WITH A PERSONAL TOUCH

"A common mistake among those who work in sport is spending a disproportional amount of time on 'X's and O's' as compared to time spent learning about people."

— Coach Mike Krzyzewski, Basketball

Preview — Coaches should get to know players beyond the field. That pursuit earns respect and inspires players to give their best.

"Coach is a jerk; I could care less if we win."

— Irritated player

As an athlete who made it to the top level, I always felt I played hard and played to win. When I liked and looked up to my coach, it pushed me all the more. Human nature takes over for most people, and they want the best for those who are good to them. Athletes who feel a connection to their coaches and look up to them tend to play with higher purpose. Athletes generally don't want to disappoint the people close to them.

A key to having a healthy player-coach relationship is having a personal connection to every player. Getting to know your athletes shows them they are more than what they do on the field. That knowledge helps build self-esteem in youth. Knowing you're on their side, win or lose, helps their confidence and gives them faith in *all* adults. Winning, losing, individual achievement, and collapse are all easier to handle with strong connections to coaches.

Here are ways that coaches can offer a personal touch.

Coaches Should:

- ➤ Look players in the eye when addressing them.
- ➤ Explain and have an open door policy so players feel comfortable discussing concerns.
- ➤ Pay particular interest in shy players and those who seem to not fit in with others. Having them feel a part of things is your job.
- ➤ Encourage and answer questions from team members. Many kids like to talk, so coaches should give them the opportunity at the appropriate times.
- ➤ Have all the coaches share stories that give insights into their background and character. Players become comfortable when they see a personal side of adults.
- ➤ Talk to players one-on-one before games to gauge their feelings and ask about any concerns they may have. When coaches notice a change in player attitude, they should see if they want to talk about anything.
- ➤ Offer affirming words to each player, not just to the whole team.
- ➤ Call sensitive players aside to provide constructive advice. Some kids retreat even more when put in the limelight.
- ➤ Give players a sports-related nickname.
- ➤ Use small talk to get to know players' interests beyond the ball field. Coaches should be aware of other family members and the schools that kids attend. Awareness and recalling the little things can show players you care about them, which helps them relax.
- ➤ Use the non-sport small talk when players seem tense and hard on themselves. Diverting their thoughts for a spell reminds players that it's just a game.
- ➤ Joke with your players from time to time.
- ➤ Bring up memorable past plays that players felt proud of having.
- ➤ Take responsibility for losses, instead of letting players feel it was on them.
- ➤ Show empathy when players are down after training.

Final Thoughts

Running into a player you coached after the season or even years later, and knowing their name is a significant boost to a kid's self-esteem, too. The more you address them by name and get to know them, the better chance of remembering them in the future.

BREEDING A DEMOCRACY

"A coach should never be afraid to ask questions of anyone he could learn from."

— Coach Bobby Knight, Basketball

Preview — Athletes work harder and follow procedures better when they have a say. Leaders must encourage input and be willing to listen.

"What do you feel we need to work on?"

— Coach to the team

The above is a question I often ask players. It's exciting to hear that, more often than not, they are right on target with their response, even young players.

Studies show that one of the most compelling questions is *"What is your opinion?"* The question makes others feel included and vital. Champion coaches use this tactic when working with teams and individuals. Players who have some input give a better effort, because, after all, it was their idea.

Often, coaches want to run the show and don't ask for or accept feedback. Do-it-my-way coaches don't inspire players like the coaches who ask for suggestions from others do. As a coach, you must put your ego aside and consult with other coaches, parents, and the team. Input from players, assistant coaches, and parents help team chemistry, effort, and performance. It also helps coaches consider details they may have forgotten. Suggestions from others helps keep everyone satisfied, because they all feel they have a stake in the team's plans.

When people have a say, they feel togetherness, power, and a deeper sense of accomplishment. Players push themselves and each other more when they work on things that they suggested. With older athletes, coaches can get feedback on codes of conduct and consequences, too. Players tend to follow rules more when they are the ones who set them and helped determine the consequences of breaking them.

Coaches Should Ask these Questions to Get Everyone Involved:

➢ *"What are our team's goals?"* These aspirations should be more about improvement than the number of wins and losses.

➢ *"What areas need the most work?"* This is vital to ask of parents, too.

➢ *"How are we going to achieve that improvement?"* This decision gives players that push to work hard and a game plan for the future.

➢ *"Do we need to practice more?"* This question can give you an idea if kids are excited and getting value out of their training with you.

➢ *"How often should players practice at home?"* When players decide this themselves, they are more likely to do it.

➢ *"What team regulations do we want?"* It's best to have parents and players involved in team policies.

➢ *"Should we have team captains?"* This is another thing players can decide. In the event teams decide to have captains, coaches can plan to allow all players to be one over the course of the season.

➢ *"Is there something the coaches can do to help everyone learn and enjoy things more?"* Outstanding coaches are not afraid to ask this and make any necessary adjustments based on the answer. This query is most important for teams that show little enthusiasm. Their response may help you plan, which may lead to increased team energy.

Final Thoughts

Asking for feedback shows that you care about relationships. Coaches who act like they have all the answers get less effort and respect.

When you get views from others, you may avoid out of line, second guessing and behind the scenes comments. Communication is best for keeping the team's chemistry.

ENSURING COMMUNICATION

"Communication does not always occur naturally, even among a tight-knit group of individuals. Communication must be taught and practiced in order to bring everyone together as one."

– Coach Mike Krzyzewski, Basketball

Preview – It helps when each player knows their role and its importance.

"Son, I'm going to drop you in the batting order for today only. I believe it will help you relax."

– Coach to struggling player

When I was playing, decisions came from the manager with no explanation. Things simply *were* because managers said so. Players accepted those decisions, often with hurt feelings. Little, if any, back and forth went on, as coaches never asked for player input. From a player's standpoint, it was uncomfortable and frustrating to be in the dark about what the plans were. Having no clue why you weren't in the lineup or why you were riding the bench for a long period didn't help player or team morale.

The coaching technique of *"command and control,"* when coaches made all player and team decisions without the athletes' input was prominent years ago. That technique doesn't work well today because someone, player or parent, will question and object to such tactics. Today's players are different for many reasons. Many athletes feel anxiety and are more sensitive than players of the past. Also, many have a sense of entitlement – the feeling that they are owed something.

When something changes with their playing status, problems may develop for the coach. Considering feelings and communicating with athletes in today's game is obligatory. Honest exchanges with players and parents are critical. They may not always want to hear your view, but it will help them know the player's status. Knowing their standing and what needs improvement gives players a chance to try to do something about it. Also, it gives people a chance to give feedback. They relax more after giving their opinion, which usually keeps them committed to the program.

Communication puts players and teams on the same page. A few words about what management is thinking goes a long way toward player and team continuity. Also, the better the interaction among all, the better the team will respond to distracting situations.

The following are things coaches should do to help the doors of communication remain open.

Coaches Should:

➢ Become familiar with all their players' personalities. Every player is unique. Some players need a lot of nudging to work hard, while others need a gentler approach. Some athletes open up about their thoughts and others do not. When you know each player's personality, you can add the right touch and notice when attitudes change.

➢ Be observant of kids' life situations and take the time to get to know players - their relationship with their parents, their goals, and their interests. The more you know, the easier it is to talk to players and treat them right.

➢ Ask the questions that need asking, and then listen to the answers with an open mind.

➢ Talk to players one-on-one. Offer constructive criticism when necessary. You should be honest about how you see an athlete's devotion, attitude, and preparation.

➢ Give the honest and unbiased evaluations in an empathetic tone. The younger the player, the more delicate the coach should be with analysis. You should never say things that could crush dreams, even if a player's hopes seem unrealistic.

➢ Provide extra talk and thoughtfulness to players in the following situations.

1. When not starting a player, especially one who usually does play with the first squad.

2. When another player has beat a player out of their usual position.

3. When making a substitution for a player in a key moment of the game.

4. When a player is too unhealthy to play.

➢ Use the most opportune time to deliver news to people face to face, when possible. After games is not the best time to talk with people. Email and text correspondence is a cold and timid way to communicate important decisions.

➢ Say things in an optimistic tone to give hope going forward. Any analysis provided with unenthusiastic talk and bad body language typically results in defensiveness and less discussion.

➢ Never rush to answer upset people. Hastiness can lead to responses you may regret later. You should take your time when dealing with angry parents and always remain in a calm manner. It's never helpful when emotions rule a situation.

➢ See the big picture. Players, fans, and the media tend to live game by game, happy when victorious and sad when defeated. As a coach, you must look at the season-long upgrade of athletes.

Final Thoughts

Today's youth want coaches to listen to them and they respect those who do because many other adults in their lives may not.

Empathetic coaching is necessary at the youth levels. It displays itself with thoughtful interaction with athletes and parents. A prominent question to ask players that's helpful is, *"What would you do differently?"* This allows players to get something off their chest without making them defensive with *"Why did you do that?"*

Good coaches help athletes learn to take criticism as a means for improvement, not as personal affronts. You should remind players with this, *"Remember, I'm here to help,"* when they get defensive and upset.

STEERING CLEAR OF PUSHING

"Managing is like holding a dove in your hand. Squeeze it too hard and you kill it; not hard enough and it flies away."

— Coach Tommy Lasorda, Baseball

Preview — Coaches can only do so much to motivate kids. When adults go too far, they risk alienating teams and athletes to the point of making them want to quit.

"You can forget any days off until you win more."

— Demanding coach to team

I regret the few times I showed disgust with players' efforts. Usually, it had more to do with me having a bad day and taking it out on the team. For many, that reaction is most common with your own child.

You shouldn't allow players to just go through the motions with little effort and enthusiasm. But, the risk of losing players forever is high when coaches go over the top with their frustration. You have to look for ways to motivate your athletes without forcing them to do things.

Here is another letter request I received. It's a model of the way many parents think in today's world. Their ambition for their kids is a form of pushing.

Jack,

I was wondering if you might be able to assist one of my girls. She is 10 and wants to get a scholarship to play college softball. Just wondering your thoughts, the best way to go about this and if there are any showcases for players that age?

It's pretty obvious from this letter that it's the parent, not the child, who wants the scholarship. If an 10-year-old is thinking that far ahead, it's because an adult has put that thought in his or her head. Coaches should not speak of scholarships and stardom at young ages. Of course, when a kid has a dream, you should not diminish it, either.

It's not hard to recognize players who've been pushed to play and work harder. They have the look of *"How many times are you going to say the same things? Enough, already."* Parents are often the source of demanding more from players. When coaches follow in that manner, the joy disappears for athletes. After hearing they're not good enough or they need to work harder too often, they begin to lose interest.

All coaches mean well when they try to motivate kids, but many go about it the wrong way. Pushing is another of those often-used terms with little definition. When you push, you place more emphasis on a certain area of a child's life (for example, sports), to the point where success seems more important for the adult than for the child. Pushing is a coaching motivational method that goes beyond standard, supportive conduct. It gives athletes no options — *"Do this or suffer the consequences"* is the message.

"If you don't practice today, you will never get that scholarship you want" is an example of placing undue importance on a kid. Pushing is never showing satis-

faction with how much players do or how they perform. Pushing occurs when adults become obsessed with victory and achievement, without realizing the toll on youth.

The possible implications of forcing athletes to do more are:
- ✓ The loss of friends.
- ✓ Unsportsmanlike or rule-breaking behavior.
- ✓ Kids rebelling with insolent behavior and lazy play.
- ✓ A lack of enjoyment.
- ✓ Burnout.
- ✓ A sense of never being able to please anyone.

Coaches should know the difference between beneficial and bad motivation techniques. A fine line exists between constructive suggestions and motivating with demands.

Pushing begins with frustrated words that give the unyielding messages of *you have to*:
- ✓ Work harder than everybody or else.
- ✓ Practice when others are not.
- ✓ Win because it's the only thing that's important.
- ✓ Do whatever it takes to get the edge.
- ✓ Suffer pain to gain.
- ✓ Never give up.
- ✓ Not let anyone push you around.

On the surface, these statements may seem minor. However, over time they can wear down players' desires and upbeat frames of mind. Athletes feel as though they are only playing to please others, and the message takes away their voice in decisions.

After mild pushy words, sometimes coaches follow with more harmful actions, like:

- ✓ Having players play to fatigue.
- ✓ Forcing players to play with injuries.
- ✓ Accusing players of faking injuries or calling them *"babies"* because they show pain.
- ✓ Threatening players with punishment for poor play and lazy habits.
- ✓ Talking too often about the necessity of striving for college scholarships.
- ✓ Insisting on personal trainers without regard for player wishes.
- ✓ Withholding things like attention, social gatherings, and playing time.

The same things said to different players have different effects. Most players feel the excess strain, but a few may get motivation from caustic coaches. The tone of the coach's voice makes the difference with how players receive messages. When you make suggestions using a matter of fact tone of voice and give options, you have the best chance of *not* alienating players. Things said with an *"If you do this, it will help you achieve your goals"* tone send the message without intimidation. Players who feel like they have a choice are much more willing to listen and try suggestions. Non-pushy coaches deliver messages with hope-filled words.

Here Are Some Examples That Motivate Without Intimidation:

- ✓ *"Sometimes you have to battle through tiredness. I appreciate your effort, but now is the time to look for that little extra."*
- ✓ *"You will be less frustrated if you put more into it."*
- ✓ *"I will help the best I can. If you need additional help, we will find it."*
- ✓ *"I know ways to improve your play if you commit to working on it."*
- ✓ *"Getting to the next level is not an easy step, but if you're willing to apply yourself, I believe you can do it."*

Final Thoughts

Occasional pushy statements may be appropriate for the college and professional levels of sports, but this style of coaching should stay at those levels.

At some point, motivation has to come from the athletes, themselves. That will only come with coaches who allow players time to gain that little extra self-push,

Coaches should apologize to kids after showing excessive frustration. *"I'm sorry I reacted that way. I just want you to be better"* is a good start to regaining a player's respect.

Continual pressure to do more leads some players to use performance enhancing drugs. This is the worst case result of demanding coaches and parents.

Often, the pushing coach is the win-at-all-cost one.

Coaches should back off a little with the instruction and intensity when frustration has set in for athletes.

Adults must treat every aspect of players' lives where effort is important with the same emphasis. Being casual about working hard in school, but being adamant about sports practice is not the right message.

The best coaches find ways of getting athletes to give more of themselves without nagging and alienating them. Adults should realize that when in doubt about what to say, less is best. When you step back a little with irritated players, they appreciate it and often figure things out on their own.

DETECTING THE SIGNS OF BURNOUT

"I'd say handling people is the most important thing you can do as a coach. I've found every time I've gotten into trouble with a player, it's because I wasn't talking to him enough."

– Coach Lou Holtz, Football

Preview – Recognizing the early signs of burnout may rescue a player from quitting.

"They love the game and love to practice; they don't need a break."

– Words from an oblivious coach

I've heard the above reasoning many times in my teaching career. My response usually goes something like *"I don't care how much they love it. Think about how they are going to feel 6 months from now when they still have 3 months to go in their season. And, how are they going to feel 2 years from now after having no breaks over that time? Sure they love it now, but later is when the effects of non-stop play will show up."*

The detrimental effects of driving kids too hard usually won't show at first, but they will later. I could not begin to count the number of talented players I coached who quit before high school. They felt like playing was all they ever did. All sports all the time took time away from friend time, social lives, and school work.

Burnout is the mental, emotional, and physical fatigue from too much. Burnout is a loss of desire and is usually the end of the line for players. When athletes reach the point that playing is no longer enjoyable, rarely does a change of mind occur. Burnout is more prominent than ever because of the stresses from little down time and specialization. The sad thing is that it happens to the most talented players.

Many athletes and parents have the mindset that more is always better. Studies of too much playing prove that is not the case. Coaches should be on the lookout for the signs of burnout. Those signs include players who lose ambition, anger quickly, and ignore team guidelines. They change from excited about playing to less interested. They never appear satisfied and don't listen, but they did in the past. The *"I've had enough"* players were the ones who never seemed to tire or lose enthusiasm before.

The solutions to avoid burnout aren't simple with today's conditions. The answers begin with having breaks from play, so athletes can maintain their competitive hunger.

Following are suggestions to keep mental and physical fatigue away

Coaches Should:

➤ Stress the importance of playing for oneself and the joy of the game, too, not just for others.

➤ Help athletes keep their self-expectations basic and reinforce that achieving more than what they wanted is a bonus.

➤ Watch for stressed athletes and try to get them to talk about their feelings.

➤ Discourage athletes from working to fatigue and explain the dangers of overtraining. Most players and parents believe athletes lose everything they worked for by taking time off. You should explain that timing and talent return quickly after time off and that having a player eager to play after a break benefits his or her development in the short- and long-term.

➤ Not set team or player expectations at an unreasonable level.

Along with these, giving players breaks from play is crucial for maintaining player enthusiasm. Here are time-off suggestions.

Game Day Breaks:

✓ Get athletes away from the game site when playing many games in one day. Even a short car ride or going to a local restaurant can help free the mind.

✓ Have players bring a magazine or book to read during downtime.

✓ Play trivia or other diversionary games between games.

✓ Have players rest in cool areas on hot days and warm places on cold ones.

✓ Recognize kids' behaviors to know when they've had enough or at least need a break. When a player's demeanor changes, you must ease up on the amount of time they put into the sport.

For In-Season Breaks Coaches Should:

➤ Give kids at least 3 days free from playing each week.

➤ Keep the joy in playing by having interesting and enjoyable workouts.

➤ Encourage kids to engage in non-athletic activities.

➤ Find a local charity to help out. Doing something for others helps everyone maintain a healthy frame of mind.

For Off-Season Breaks Coaches Should:

➤ Give 3 to 7 months away from playing, depending on the age of players.

➤ Encourage the playing of other sports during the offseason.

Final Thoughts

Coaches should inform parents of the signs of burnout.

Coaches must encourage and accept an occasional personal break when their personality and attitude change from too much play.

Having an extra player or two on the team from the beginning helps you avoid using athletes to exhaustion.

It's worth repeating that even short mental breaks on game days can revitalize players.

CHAPTER 8

~

Creating Meaning beyond
the Playing Fields

Along the way, coaches have the opportunity to provide life lessons. The life teaching moments turn coaches into the role model kids need.

Here is the story of one of my proudest coaching moments, which shows the powerful influence coaches can have on players.

One of the finest players I ever worked with came in to see me after many years of not being in touch. He was playing professional baseball. After reminiscing for a spell, he posed this question. *"Many of my teammates have taken steroids, and I am wondering if you think I should?"* Taken aback at first, I explained that I knew what a powerful pull the major leagues were. The message I went on to convey was that he had to live with himself long after making the choice and after playing baseball.

He seemed to nod in agreement, but I wasn't sure he was convinced of what to do until I noticed he retired later that off-season. I was happy that he made the right decision, and was proud of him for having the courage to ask the question. The memory of him respecting me enough to discuss such a decision is a humbling one. Our years of working together built up a trusting relationship. He knew I cared not just about his athletic career, but for him as a person, too.

TOM IZZO

Another of the finest coaches is Michigan State University basketball coach Tom Izzo. Coach Izzo has developed a winning culture with a philosophy that revolves around player accountability.

Before the season, Izzo has his players write down their goals for everything. Those areas are for on the court, in the classroom, and off the court. Coach Izzo has players give him their responses so he can keep track of things. As the season proceeds, Coach Izzo compares how players are doing with their objectives. When he feels like a player is not meeting their intentions, he points that out to them. He also helps them figure out ways of improving upon reaching their ambitions. Tom believes that if they were goals in the first place, they should remain that way. He believes a coach's job is to find ways to help players reach their stated purposes.

Coach Izzo teaches that being a good teammate is as praiseworthy as being a star player. Few athletes are the elitist of players, but all can be exceptional teammates.

Also, Coach Izzo tries to build strong leaders on the team. He knows that leadership comes not only from the coaches but from other players, too. Players may ignore the coach at times, but they will think long and hard before challenging a peer.

Lessons Learned from Coach Tom Izzo:

1. Having goals for the right things help keep focus.
2. Holding players accountable is imperative. Of course, there is a difference between the college level and youth level in regards to the amount of accountability.
3. Helping players learn to prepare and give their best gives them the chance to reach their ambitions.
4. Developing leadership qualities is another coaching task. The leaders do not have to be the star player, just one of exemplary character.

DEVELOPING LEADERS

"My responsibility is leadership, and the minute I get negative, that is going to have an influence on my team."

– Coach Don Shula, Football

Preview – Leadership begins with the example of the coaches.

"Way to take charge out there."

– Coach to a player

A young ballplayer I coached had an unusual habit. Although in the game, he went to the players who were not in the game at the end before congratulating the ones on the field. That was quite a display of leadership. That behavior made an impact on other players who began the same ritual. Nothing teaches like example does.

The famous quote from John Wooden's book says so much. *"No written word, no spoken plea can teach our youth what they should be, nor all the books on all the shelves, it's what the teachers are themselves."* (Anonymous author).

When coaches display leadership qualities, players see first-hand how leaders behave. Coaches with self-control, consistency, enthusiasm, and pride give athletes an excellent picture of guiding others. Some players have natural leadership abilities, and coaches can enhance those and more. You can help develop management skills in all athletes.

Following are the leadership traits coaches should have, look for, and develop in others:

- ✓ **Humility**. Coaches should not take the credit for prevailing or other's success. You are just another cog in the wheel. You can explain that it's the efforts of all that leads to individual and team triumph.
- ✓ **Passion**. Having a spark with words and actions above and beyond others is a sign of a leader.
- ✓ **Understanding**. Coaches know that sports proficiency comes and goes, but they must be willing to work with all players whether they are successful or not.
- ✓ **Empathy**. Coaches should act with the realization that sports are just *one* aspect of players' lives, and not the main one. You can showcase schoolwork and family relationships as a case in point of things more important.
- ✓ **Commitment**. By giving a solid effort, day in and day out, coaches display the work ethic they want kids to develop.
- ✓ **Accountability**. People have a higher opinion of those who are willing to take the blame for bad performances. Coaches are the ones to do that with youth athletes. *"We have to prepare you better the next time"* is one way you can deflect the fault from the team.
- ✓ **Optimism**. The best coaches are able to teach others to have faith that things will turn around when growth does not show.

✓ **Altruism**. Coaches should applaud kids who sacrifice personal goals for the betterment of the whole.

✓ **Resilience**. Leaders bounce back from any hardship and help others do the same.

✓ **Acknowledgment**. Good coaches give credit where it is due, even if it means recognition of an opposing player or team.

✓ **Curiosity**. Influential people never feel as though they have all the answers. They ask questions and seek out knowledge to further themselves and their team.

✓ **Honesty**. Coaches who admit they do not have the solution to something gain respect more than those who pretend to know everything.

✓ **Obligation**. All athletes ought to learn they represent more than themselves and that their actions exemplify the whole.

✓ **Consideration**. Coaches, who allow athletes to speak and listen to them, display an essential ingredient of leadership.

✓ **Gratitude**. Leaders let others know how appreciated they are. They make people feel like they are somebody.

Final Thoughts

Any time coaches notice players showing any of the above qualities, they should make a point of mentioning it to everyone.

People often associate leadership with the best player. But the star players who do not work hard will not be the team leaders, at least not for long. Without passion and a consistent work ethic, others will not follow. You must point that out to those who do not work hard but believe their success warrants them to be the team voice. Of course, the ideal coaching situation is when the most talented players have the highest character.

At the higher levels of sports, it's hard for an athlete to be a team leader without having personal success. However, leaders at the youth level do not have to be the best players. An athlete with an infectious personality may fill that role. Coaches should encourage players to be themselves, allowing characters to emerge and encouraging others to follow those who display leadership.

A useful method for teaching leadership is putting players in a leadership role. The *"Captain of the Day"* can do just that. Coaches can choose a different player each day and have that player make some decisions for the team. Captain for a Day helps players develop assurance, self-esteem, and responsibility.

Coaches should point out the positive sports leadership stories that are in the daily news.

MATURING YOUTH WITH DISCIPLINE

"Discipline and demand without being demeaning."

– Coach Don Meyer, Basketball

Preview – Things can get out of control quickly without consistent and immediate action for disrespectful conduct. Establishing appropriate control does not make you a bad or negative coach.

"You are not going to humiliate my child like that."

– Irate parent warning

I will never forget the young ballplayer who karate kicked a base stealer at one of my baseball camps. The karate kid said he was following coaching instructions of, *"Do not let the runner steal."* This instance was funny on one level, but it's a good reminder that many athletes let their emotions get the best of them.

If you coach long enough, you'll encounter the player who's ready to fight or challenge others verbally at the drop of the ball. A fine line exists between competitive athletes and those who cannot control their actions. Some sports have and allow more aggression than others, but whenever players are out to intimidate or fight, regardless of the sport, coaches must act. You must not allow things to get out of hand when players are in physical or emotional danger. Your job is to ensure that all players are safe and can play without fear of others.

It was never an enjoyable experience when I felt the need to bench a player or call their parents about behavior. But, when a player's actions disrupted others beyond normal, I felt I had no choice. I always appreciated when parents were all for the actions I took. But, some parents were upset about them.

Discipline can be a dangerous area for coaches. Athletes may not feel the need for it, and parents may not see it the way you do. Many parents believe their kids can do no wrong, which adds to the problem. Before any punishment, coaches must be careful of creating bigger issues. Even running extra laps may upset people. Coaches must discuss behavior expectations in the preseason meeting with parents and athletes. That discussion leads to the regulations that will make future disciplinary moves much easier. Team leaders can help coaches keep players in line with upper-level teams. With youth teams, getting parents on board with any team rules helps with player discipline.

When players show disregard, are disruptive, or ignore team policy, engagement is necessary. It's mandatory that you respond to those, no matter who the culprit is. Letting even one incident slide will make corrective measures in future similar cases difficult. Selective punishment will cause people to lose respect for the coach. Action is also compulsory when something causes physical, emotional, or psychological harm to others. If you feel the need to impart a life lesson, you must proceed.

These tips help coaches to maintain consistent control. A trial and error process may be necessary to find a solution.

Coaches Should:

> ➤ Review the training procedures. Sometimes, goofing around and short attention spans are signs of boredom, not disrespect.

> ➤ Have stated and fair rules based on player and parent input that are appropriate for the ages of players. Those policies involve interactions with others, so players learn to treat others with acceptance. Reviewing what respect for the game and sportsmanship are is necessary.

> ➤ Say it and say it again. Penalizing kids for mistakes is hard when they have not been told right from wrong actions. Older youth should know correct behavior, but coaches should not take for granted that every child knows how to conduct themselves.

> ➤ Gather all the facts before making a decision on what to do.

> ➤ Talk about the importance of self-control and that it's something kids can work on and improve.

> ➤ Act immediately and every time an athlete's emotions gets the best of them. When allowed to get away with antagonistic measures, players tend to become bolder. Escaping discipline from the beginning makes it harder to get them under control later.

> ➤ Remain as calm as possible and don't respond with aggression. Aggressive behavior is what some players know and usually expect. When you act the same, it reinforces the idea that it's OK to solve encounters in that way.

> ➤ Explain to players exhibiting bad conduct that they always have a choice to do the right thing. After that explanation, you should offer options for moving forward.

> ➤ Make clear the reasons for any disciplinary measures. When kids are not sure why they've been chastised, parents may be told a different story. Story variations can lead to upset parents more often than not.

> ➤ Be on the alert for acts of swearing, harassment, or dirty play towards others. Immediate discipline is mandatory for these transgressions.

➤ Meet with the offenders only when a player or two are out of line. You should not scold the whole for the acts of a few. This meeting should be away from others but with another coach on hand, if possible, so it doesn't disgrace players in front of teammates.

When meeting individually doesn't seem to be effective with older players, you can try reprimanding the whole team. This method may not be fair, but it stresses the importance of *"we're a team,"* and what one does as a member of the team affects all. Often, players will get the offending player in line when the whole team has to do something unwanted. Sometimes, peer pressure works best for keeping team policies.

➤ Give problem players more responsibility. Naming them a captain for the day or leader of something may get them in line. A prominent role may help them feel like they're part of something bigger than themselves.

➤ Use a lap or two or a few push-ups to make a quick point to disruptive athletes. That small measure gives them a few minutes to think about their behavior and they may calm down.

➤ Sit a player down. The *"time out"* penalty may give players time away from others to relax and change their outlook.

➤ Discuss player attitudes. You must inform players that refusing to hustle, showing disgust, and disrespecting others are reflections on the whole team and you must penalize them if warnings don't work.

➤ Have a heart-to-heart talk with players. Sometimes, a one-on-one session goes a long way. You should listen and then tell them why their actions were wrong. Ask the player what they can do the next time they feel the same way.

➤ Not allow athletes to blame others for their actions. You must explain why players were in the wrong and the necessity for consequences.

➤ Have the inappropriate player give a sincere apology to anyone they offended, and to the team as a whole if necessary.

➢ Use the bench for players with continual bad attitudes, a lack of hustle, and quarrelsome behavior. This tactic is only appropriate at the advanced levels of play. For young athletes, sitting a player down is only an option when the athlete's behavior is a danger to others. When possible, you should inform parents beforehand if you feel a player must sit out a game. The parents may not agree with the punishment, but you must explain why it is necessary. It's not fair that parents show up to a competition only to find out that their child is not playing for disciplinary reasons.

➢ Never forget to praise players who act under control. Out of order players may learn the desirable behavior in that way.

➢ Meet with a player's parents when nothing seems to help out of line behavior and rule-breaking. This meeting is the last resort and may include the athlete, too.

➢ Continue to coach the penalized players as if nothing happened after their punishment. You may see players change their state of minds when they notice the coach still cares about them.

➢ Discourage the *"tougher than the other person or team"* attitude with players. Coaches should explain that there's a difference between playing hard and hard play.

➢ Have consistent methods of dealing with players. Letting some players slide and others not is the best way to cause dissent and lose respect.

➢ Set limits and inform athletes that repeat offenders will suffer greater consequences.

➢ Follow up with confrontational kids with reminders that they need to practice self-control and explain the coaching staff's expectations of their future conduct.

Final Thoughts

Coaching patience is mandatory, especially in the beginning, in order to have a chance with a troubled player later. The ability to reprimand in a commanding but empathetic tone works best. Keep in mind, the sports venue is rarely the only place some kids will act out, and an anger issue may be the result of harsh family life. A coach may be the only person the troubled player has to look up to, so it's important to work with them the best you know how.

For minor acts of disobedience, informing the players' parents may resolve the issue. Parents may be able to stop the situation before it happens again.

Coaches must be careful of using physical training, like running, for discipline. When athletes interpret physical activity as punishment, it may undermine conditioning.

You must never forget that youth players are not adult athletes when it comes to penalizing, but sitting them on the bench for a short spell may be a needed wake up call.

The penalty for first offenses must be the same for all players. The degree of punishment changes for repeat offenders.

The consequences should never be something that humiliates kids.

Coaches should not abuse their authority with discipline and should only use harsher measures when initial warnings do not work. Once players have animosity towards the coach, other problems may come.

You should always recognize and thank players who make behavioral adjustments.

Coaches should never chastise players for poor play or because they do not like a player.

NURTURING THE COPING SKILLS AND RESILIENCY

"Never give up! Failure and rejection are only the first step to succeeding."

– Coach Jim Valvano, Basketball

Preview – Having a team of fearless players is another coaching goal.

"Do not be afraid to make mistakes, let's just learn from them."

— Coach to team

I remember most of my high school class laughing when I said I wanted to be a professional baseball player. I would love to run into them again, not to say, *"I told you so,"* but to thank them for the motivation they provided. William Arthur Ward said, *"Adversity causes some men to break, others to break records."*

I know there's no crying in baseball, as the famous line from *A League of their Own* says. But, there is. I was a grown man, bawling away in the bullpen during a game one Spring Training day. Earlier that day, I had been demoted to the minor leagues after having spent the previous season in the major leagues. It was a blow, even though I expected and deserved the demotion. If things can affect adults in that manner, just think of how disappointment can hit young people trying to handle tough moments.

Kids may not have the experience or wherewithal to deal with disappointments like:

1. Getting cut from a team.
2. Getting benched.
3. Being told they are no good.
4. Having friends cut from their team.
5. Seeing a teammate treated unfairly.
6. Seeing a teammate's parents treat their friend in an abusive way.

All of those are difficult things for youth, and can even be overwhelming enough for them to want to quit playing. If sports do nothing else, they challenge athletes to learn how to handle defeat. Coaches must help players deal with disappointment in a productive way.

What often separates the top tier collegiate and professional players besides their unique talents is that they display the courage to risk failing. What coaches should explain to young athletes is that a player does not have to be a brilliant athlete to be fearless. Teaching players to have courage takes time, but it is something that will develop as kids learn to cope with misfortune. That learning process helps them grow as athletes and people.

Following are the things coaches should do to bring about a daring attitude and mental toughness.

Coaches Should:

➤ Make sure players know that no one expects perfection from them.

➤ Tell players they can limit disappointment with dedication to training. Let them know that failure is a setback only when they do nothing about it.

➤ Encourage players to embrace challenges and take chances.

➤ Help players realize they cannot change past plays and that dwelling on them does not help.

➤ Help kids learn how to use hard times as motivation.

➤ Assist players in learning ways of keeping their mind in the present. A fearless demeanor is difficult when thinking of past and possible future failures.

➤ Enact clutch situations in practice, which gives players a sense of "*been there before.*" Experience helps kids focus, relax, and execute the next time.

➤ Inform players that you believe they will give their best and that's all you ever expect from them.

➤ Show little emotion after mistakes. Players are brave when they feel like they won't disappoint the coach.

➤ Separate what players do on the field and "who they are" by treating them as more than athletes.

➤ Tell players that every play and game's outcomes are independent of previous ones.

➤ Remind athletes that they are part of a team and that no one player determines the game's results.

> ➤ Inform players that other team members are there to pick them up when they fail.
> ➤ Remind players that games involve many plays, and no one individual play causes a loss.

Final Thoughts

Often, kids are more resilient than the adults. As long as coaches don't make too big a deal out of struggling times, kids tend to bounce back on their own. Sometimes, it's best to be silent and let the rough time run its course. Coaches may have to remind parents to keep an even keel, too.

Discovering ways to deal with bad luck builds strength in teams and is valuable in all phases of life.

BUILDING OPTIMISM

"A good coach will make his players see what they can be rather than what they are."

– Coach Ara Parseghian, Football

Preview – Teams often take on the coach's mentality. One of the best character traits you can pass on is optimism.

"They may have beat us the last time, but I guarantee if you keep your heads in the game, things can be different this time."

– A coach, trying to give the team hope

Despite making it to the major leagues, I never had much self-confidence in my playing ability. Deep down, though, I always felt optimistic that my career would go the way I wanted. A major part of that optimism came from my parents and youth coaches. Of all the things I try to do as a coach, keeping players hopeful is at the top of the list.

It is common for players and parents to become pessimistic if players do not perform well or when the team loses. It can be a difficult undertaking to remain hopeful when people get down on your ability or the team's success rate. When coaches feel that weight on them, they have to fight the urge to get down themselves.

Despite the sense of doom all around, coaches can, and should, instill a hopeful outlook in all individuals and teams. Optimism is a way of life that coaches should practice no matter their personality or the circumstances. Here are things you can do to try and help everyone remain encouraged during the difficult times.

Coaches Should:

➤ Stay optimistic no matter how bad the team plays.

➤ Remind everyone they should play for the enjoyment and improvement, and that winning and immediate success should not be the top priorities. Keep teams centered on long-range development.

➤ Not make excuses for anything or anyone and discourage players from making them, too.

➤ End sessions with a good play outcome. The last memory players have is important.

➤ Point out the skillful things teams do, regardless of a game's outcome.

➤ Encourage players to believe the next game will be better.

➤ Explain to players that the coaches will not accept the word can't. *"It's too hard, I can't do it"* is a pessimistic outlook that is self-fulfilling. Instead, have players say out loud the best case scenario they see for themselves.

➤ Inspire players to try new things. I often tell athletes that any piece of advice is worth a try. Experimentation helps them find what works and what doesn't. Hope comes from believing a new way may be the answer they've been seeking.

> ➤ Communicate hope by saying things like, *"There is a way,"* and *"We will find that way"* and *"That way starts now."*
> ➤ Remind players it's only a game and the real winners are those who give as close to their best as possible.
> ➤ Laugh off bad games as anomalies, not the team's identity.

Final Thoughts

It's natural for players to grow weary when the season is not going as planned. During those times, I try to get players to clear their minds and start over. *"The season starts anew today"* is one of the mantras I give them. I find myself saying the following a lot when things do not go the way they wished:

"That's part of the game."
"You will never be perfect."
"You'll get it next time."
"Hang in there, things will change."
"Forget about it."
"We will do better."
"It's never too late to improve."
"Believe in yourself."
"Believe in each other."
"I will never give up on you."

You should keep expectations reasonable without pressuring teams to win. That process helps players stay optimistic.

TEACHING ACCOUNTABILITY THROUGH WINNING, AND LOSING

"I've learned that something constructive comes from every defeat."

– Coach Tom Landry, Football

Preview – One of the best times to teach is during the post-game talk.

"It's great that we won, but how do you feel about the way we played?"

– Coach to team

One of my most memorable scenes from my youth is of lined up cars at the ball field parking lot 30 minutes after the game. Our coach was lecturing us on what went wrong and how to play the game. Although well-intentioned, my memory recalls nothing of what he said. But the picture of the waiting and anxious parents in the cars stayed with me.

Many people think that today's emphasis on winning has made things too competitive, that it's become a bad thing. Given the current state of youth sports, they have a point. But we must keep in mind, whenever groups are trying to outdo the opposition, score-keeping is part of the process. The problems aren't with the idea of keeping score – rather, they arise with how people *deal with* the triumph and loss.

The post-game discussion provides the opportunity for coaches to communicate about accountability. After games is the time to instill the idea that victory is just one gauge of achievement and that preparation, effort, and responsibility are of greater importance. You should be honest about how the team played, as sometimes teams will win after not having played well and other times they will lose after having played a great game. You should always help your team understand the things they can control – training, energy, and determination. Coaches can address what went wrong on the field, without focusing on winning or losing but on the preparation, energy level, and mental game. When wrapping things up, you should make the point that continuing to work hard is best.

That doesn't mean you should give a post-game lecture. Think of it more like a conversation with the team. Questions help players reflect on their thoughts and actions. Responses help players, coaches, and parents figure out what all can do to reach his or her individual and team potential, and not just on the playing fields.

Here are 3 post-game questions you should ask to help kids distinguish the significant things.

Question 1 – "*How did we play today?*"

After kids respond, you can detail the highlights of the game. Then, follow with the lowlights, but be careful to not single out individual players for ineffective play. You should speak as if the whole team made both good and inefficient plays, and not anyone in particular. You don't have to sugarcoat things after poor play, as long as you mention the positives.

Observant coaches know how to separate the mental mistakes from the physical ones. They should help players understand that the mental ones are the ones they can control.

Question 2 – "*Are you happy with your preparation before the game and with your effort during it?*"

Give your honest response to this issue after players have a say. When players and coaches agree they trained well and played hard, that's a victory. If everyone agrees they did not prepare the way they should have, or they failed to play hard, don't be afraid to let the team know they should not feel too satisfied, even if they did achieve a win.

Question 3 – "*What can we do to play better next time?*"

Athletes usually have a pretty good idea of what needs improving. You can add to that analysis and develop a plan from the suggestions for the next practice.

Final Thoughts

Coaches must help players maintain a balanced viewpoint of not getting too high or low after victories and defeats.

Many coaches go on a rant after losses and blame players for failing. Any outburst makes winning more important than it should be and gives players the message that assessing blame on others is acceptable.

It is never a bad idea to end your analysis with a reminder the athletes committed themselves to hard work in the beginning, no matter the score.

CHAPTER 9

$\sim$

Creating Sense and Integrity

Coaches who handle threatening situations with class and integrity deserve accolades. They are the people sports need more of and the ones who should coach youth for as long as possible.

Here is an event that occurred at a local playing field as relayed to me from a friend. It shows the type incidents that have become more common in the current youth sports environment.

My friend and his daughter were sitting on the sidelines watching his son's game. Another father of a player on the same team was roaming the same sidelines. This roaming father was starting and stopping, obstructing the view of many. Finally, my friend politely said to the wanderer, "*If you don't mind?*" suggesting that they couldn't see the action because the guy was in the way. His response wasn't something one would expect like "*I'm sorry*" or even, *"This is my usual routine."* No, he immediately came back with *"Any place, any time."* This fellow was unapologetic and ready to fight another parent of the same team.

JOHN WOODEN

You have seen this name quite a few times already. I would be remiss not to write more about UCLA basketball coach John Wooden, *"The Coach."* Coach Wooden wrote the book on coaching, literally and figuratively. His simple definition of a coach is a teacher. If more coaches looked at coaching in this way, our games would be better off.

Anything you read about coaching philosophy will likely discuss his leadership and coaching methods. It seems nearly all esteemed coaches since him have incorporated many of his values and techniques, as well they should. His principles were impeccable – he was a model for how positive coaching works. It's not hard to see that he believes coaching is teaching life as well as sport.

I hope it's clear that John Wooden's philosophy influenced my coaching viewpoint. Following are many of his thoughts on coaching and life. I offer just a little bit of analysis and reflection, even though his words really speak for themselves.

1. *"People want to believe you are sincerely interested in them as a person. Not just for what they can do for you."* The key ingredient of coaching – caring, and that kids are more than what they do on the field.
2. *"Target the things you can control."* Players and coaches often waste a lot of time with things they shouldn't be concerned about, like making winning the primary goal and satisfying personal egos.
3. *"Flexibility is the key to stability."* The best coaches adjust to their team's personality and talent levels. Coaches who get stuck in their ways and try to make players something they are not will ultimately fail.

4. *"It's what you learn **after** you know it all that counts."* Coaches must never think they have all the answers or stop their study of the game.

5. *"There is no progress without change, so you must have patience."* Patience — another of my must-have essentials to coaching youth.

6. *"It's the journey."* Victories are sweet, but the preparation and competition are what sports should be about.

7. *"It can be done in a way that's also helping them develop in other ways that will be meaningful forever."* Empathetic coaching works best and can impact kids for years to come.

8. *"We can agree to disagree, but we don't need to be disagreeable."* Sportsmanship is possible in all situations.

Coach Wooden always wanted his teams to acknowledge the player who assisted another. One player asked, *"But what if they are not looking when I point to them on the court?"* He said, *"That's OK; I guarantee I will see it."* His attention to detail is legendary. At his first practice of every season, he showed college aged players how to put their socks on correctly to avoid blisters.

Lessons Learned from Coach John Wooden

1. Sports, like life, are all about doing the right thing.
2. Coaching is best when done in a way that helps, not harms.
3. There is a way to disagree with civility.
4. Dignity and class should rule every coaching decision.
5. Sports are a journey taken with others, never alone, and the journey is one you should enjoy.

TEACHING THE PARENTS, TOO

"As the leader, part of the job is to be visible and willing to communicate with everyone."

– Coach Bill Walsh, Football

Preview – Parents who teach the same things as the coaches help player advancement.

"If you are telling them one thing and I say something different, the players get nowhere fast."

– Coach to parents

When I began coaching years ago, I didn't want parents around. I had the mindset of, *"Hey, give your kids some space and let them fend for themselves."* Furthermore, I felt like I knew the answers, and I didn't want others to know them. It didn't take long before I realized the errors of my ways. When I began to share my knowledge with parents, coaching was easier. After sharing, people trusted me more, and that led to the parents leaving the teaching to me. The best scenario is when parents trust that a coach knows their stuff. Then, parents allow the coaches to do their thing more often than not. Also, at-home practice became more pleasant for the athletes after sharing knowledge with the parents.

"How to" suggestions from too many sources lead to confusion and player disenchantment. When everyone teaches the same basics, athletes improve at a quicker rate. Players who hear the same terminology and practice the same drills with everyone have less confusion.

Most coaches want parents to stay as far away from the day-to-day coaching as possible. When coaches feel secure in their knowledge, they should do the opposite. Having interested parents learn and reinforce the same instructions will foster players' talents.

Also, many of today's parents *want* to be involved. It's OK for you to include them, as long as there are boundaries. Parents must be told that games and practices are the coaching staff's time with players, and interested parents should just listen during these structured times. However, setting aside some time to have parents listen in is good. Teaching the parents may take extra time, but it is well worth it. Coaches don't have to show parents everything, but a few of the basics can be beneficial for at-home practice with their child. It bears repeating, making sure everyone teaches the same things benefits the players and you.

If you have the faith in your knowledge and the time to implement this, you can help get all on the same page with the following plans.

Coaches Should:

➢ Encourage parents to listen in on instructional team talks.

➢ Ask for questions from parents about which techniques to reinforce. If time doesn't permit these discussions right after a game or practice, encourage parents to follow up later.

➢ Finish each session with demonstrated homework that parents can work on with players at home.

When there is time, coaches can also try:

➢ **A parent training day near the beginning of the season**. Parents get together with the coaching staff to learn and discuss the fundamentals and drills for home use. Some parents may feel they know better ways of doing things, and this is the time to talk about the most optimal ways of teaching players.

➢ **A parent/child practice**. All learn the game together, and parents work with their child with coaching oversight. Each player has different needs. These sessions offer an opportunity to find those variances.

Final Thoughts

You should remind parents to reinforce what the coaches teach. Reiteration of the same things help, but its' also important to ask parents to back off when players seem tired of hearing the same things

You can also **inform parents of informative websites** that you visit that have solid coaching advice and playing tips. It's refreshing for coaches to have players, who were once unwilling to listen to their parents, now pay attention to them because they hear the same instructions as the coach teaches.

Coaches should never have closed workouts at the youth levels as long as parents are willing to just observe. However, asking an attending parent for teaching assistance when short of coaching help is a good thing.

Coaches should discuss any differences of opinion with parents away from the players.

It's always best to express the importance of everyone having patience.

Coaches can send practice tips to parents in emails, too.

Some parents may not want to be involved, and that's OK, too.

The parental-involvement coaching technique may not be for teenage and older players. Often, older athletes prefer not to have parents around.

ELIMINATING THE VERBAL NON-MOTIVATORS

"I have learned over the years how to hold a team together. How to lift some men up, how to calm others down, until finally, they've got one heartbeat, together, a team."

– Coach Bear Bryant, Football

Preview – One self-esteem damaging statement may affect an athlete's career. At the least, it can cause a sleepless night and spoil the pleasure of competing.

"You should be embarrassed with your play, today. You guys stink."

— Unhappy coach statement

Anyone who wants to see the negative coaching style simply needs to hang around a sports facility or field for a short time. I see it all the time. Similar to a previous story in this book is this occurrence. I was working with a student and an adult was working with a young player about 10-years-old in the adjacent batting cage. After most pitches, the adult's comments were, *"Terrible,"* *"That's bad,"* or just a head shake *"No."* After a well-done play, the coach was silent. There are just so many times a player can hear words like terrible and bad before they believe that is what they are.

It's normal to sometimes be frustrated with athletes. But that frustration is never an excuse to use words or displays that attack a player's character. After a while of hearing the same words, an athlete will wonder if playing is even worth it. For sensitive kids, it only takes one bad experience with a coach to lose desire.

You must learn to say things that describe the action, without wounding a person's self-worth. Words that attack make players defensive, less willing to listen, and timid. Desire-killing statements start with digs at a player's effort like:

"Why did you do that?"
"Why don't you ever do what I tell you?"
"You will never get anywhere doing it like that."
"I can't believe you cannot do it the right way."
"Do you want to be here?"
"We are going to run and run when this game is over."

Hearing statements like these too often will wear on kids. Worse yet, the derogatory comments often escalate into more serious declarations over time, like:

"I thought you wanted to play?"

"Forget it; you are not worth my time."

"It's disgusting to watch you play like that."

"You are a head case."

"I am wasting my time here."

"You stink."

"You are embarrassing yourself and me."

Notice the word *"you"* is in just about all the statements. The word pierces players' pride when used in these ways.

This section could also be in the description about negative coaching because that's what it is. But it was necessary to go into it further, so coaches don't end up saying that one thing that may turn an athlete off forever.

Mocking players will lessen a coach's character in the eyes of athletes and negatively affects players more than they may let on. Staff coaches should monitor each other for how they say things because it's easy for some to fall into a cynical style without realizing it.

Following are some strategies that keep kids engaged and not under attack from the coach.

Coaches Should:

➢ Describe the action, *"That move was incorrect and doesn't seem to be working. Try this instead; it will help."*

➢ Explain the possibilities, *"I know you can do it, I have seen you do it before, keep working."*

➢ Give a positive thought first, *"I know you are trying, but that is not what I am looking for."*

➢ Keep a fresh point of view. Sports are only one aspect of a child's life. *"Hey, it's only a game."*

➢ Smile. Coaches should learn to smile when they feel frustration. It is hard to say something that hurts another person after smiling.

Final Thoughts

Too often, coaches just assume players know what they mean. Coaches must realize, inadequate teaching practices are often the reason for poor play.

Frustration is a desire killer in kids when it comes from the adults.

DEALING WITH GAME OFFICIALS

"If you are going to make every game a matter of life and death, you are going to have a lot of problems. For one thing, you'll be dead a lot."

— Coach Dean Smith, Basketball

Preview — Having a supportive relationship with game officials is crucial. It not only sets an example, it may give coaches the necessary, mutual ally when a lack of sportsmanship arises.

"You cost my team the game."

— Upset coach to referees

It's not uncommon to hear one of my students claim the umpire blew the call. They'll say it's why the team lost or why they failed to get a hit. And sometimes, they may be right, but players should never use this as an excuse. That response often occurs because adults blame the umpires, and then they allow the kids to do the same. Blaming others instills the wrong lesson to youth. With this mindset, players begin to believe that it's always someone else's fault when things don't go as planned.

Treatment of officials is another example of professional games affecting youth coaching. Some youth coaches see how the coaches on TV act towards the umpires and begin to think it's OK for them to behave the same way. Other coaches just take the game too seriously and are only out to win. They pester the referees when things do not go their way. Whatever the case, a lack of perspective usually means ugly incidents will follow.

First, you shouldn't expect youth officials to be even close to perfect. Next, there is no excuse for not showing appreciation for referees at all times. When coaches treat officials with contempt, others tend to follow suit. Before long, fans and players will begin to ride the officials, too. A free-for-all ensues with everyone ganging up on the referees, and that is a recipe for trouble. Many of the unfortunate, extreme occurrences in sports stem from people getting upset with the officials.

A sense of *gratitude* for their effort is mandatory and sets the standard for your team and fans.

These are ways coaches should deal with game umpires.

Coaches Should:

➤ Begin every game by reminding themselves that the games are about the kids, and not about you or winning.

➤ Know the first names of the refs and address them with that name.

➤ Shake hands before games and thank them for their time.

➤ Have only one coach, usually the head one, talk to the refs and only for rule clarifications.

➤ If necessary, talk to officials nearby and in a calm manner. Yelling from a distance, for everyone to hear, leads to problems.

➤ Never get into an argument or say anything that questions an official's ability.

➤ Not speak in a derogatory way under your breath just enough for officials to hear.

➤ Not slam things down and show disgust over calls.

➤ Never allow parents to talk to the umpires at any time, unless it's to thank them for their work.

➤ Not let players talk to referees unless greeting or thanking them.

> ➤ Alert the officials at the first signs of disrespectful conduct by anyone.

> ➤ Ask the officials to speak to the offending party when disruptions occur.

> ➤ Remind everyone that the officials are not professional ones or to blame for individual and team outcomes.

> ➤ Encourage people to thank the officials after every game.

Final Thoughts

The best ally a coach can have when dealing with obnoxious people and unsportsmanlike conduct is the game referee. Coaches who treat the officials with esteem usually get the help to handle out of line people.

Coaches should consistently recommend that leagues have ongoing training and evaluations of officials. Most officials welcome input when it's given at the appropriate times. In that way, leagues can weed out the weak officials and address in-season issues as they see fit.

A shortage of officials is showing up in some areas of youth sports. Part of the reason for that is the abusive behavior of the adults towards them.

When the official is a teenager, be especially mindful if anyone mistreats them, and step in to help the youngster as if they were your own child.

HANDLING GAME PRESSURE

"Pressure is something you feel when you do not know what you are doing."

– Coach Chuck Noll, Football

Preview – Coaches must be careful of behavioral changes that affect teams in unintended ways.

"Coach is acting like a madman today."

– Player-to-player exchange

My major league playing experience helped me in several ways when it came to coaching. I believe where it helped the most was in big rivalry and championship games. Having played at the highest level, I didn't get overly-excited when my youth teams made it to the big games. At least, I didn't show the team that I was feeling the strain of the moment. I believe that my lack of emotion helped the team perform well in the biggest of games.

Coach John Wooden said that early in his career he wanted to win so much that he hindered his team. If even a coach with Coach Wooden's character could be a deterrent to his team's championship, it's bound to happen to many others. Coach Wooden was humble, so I would guess he was exaggerating some. But, he makes an excellent point because coaches often get in the way of their team's progress.

Coaching anxiety turns up the most in playoff games, against biggest rivals, and in tight games. Many coaches display panic behavior before players have even thought about the gravity of situations. Adults add an emphasis, intentional or not, by changing their mannerisms. The problem is that when coaches show a sense of urgency, players become tentative and play not to lose. The added tension often leads to mistakes that make coming out ahead difficult.

Although it's natural to want to win, don't let your behavior affect your team's chances of winning. Calmer coaches have the best chance of having confident and relaxed athletes, especially with the younger aged teams.

To Avoid Putting Undue Stress On Teams, Coaches Can:

➤ Be organized. Running around at the last minute puts everyone on the edge.

➤ Keep the same personality and routine for every game, and for the entire contest.

➤ Mentally prepare themselves for the close games and tight situations. In practice, coaches can have players visualize the big games. Coaches should picture their behavior in them, too. It helps everyone to see themselves in intense games, game-ending plays, and nail-biting situations beforehand. That mental rehearsal leads to confidence in making the right calls under pressure.

➤ Read the team's mood and act accordingly. Players know when games are big, so coaches don't have to over stress them. With uptight players, coaches can act carefree and use humor to calm them down. When coaches relax, players can be themselves and just focus on playing. On the flip side, when players seem too casual, coaches can stress a little more urgency to them.

➤ Express how proud they are that the team has made it this far.

➤ Stress the importance of competing for one play at a time. Coaches must do their best to keep players' minds in the present and not on the outcome or the thought of possibly losing.

➤ Prepare players for the tight situations in practice by encouraging them to want to be the player on the spot at the end of the close games.

➤ Remind the bench players of their importance and to stay ready because their time will come.

➤ Stay cooler than the opposing team's coach. Players appreciate playing for the *"under control"* coach and not the wild one on the other side. Calm coaches bring poise to athletes more than the excitable coaches do.

➤ Remember to not be afraid to smile and laugh, even during the tense moments. Expressing and showing others how much fun you are having relaxes others and is contagious.

Final Thoughts

It's natural for coaches to act a little more excited than normal before championship games. But, you should do your best to not change your personality or your usual game demeanor.

Coaches must never forget that being too up tight can cause the same in players, which hurts performance and fun.

MANAGING SPORTSMANSHIP ISSUES

"One man practicing sportsmanship is far better than 50 preaching it."

– Coach Knute Rockne, Football

Preview – Coaches should recognize unsportsmanlike conduct and deal with it.

"Wow, I cannot believe they would intentionally walk a 9-year-old."

– A bewildered baseball coach

I have seen many unfortunate incidents occur on the playing fields because of situations mentioned by this surprised coach's statement. What one coach may view as good baseball tactics, another may feel is a lack of fairness for that age of players. Many fairness rules are open to a never-ending debate, as to whether they are displays of bad sportsmanship or just part of the games. Part of the problem is many coaches lack training and expertise in the finer parts of the game. Even though most volunteers have a background in the sport, they can be unaware of the unwritten rules.

The other scenario, much more troublesome, is the coaches who know the rules of good sportsmanship but choose to ignore them. They have the *"winning is everything"* or the *"beat the opposition as bad as possible"* mentality.

The first step to making sure everyone displays sportsmanship is making sure they know the definition – *"ethical, appropriate, polite, and fair behavior."* There's one word that really exemplifies the difference between the top levels of sport and the youth levels: "*appropriate*." What may be proper at the pro levels is not necessarily acceptable in the amateur ranks. Often, players regulate themselves at the highest stage. Players and teams at the professional level may use retaliation and other questionable moves that shouldn't be a part of the youth games.

Youth coaches must never allow or use retaliation. The adults must act in ethical ways, but point out the unfair moves at the appropriate time. Understandably, young players do not know these unwritten fairness rules, so it is mandatory that you teach them.

Every sport has actions that cross the line of fair play. Common to all are:

- ✓ Running up the score.
- ✓ Overly aggressive coaches.
- ✓ Dirty play.
- ✓ Taunting the opposition or the officials.
- ✓ Excessive celebrations.

Often, these actions create bad feelings and lead to further unfortunate events. Unprepared coaches react in ways that escalate situations.

Following are suggestions to deal with poor conduct.

Coaches Should:

- ➢ Stay up to date with their sport to know what makes up fair play and what does not. Things change over time and what is OK behavior at one level may not be for another. Coaches are responsible for knowing right from wrong behavior.
- ➢ Recognize a lack of fair play and pick the right time and place to deal with it. Willpower and restraint are necessary at first. When coaches are unprepared or act impulsively, situations can escalate, and you must avoid this.
- ➢ Keep their teams absorbed in the game and not on the other teams' actions.

➤ Explain to young athletes that professional sports are for entertainment purposes, too, and that youth sports are not. Coaches must help their players understand that some of the behavior they see on TV isn't acceptable at their level.

➤ Address any predictable issues before games. Some coaches have behavior that's notorious and their reputations precede them. If you're aware of a coach's known behavior, you can discuss sportsmanship before the competition. For instance, some coaches are over the top with their celebrations of good plays. It's understandable for players to show excitement. But, when coaches go overboard, it can be unpleasant for the opposition. At the least, discussing the potential for this type of behavior beforehand may get coaches thinking about their conduct.

➤ Mention any concerns to game officials immediately. Some game officials may be able to put an end to impropriety, which is the best case scenario.

➤ Never stoop to the offending team's level. When the opposition has excessive celebrations, it doesn't mean your team should be allowed to follow suit.

When coaches feel the opposition is acting in an improper manner, they may be able wait to bring it up at a time where it will be less likely to affect their team. When things can wait, the post-game handshake is a good time to tell the opposition coach of their unsportsmanlike concern. That conveyance should be in a non-confrontational way. Some coaches are unaware of the unwritten rules of sportsmanship and learn as they go. Bringing inappropriate actions to their attention may help stop it down the line.

In addition to talking with the out of line coach, league or tourney officials should be informed of the situation afterward. You can ask them to discuss it with the offenders so it doesn't reoccur. One of the problems with travel sports is there may not be a central board to give concerns. You can recommend to tournaments and leagues to not invite inappropriate coaches back the following year.

➤ Treat the unsportsmanlike behavior as a teachable moment. Coaches should explain to their own team what poor sportsmanship is, what behavior is wrong, and that it will not be allowed.

Final Thoughts

Coaches cannot discipline players from other teams but, if the out of line players are on the opposing team, coaches should talk to officials. If things don't change, coaches must be prepared to speak to the opposing coach. Taking a team off the field before the end of a game should only be a last resort, and should only occur if the safety of players is at risk.

It is never a bad idea for you to try to spend a few minutes before the game to get to know the opposition's coach. That friendly gesture could pay off if any unpleasantness appears later.

The post-game handshake should be a rule at all youth sporting events. Coaches should teach their team to be sincere with their congratulatory words and actions after a loss, just as they should be compassionate towards the opposition after a win.

To reiterate, coaches should never use a lack of sportsmanship from an opponent as a reason to retaliate against them.

Running up the score is a typical lack of fairness act. Coaches should never embarrass another team by running up the score. You must find ways to avoid pouring it on, especially when a no "*mercy rule*" exists for the game. Sometimes, a runaway is unavoidable and coaches of the dominating team must tell the opposing coach they are not out to embarrass anyone.

Coaches should recommend a mercy rule for the league and work to that end when they fail to have one. That regulation limits the score differential so the losing team won't be embarrassed. Also, when posting scores, there should be a mercy rule score, so as not to embarrass another team. For example, a lopsided baseball score after four innings of play could be a 9 – 0 game, not 23 – 0, the real outcome.

A fine line exists between aggressive play and unsportsmanlike conduct. Coaches must try to distinguish that difference before acting on situations.

CONTROLLING OBNOXIOUS ADULTS

"Coaches don't sleep for a reason. They don't sleep because it's a danger zone every night... The lifestyle of coaching in the NBA is a tremendous challenge that gives you tremendous highs but also tremendous lows."

- Coach George Carl - Basketball

Preview – Unfortunately, the increase in unsportsmanlike behavior comes from the sidelines, now. Coaches must do something about rude people. Of all the coaching tasks, this one is the most difficult, but also the most necessary.

"The best youth games are the ones when no one notices the adults."

– A wise fan after enjoying a game

I was at a youth game recently and left disappointed with what I saw. With every decent play by their team, this one parent sprinted around high-fiving the other fans. Cute. As one would guess, with every dash, players' and fans' eyes went to him the whole game.

Youth sports aren't the place for attention-seeking adults, but they seem to be everywhere now. Adults who feel they have the right to do whatever they want is one of the most obvious changes in youth sports from years ago. It's a shame that things have come to that. All youth leagues may eventually have to implement a written code of conduct for adults to sign before they attend games if things don't change.

Often, the disturbing actions are in the form of vocally slamming someone. No one is immune to the obnoxious fan – the opponent, a coach, the referee, or even their child – can all be targets. Someone needs to point out these immature and unruly acts and try to put an immediate end to them. Doing so, without escalating the situation, can be challenging. When the game and league officials do nothing, the coaches are responsible for control of the games. This duty is most appropriate when young, inexperienced officiating crews run the games.

When the offensive party disrupts the players' experience, you must try to put an end to it. If you're unsure of how much it's affecting players, discuss the situation with other coaches. If others agree that the situation is unhealthy, you must do something. Anything meant to embarrass another team or player demands action.

Here are some of the inappropriate behaviors that coaches must be prepared to act on:

- ✓ Opposition parent verbally "getting on" one of your players.
- ✓ Excessive "*riding*" of one's own son or daughter by a parent.
- ✓ Laughing at or deriding the opposition.
- ✓ Ridicule of officials.
- ✓ Any tough talk or threats to their team or the opposition during play.
- ✓ Over the top screaming to rile the other team.
- ✓ Repeated gestures that take spectator interest away from the game and to the sidelines.
- ✓ Over-celebrating during or after games.
- ✓ Any attempts to intimidate others before or after games.
- ✓ Any talk from adults that suggests players should retaliate against the opposition.

Coaches should deal with out of line adults without intensifying the situation, if possible. Following are some things you can try to address situations without making them worse.

Coaches Should:

> Wait to discuss things if they feel like the immediate discussion may provoke further problems or when they feel it's something that can be put off until after games. After games, they can bring up any issues to the opposing coach. Coaches may want to look for and talk with an opposition coach who seems the least involved when the head coach is too intense. Coaches should never confront the opposing team's youth athletes, only a superior.

> Remind parents that the benching of a child for out of line parents is a possibility, as long as that was set as an option before the season. Coaches should warn any unruly parent of this possibility before games by telephone or in person and follow through with the benching if their conduct does not change.

> Express to referees the games should be about the kids. Coaches can ask the official to try and talk to the offender or the other team's coach about an out of line fan.

> Call for an available league supervisor to discuss the inappropriate acts.

> Talk to the opposition coach when an opposing fan creates a scene. Hopefully, they will do something about the annoying person.

> Give a written note to the other coach to avoid making a scene. This letter can state something like: *"I'm trying not to make a big deal out of this because I don't want to take the focus away from the game. But, we do not appreciate the behavior of so and so. It reflects on you and your whole organization. If that is not what you want, you should talk to the individual now, so the appropriate sportsmanship displays itself."*

Final Thoughts

Some of your parents may offer excessive encouragement to players but that can be too much, too. You know they mean well but you may have to talk to the offenders afterwards in private about overdoing it.

Coaches should do their best to keep the players fixated on the games.

You may have to remind your team parents, when they appear upset over the opposition's behavior that you'll deal with any extreme stuff at the right time.

The opposition coach may get defensive about any mention of dishonorable behavior and do nothing, or they may act upon it, which is the best case outcome. At the very least, by pointing out the poor conduct, it may make the coach think about their side's behavior in the future.

Failing to make a point of offensive behavior means it will likely continue.

As much as people may want to help the child of the harsh parent, it may not be their place. When a situation involves a player and their parent, it can get very tricky. When coaches get in the business of telling others how to raise their kids, trouble often follows. You should try to only approach a parent when behavior is negatively affecting more than just their child. Talking to the aggressive parent's spouse may be a possible line of action. A personal call later on when cooler heads prevail may work. No matter what course of action is taken, these situations can provide you with teachable moments. Let the offended child who appears upset or embarrassed that you're aware of the situation, you don't agree with it, and you're trying to help.

It's mandatory that coaches address game day behavior with team parents at season's start. An occasional reminder of the proper conduct during the season is essential, too. Letting everyone know that their behavior is a reflection on the whole team and organization is important.

You can also work for and encourage the sports facilities in your area to have a fan *code of conduct* sign placed at all venues.

CHAPTER 10

Creating Inspiration

Words have tremendous power. Coaches must use them wisely.

Often, the best way to teach and motivate is with stories. This is an example of one of the stories I tell my students.

"Listen up everyone. Each year for the past many, I have trained for a marathon. As you know, the weather can be inclement with 90- and 0-degree days. On those days, I have a choice to make, run outside or run on a treadmill in the comfort of the house. More often than not, I choose the outside venue."

At this point, I have the players' attention. I proceed.

"You see, there is no way I can reach my goal of 26 miles without embracing and overcoming the smaller challenges along the way. Every time you conquer one obstacle, it makes you stronger for the next one. This game is hard and you are going to fail a lot, but every time you get back up, you'll be better prepared the next time. Look forward to the challenges. When you get to that hill on your path, you have a choice. You can run up it, walk it, or turn back. I hope you do not choose that third option because others will pass you by and you may regret it for a long time."

DAVE BELISLE – A LITTLE LEAGUE LEGEND

It may be unfortunate that youth games get television coverage. The media attention at such a young age can add considerable pressure. The commercialization of kids is another new debatable issue that society must deal with.

Even though it can be overwhelming for the young ones, some good can come out of having the spotlight. With the cameras running, coaches and parents usually show their best sides. Adults tend to display a passionate, but caring manner. That's the way it should be. Fewer people may reveal their worst side because they know the whole world is watching.

Many unfortunate incidents also find their way on the internet now. Maybe the televising of all youth games is one idea to keep people under control. I'm wrong again! Some TV reality shows already exist which show the worst of youth sports and seem to promote borderline child abuse behavior. I do not want to give them any credibility by mentioning their names here.

Still, the televising of displays of high character can inspire others. That was the case with Rhode Island Little League Coach Dave Belisle. It's clear that he *"gets it,"* and is cognizant of what youth sports are. Coach Dave proves that one doesn't need to be a superstar coach to make a huge difference, just a caring person. This is his inspirational post-game message after his team's loss and last game together.

"Heads up high. Heads up high. I've got to see your eyes, guys. There's no disappointment in your effort – in the whole tournament, the whole season. It's been an incredible journey.

"We fought. Look at the score – 8-7, 12-10 in hits. We came to the last out. We didn't quit. That's us! Boys, that's us!

"The only reason why I'll probably end up shedding a tear is that this is the last time I'm going to coach you guys. But I'm going to bring back with me, and the coaching staff is going to bring back, and you guys are going to bring back something that no other team can provide – that's pride. Pride.

"You're going to take that for the rest of your lives, what you provided for the town of Cumberland. You had the whole place jumping, right? You had the whole state jumping. You had New England jumping. You had ESPN jumping. OK?

"You want to know why? They like fighters. They like sportsmen. They like guys who don't quit. They like guys who play the game the right way. If everyone played baseball like the Cumberland Americans, this would be the greatest game.

"The lessons you guys have learned along the journey, you'll never forget. We're going to have some more fun. We have two more days of fun. When you walk around this ballpark in the next couple of days, they're going to look at you and say: 'Hey, you guys were awesome!'

"Everybody has said: You guys are awesome. Awesome. Awesome. Absolutely awesome.

"It's OK to cry because we're not going to play baseball together anymore. But we're going to be friends forever. Friends forever. Our Little League careers have ended on the most positive note that could ever be. OK? Ever be.

"There's only going to be one team that's going to walk out of here as World Series champions. Only one. We got down to the nitty-gritty. We're one of the best teams in the world. Think about that for a second. In the world! Right?

"So, we need to go see our parents, because they're so proud of you. One more thing. I want a big hug. I want everyone to come in here for one big hug. One big hug, then we're going to go celebrate. Then we're going to go back home to a big parade.

"I love you guys. I'm gonna love you forever. You've given me the most precious moment in my athletic and coaching career, and I've been coaching a long time – a looooong

time. I'm getting to be an old man. I need memories like this; I need kids like this. You're all my boys. You're the boys of summer.

"*So, for the last time, we're going to yell Americans: 'One, two three – Americans!*

"*OK. Good job. Let's go. Time to go.*"

National championships and youth travel sports often get a bad rap because of the money and time involved. But moments like the one above are priceless for athletes in terms of their education, memories, and maturation. An upside to the increase of games in the travel ball age is the formation of deeper relationships and the opportunity to meet people from other areas. Many athletes get the opportunity to see places they may never have without sports. Kids may get their first taste of independence from mom and dad, which helps the maturity process, too.

Lessons Learned from Coach Dave Belisle:

1. Having the right approach is vital – it's not just about winning and the love of the game, but about the love for people.
2. Coaches must seize the opportunity to inspire kids.
3. Sports are about doing your best and the pride that comes from that pursuit.
4. The lifelong memories and friendships are the most valuable things.
5. Life goes on after the games; it's time to go. Helping kids overcome adversity is a top priority for coaches.

PROVIDING MOTIVATION

"***Don't ever ask a player to do something he doesn't have the ability to do. He'll just question your ability as a coach, not his as an athlete.***"

– Coach Lou Holtz, Football

Preview – Having a daily purpose is a beneficial way to help your whole team's and your individual players' needs. Kids often remember these more than any how-to information.

"Here is the one thing I want you to focus on today."

– Coach to player

My students used to seem a little intimidated by me, even though I don't think I'm an intimidating person. It's natural for youth to feel a bit cautious around adults. But once I begin telling stories with a message, kids act like they trust and know me more. Soon after I tell them some of my stories, they always seem more comfortable around me. Cool! The other interesting thing is they are always disappointed if I don't have a short story for them.

Even though parents should not expect volunteer youth coaches to be experts at strategy or with coaching skills, some will and coaches have to accept that fact. Whatever their knowledge level, all youth coaches should realize they have the opportunity of a lifetime to inspire kids.

Many of Coach John Wooden's players thought his philosophy outlined in his *"Pyramid of Success"* was corny when they originally heard it. The Pyramid was a diagram for the ingredients Coach Wooden felt were necessary for obtaining success. Over time, many of them began to realize its importance to their lives.

Coaches should not be afraid to inspire and use some originality to do it. Kids may roll their eyes at inspirational attempts, but their efforts may have a powerful effect later.

Here are ways that coaches can stimulate youth.

Coaches Should:
  ➤ Have themes for the day. Simple one-word ideas like *teamwork, desire, hustle,* or *resilience* work well. Discovering new words and concepts are educational for youth. Short phrases like *"the will to prepare,"* or *"practice as you play in a game,"* can make a difference. You can give def-

initions and examples of the day's words. When kids find out how to exemplify the theme of the day, it's useful for character building.

➢ Tell inspirational stories about athletes' feats or personal ones from your past.

➢ Encourage the team to come up with a theme for the day.

➢ Have players look up inspirational sports quotes online and bring a copy of them for each player on the team. A season-long list gives players an excellent volume of inspirational quotes.

➢ Give the athletes inspirational words to learn and showcase instances of each in the sports world.

➢ Provide each player with a specific area of direction, too. That assignment acts as a valuable, motivational tactic. This area of individual concentration can be a word or phrase, or it may be a drill for skill development. For example, for aggressive players, coaches may assign the word self-control. Many words work for all sports. *Balance, focus, strength, determination, positioning, vision, communication, readiness, aggressiveness*, and *control* all apply. Simple things like *eyes, ears, head*, and *feet*, also work to give players an area of dedication. Having a daily purpose is an excellent way to further players' knowledge of certain actions and plays.

➢ Ask players what their inspirational theme is and why or how it applies to them. This question and answer helps coaches make sure players appreciate the essence of their topic.

➢ Give kids ways of working on their area of focus.

➢ At the end of the session, you can ask players to define their field of concentration and what they did to improve it. Have players explain their concepts to the whole team.

Final Thoughts

Coaches should give thought to each player's needs before assigning them a topic. The list of possibilities is vast.

Coaches may never know the inspiring effect the above have on athletes. If it helps one player at some point, it will have been worth the coaching effort.

The neatest thing is when players start asking coaches what their theme for the day is.

Coaches must never forget the 3 best ways to motivate – attention, approval, and knowledge.

A smile and high-five always inspires.

Parents love hearing positive words, too. You should make a point of mentioning what a nice job their son or daughter did that day.

RALLYING WITH THE PEP TALK

"You were born to be a player. You were meant to be here. This moment is yours."

– Coach Herb Brooks, Hockey

Preview – It only takes a few words to give hope and energy.

"Situations like these are why we worked so hard; I know you are ready for this."

– Coach to the team

At times, I feel like I play the role of a sports psychiatrist. I am always looking for the words to boost desire and conviction. Those inspiring words can build character in maturing young people, too.

Inspirational pre- and post-game pep talks have their role. During games, pick-me-ups are decisive, too, as players often need a boost. A few quick words that give players the guts to keep going are essential. Saying the right thing helps players persevere and play with determination. Energy-

223

boosting comments help players develop the resiliency to fight through misfortune.

These Are the Character Traits That Emerge from Inspiring Words:
- ✓ **Pride**. *"Play for the name on the front of your jerseys not the name on the back – we are one."*
- ✓ **Effort**. *"Do your best; that's all anyone expects."*
- ✓ **Empathy**. *"I know it's been a long day; hang in there, you can do this."*
- ✓ **Courage**. *"Do not be afraid of making mistakes, go for it."*
- ✓ **Trust**. *"Believe in yourself."*
- ✓ **Honesty**. *"Your hard work will pay off; I guarantee it."*
- ✓ **Gratitude**. *"Thank you for your effort. I am proud of you."*
- ✓ **Loyalty**. *"Trust in each other."*
- ✓ **Contentment**. *"We love watching you play."*
- ✓ **Humility**. *"You make us coaches look good."*

Putting those together at one time gives coaches the pep talk before the big games. You can touch a little on each of the above with a speech like this:

"You have earned your way here; no one gave it to you. I know you will give your all, and that is all anyone can ever expect. Things will get tight out there, play with courage and trust in each other. Your preparation will pay off. As long as you give your best effort, you have succeeded. I want everyone to know that the coaches are already proud of you. Your parents will be proud whether we win or lose, too, if we give our best. Have fun out there and represent yourselves with that sense of pride inside of you."

And for the post-game:

"We are proud of you. You gave your best, and that is all we ever ask of you. I hope you feel the same way. If you aren't sure, that's OK – as long as you make the choice to give a little more the next time. We must learn from this experience. No one expects you to have everything figured out at your age. If you put the same effort into your school work and everything else, you will go a long way in life. Walk out of here with your heads high and enjoy

what we have accomplished. Remember, we are here for each other no matter what. The coaches want to thank each and every one of you."

Final Thoughts

Coaches should not dwell on the victories and losses. Players may be happy, or they may be disappointed after games, but coaches have done their job when youth learn about the pride that comes from the energy given.

It's hard for athletes to stay involved when tired and hungry. Coaches should remind players to stay hydrated during and to eat before games. Sometimes, rest, water, and food are the best energy boosters. Thirst and hunger are energy zappers. On long game days, coaches should have healthy snacks available. The concession stand food may not be the best energizing foods.

Coaches should encourage parents to have players eat healthy foods at home and when away from it, too. Unhealthy fast foods become a way of life for travel team players when not watched by adults.

GROWING CONFIDENCE AND POISE

"Each person holds so much power within themselves that needs to be let out. Sometimes they just need a little nudge, a little direction, a little support, a little coaching, and the greatest things can happen."

– Coach Pete Carroll, Football

Preview – Playing with confidence is best. Poise is even better; it helps players through when self-assurance may be absent. Coaches can develop both in kids.

"No one else I would rather have in this situation than you."

– Coach to a player

I suppose I was one of those rare athletes who made it to the highest level with little self-confidence. At the highest level, I had trouble believing I belonged. However, I felt I had a calm come over me in the tensest of moments. Poise came, and that feeling of belonging was comforting.

Playing with confidence is the best way. Belief in self allows players to trust in their ability, which leads to relaxation and focus. Without certainty, players may feel as if they have no control, which is not a comfortable feeling. A lack of faith adds strain on athletes, which inhibits instinctual play. However, confidence levels are variable with all athletes, and they come and go. Coaches must work to help players maintain them, so they can play with confidence more often.

Poise is one of those things that many people recognize when they see it, but it's often difficult to define. Poise is a state of balance - having control when circumstances make it easy to feel out of place. It's feeling comfortable under tougher than ordinary conditions. Some players have grace under pressure from the start, and some do not.

Poise is another thing coaches can teach and players can develop. The enhancement of skills, optimism, and experience can bring calm for many athletes.

Following are ways coaches can develop a belief in self and composure.

Coaches Should:

➤ **Develop the skills**. Having physical stability is the beginning of mental equilibrium. The more under control one's body is, the more relaxed and confident they can be. There is no substitute for doing things the right way. Coaches must commit to the fundamentals the whole season long. Advancing players' talents is a tedious but obligatory task.

➤ **Explain the value of preparation.** Hard work leads athletes to the belief that they geared up in the right way. Proper training helps athletes expect good outcomes beyond just having hope. Poised athletes believe things work out for the best more often than not because of their preparation.

➢ **Reaffirm players with statements like,** *"Right player, right time."* Affirming statements give kids hope, and this type dialogue works to develop comfort and composure.

➢ **Teach self-awareness.** Poise comes with knowing oneself. Athletes who have a good perception of their strengths and weaknesses do not overextend in difficult situations. Composed players realize if they stay within themselves, good things will follow. The ability to stay in the moment during tight situations blocks out pessimistic thoughts, allowing for focused play.

➢ **Explain the effects of facial expressions and body language.** The capacity to look composed even when the hearts are pounding comes with experience. Players who look like they are under control often gain a mental edge over the opposition. Upset players kick the dirt, throw things, swear, glare, pout, and fail to listen. Those players lose concentration. Coaches can help players cut anger and disappointment displays.

➢ **Help athletes maintain the same breathing patterns.** Consistent breathing aids players' ability to observe things with a clear mind. Teach players to take a deep breath before the action.

➢ **Teach visualization skills.** Having players mentally rehearse seeing themselves perform plays before the action helps confidence.

➢ **Maintain balance, too.** By not getting flustered in tight situations, coaches show players how to have poise and confidence.

Final Thoughts

Poise and confidence have the best chance of showing up with patient, adult guidance. Impatient adults develop the opposite – tense and out of control players.

Players who act under control are a model for stressed teammates.

UNITING WITH THE HUDDLE

"Individual commitment to a group effort – that is what makes a team work, a company work, a society work, a civilization work."

– **Coach Vince Lombardi, Football**

Preview – Coaches have one of the best motivational tools available with the team huddle. Using timeouts and group gatherings at the most opportune time unites players.

"OK, gather around, here's the plan."

– Coach to the team

The best coaches I ever played for had a sixth sense for knowing when to call a team meeting. They knew when things were slipping away. They read their team's state of mind and gathered all before the ship sank too far.

Knowing when teams need a boost, when to let them relax, or when to pass on information at the right time can be game changing. The best coaches use the huddle just enough, without overusing it. Using the group summit too often defeats the inspiring purpose of it, so the timing is crucial.

A team gathering for game instructions is often the case. But, the best use of the huddle is for rallying the group. The *"huddle up, gang"* is an excellent bonding tool, as it gives players a feeling of togetherness. The cluster provides a unique sense of team and gives players a power-in-numbers sensation. Assembling the team into a circle helps rally and refocus individuals. Calling game timeouts at the most opportune time can change momentum and refocus teams.

Coaches Should Use the Assembly and Timeouts to:

➤ **Have players focus on the process.** Coaches can ask players to execute and do so without fear of what may happen.

➤ **Give short-term adjustments.** Huddling players when they seem to have lost their way in games can be significant.

➤ **Increase energy levels.** The break is not the time to dwell on mistakes but can be used to give a quick dose of spirit. *"Forget about what happened; now is our time to go."*

➤ **Provide instructional points.** A few quick tips can help players deal with situations and improve. When coaches notice something that will assist, gathering everyone is the best way to let all know.

➤ **Relieve stress.** A few funny words can help players relax. *"Now we have them right where we want them,"* is an example.

➤ **Offer teachable moments.** Coaches can communicate and motivate when faced with difficult circumstances. Examples of these moments may be the times when the team is losing badly, or when they experience a lack of sportsmanship by their foe.

➤ **Give the last push.** Bringing the team in toward the end of the game can give teams that extra rest and push to give their all.

➤ **Explain long-term focus.** Sometimes teams seem to lose their way during the season. Coaches can have a team meeting to figure out what to do from that point. At the higher levels of sports, the players themselves may assemble the team to hash things out.

Final Thoughts

Coaches can end each team session with a huddle for a "go team" cheer.

Coaches can encourage one of the team leaders to give a few inspirational words, too. Teammates can motivate better than coaches, sometimes.

As mentioned, having too many team assemblies takes away the desired effect of them.

CHAPTER 11

~

Creating a Team Atmosphere

Getting individuals with different personalities, backgrounds, and skill levels into a cohesive unit takes expertise.

Following is a personal short story which attests to the importance of coaches letting players know what is expected of them.

My *welcome to professional baseball* moment came on the first day of arrival. After getting there too late to play in the game that our team lost by a huge margin, I got on the team bus to head to our next stop. Our manager, who I had yet to meet, was disgusted with the game, with my new team's play, and with a lack of togetherness among the players. He broke into an expletive-filled tirade about the importance of working as a team. The coach spewed more 4 letter words together than I had heard my whole life. Even though I was shaking in my shoes, I marveled at his linguistic abilities and abruptly realized I was no longer in college.

He threatened that changes would be made if things didn't improve. I quickly became enlightened to a simple fact: baseball was now a business. Things were taken seriously, and people's livelihood depended on performance.

Changes on that team *were* made, and soon after. The next day, two of the team's players were released – another went back to a lower level, and still another moved into a utility role. I believe that was the best introduction to pro ball I could have had. I gained the understanding that it was either produce, work together, or "*get lost.*"

Not much about this coach's actions would be suitable for youth sports, except what I learned that night on the bus. In a different way of expressing it, every player should know what is expected of him or her from the very beginning. They should know that "*team*" is important. At the youth levels, too, everyone needs to know the expectations, including the assistant coaches and parents, as well as the team members.

BRUCE BOCHY

The San Francisco Giants have won 3 championships in 6 years with players most experts felt weren't the most talented. A leading reason for that consistency is Giants manager, Bruce Bochy. The ironic thing is that most people would not recognize him. With his unassuming personality, Bruce is a worthy role model to youth coaches. He keeps the emphasis on the players, and not on him. Also, he is adept at keeping his players' hearts in the games and the coaches focused on the team. Like many of the best leaders, Bochy does much of his work behind the scenes.

Also like other prominent coaches, Bochy expects commitment, accountability, and acceptance of each other. Blending those traits brings harmony, and winning often follows. Bochy has shown that teams who stay together and play the game the right way can beat even more talented teams.

His coaching style allows players to be and enjoy themselves. Often, his adult athletes rally together like a high school team. It's a refreshing sight to see a professional team pumping up the fans when it's usually the other way around.

The champion managers have ways of keeping the weight of the moment off the players. Bruce Bochy knows that the best performance comes when players are happy and play with courage.

Lessons Learned from Coach Bruce Bochy:

1. The games are about the athletes, period.
2. It has to be enjoyable.
3. You don't need to have the most talented team to win.
4. Pressure is a performance killer more often than not.
5. Behind-the-scenes leadership is more effective than showing off during games.

ACTIVATING A TEAM-FIRST APPROACH

"Good teams become great ones when the members trust each other enough to surrender the 'me' for the 'we.'"

– Coach Phil Jackson, Basketball

Preview – If players learn nothing more than the value of being part of a group, playing will have been worth it. More exists to team chemistry than winning.

<u>T</u>ogether

<u>E</u>veryone

<u>A</u>chieves

<u>M</u>ore

<u>T</u>ogether

<u>E</u>veryone

<u>A</u>ppreciates

<u>M</u>ore

<u>T</u>rust

<u>E</u>ffort

<u>A</u>ttitude

<u>M</u>atter

— My definitions of what a team is about.

Many of my most memorable sports memories are of the joy and camaraderie I had with my teammates. The friendships and day-to-day experiences are what I and most retired athletes miss. I have been part of teams that won, but that had internal turmoil. Some teams thrive without chemistry because talent overcomes many obstacles. I have been a part of teams that lost, but that had consistent team unity. The seasons with the latter seemed to fly by and were more enjoyable even when the victories were elusive.

One of the usual statements from players and coaches of championship teams is about how close the players were with one another. People often believe winning produces chemistry. That's not always the case, even though it helps.

Coaches should want personal success for players, but they also have to think of the whole team. Molding individuals into a team is not an easy thing at any level of competition. Players are different and the worries to do well can create a *"me-first"* mentality. Also, at the youth levels, coaches have to deal with parents who have various ambitions for their kids. Different goals for playing add to the complexity of everyone working together.

Athletes may not sense it, but those who are out for personal glory only, have less joy. Players only out for themselves get in the way of team progress.

Players who believe it is about the team feel best after games. A team-first outlook helps athletes learn that teamwork and striving together for group goals trumps personal achievements. Also, working with others on group goals creates stronger bonds among teammates. Both individual and team happiness come when coaches promote the value of the whole.

Team chemistry begins with the head coach and their relationship with the other coaches. When coaches get along well, athletes recognize that and learn from it. Coaches with ethical behavior and moral character set the stage for the players.

Following are ways coaches can create a unified team atmosphere.

Coaches Should:

➢ Find assistants and players with exemplary character. When coaches draft teams, they should watch for players who display impressive character. Athletes with integrity help player interaction and team harmony.

➢ Address any in-team turmoil or gossip as soon as possible.

➢ Explain that every player is a critical part of the team, and that the team is dependent on one another. Chemistry begins when players buy into team aspirations and accept their roles.

➢ Avoid displaying individual statistics. Personal numbers endorse individuals over the team.

➢ Praise players who sacrifice their statistics with team plays.

➢ Identify individual accomplishments with praise, but emphasize group achievement with genuine excitement.

➢ Applaud players who are willing to play positions that are not their best ones or their favorites.

➢ Commit to finding ways to help players feel part of the group. Players who feel they contribute tend to trust each other and pull together, so focusing on their development helps that.

➢ Commend role players and hard workers who do not have as integral a part as the star players do. Using high energy players as examples helps encourage others to do the same.

➢ Never neglect talking to the players on the bench. You can and should tutor them as if they were in the game.

➢ Praise players who own up to their mistakes. People with honor do not blame others. Coaches should create the slant that the team wins and loses together.

➢ Show appreciation for players who never miss practice. No better sign of team loyalty exists.

➢ Compliment players who pull for others.

➢ Have team members pair off with different players instead of always the same ones when doing drill work.

➢ Help all players feel a part of the team's successes, no matter how bad their individual performances.

➢ Point out that personal accomplishment only comes because of contributions from others.

➢ Encourage players to do things together away from the games. Deeper friendships result from time together. Relationships give kids a greater purpose than just playing.

➢ Explain that teams and players handle hard times better as a group.

➢ Encourage others to follow the lead of the players who assume a team leadership role.

➢ Watch for players who may be a bad influence on other team members and try to talk with all about doing the right things.

Final Thoughts

It's an incredible accomplishment and feeling to see players blend into a cohesive unit. Once a team believes the whole is better than the parts, coaches should feel a sense of triumph.

It bears repeating that a harmonious team will have the most fun — which is the overall goal of young players.

Developing a cohesive team environment can lead to teams having a superiority complex. Coaches must not allow an elitist line to grow, but only one of pride.

Coaches should ask bench sitters to keep their heads in the game and stay ready, but let them know it's OK to enjoy themselves, too.

Close-knit teams have players who wish to remain on the same team year after year. Longevity of playing together builds even stronger bonds among people, both youngsters and adults.

For teams that win championships, even stronger bonds develop. Something extra special exists when teams make it to the top.

Teams with chemistry make it less likely for parents to become disenchanted. Parents recognize the joy and camaraderie their kids have and will hesitate to rock the boat.

REWARDING THE RIGHT THINGS

"We try to stress the little things because little things lead to big things."

— Coach Steve Alford, Basketball

Preview — Rewards are OK when used for teaching the right lessons, like those of dedication and teamwork.

"Win today and I will treat everyone to pizza."

— Coach to the team

At the end of my baseball camps and clinics, the coaches handed out awards. Many kids became sad when they were not chosen. Those upset athletes led to unhappy parents who had to deal with their disappointed children. I understood their concerns. However, I believe the awards had their place when they were for the right things. The honors were not for being the best players, but for life lessons. The initial lesson was that not everyone wins and gets an award. That's a reality that young people need to learn, even if it means a few tears.

We recognized players daily for things like best attitude, most coachable, best hustle, best teammate, most improved, and best play of the day. Those things served to motivate players from day to day. Also, those were the things coaches wanted kids to understand were the essential attributes of sports.

Having rewards for statistics and winning sends the message that sports are only for the best players. They lead to athletes playing for awards, personal marks, and victories.

That Procedure is Harmful Because It:

- ✓ Takes the point away from the concept of team play and improvement.
- ✓ Rewards kids for things they cannot always control. Triumph and favorable statistics depend on many things, with good luck a major contributor. Just because a team loses does not mean they played poorly. Athletes should feel proud after well-played and hard fought matches, even after losing.
- ✓ Usually recognizes the same and best players most of the time. Other players lose desire and self-esteem when they do not get recognition.
- ✓ Establishes a precedent that's hard for coaches to get out of because kids expect something all the time.
- ✓ Puts coaches in awkward positions with children and parents who feel slighted by the coach.
- ✓ Leads to negotiation that may turn into hurt feelings.

However, rewards for teamwork, improvement, and socialization are beneficial. A system of awards that motivates kids to work hard in practice and on their own is valuable. Here are ways of rewarding youth, so they learn the things that are important.

Coaches Can Honor:

- ➢ **Attendance**. Players who show up all the time deserve acclaim.
- ➢ **Teachable athletes**. Recognize the kids who listen and are willing to try the things taught.
- ➢ **Hustle**. Players who move with enthusiasm in their step deserve credit.
- ➢ **Helpfulness**. Athletes deserve approval when they help set up before and clean up after games.
- ➢ **Consideration**. Players who root for teammates warrant appreciation. A special mention should go to those who cheer on their team even when not in the game at the time.
- ➢ **Respectfulness**. Athletes who show regard to all deserve tributes.
- ➢ **Improvement**. When players figure out something they've had a hard time getting, they earn praise.
- ➢ **Character**. Kids who are able to accept tough situations deserve mention.

Final Thoughts

Coaches can give players some small token for the above things or special mention at team events.

All kids like accolades, whether they show it or not. You should do your best to spread out awards over the season. The right rewards often lead to motivated, hopeful, and willing-to-learn players.

Having league awards for winning the championship and most valuable players is fine. Striving to be the best is inherent in competition, and that is as it should be. But, you can still teach life beyond victory and achievement with appreciation awards.

FINDING CONFIDENCE LEVELS

"Persistence can change failure into extraordinary achievement."

– Coach Marv Levy, Football

Preview – Asking for volunteers allows coaches to find players' confidence levels. That information helps managers make game decisions.

"OK, who wants to show everyone how to do this?"

– Coach's question to the team

I'll never forget the player I asked to demonstrate a few drills to the team for me. She struggled with one of them. After thanking her, I set up stations with the same drills. The players got to choose which station they wanted to start at. The struggling player immediately went to the exercise she didn't do well at. I knew then that she would go far in sports and life.

I love asking for volunteers. It's a fine way to learn who the confident and fearless athletes are. The surprising thing is that many of the players who volunteer aren't the best athletes. Some players have the faith and courage to handle the tense situations better than others. As a coach, knowing who the self-assured and fearless players are can help you when making lineup and game decisions.

Watching kids demonstrate skills in front of others shows coaches a lot. It can indicate which players have confidence and which ones need self-assurance. It can also help players learn to handle pressure and adversity when their demonstrations do not go well.

Following are ways coaches can help players recognize and build courage, resilience, and trust in themselves.

Coaches Should:

➤ Ask for volunteers to demonstrate a skill – this allows a coach to see which players have the confidence to display their skills in front of the team.

➤ Challenge players with drills and tense game situations to see how they perform.

➤ Ask players to work on the things they struggle with on their own and observe which players do that.

➤ Watch player body language before and after demonstrations.

➤ Have players with little certainty show the easier moves. Once they prove to themselves that they can do it and do it under the spotlight, their courage grows. In due time, coaches can have them show the advanced techniques.

➤ Have the more resilient athletes show the most challenging things. Even if they fail, they tend to not take it too hard. Their healthy outlook helps the less confident players see how to handle failure.

➤ Always praise and thank players for participating in demonstrations.

➤ Never make too big of a deal when volunteers don't perform well. Coaches should act calm, explain what can be better, and have them try again. A patient reaction from the coach is mandatory. Coaches should not let players get frustrated by explaining, *"That is why we practice."*

Final Thoughts

This technique may spur some to practice at home, too, so they will be ready the next time they demonstrate something.

Sometimes, coaches may have to or want to nominate a player to show something rather than asking for volunteers. Over time, coaches should have all team members show something under the spotlight.

Many coaches think confidence comes from telling kids they can do it. That may help, but it won't stay for long without sweat and accomplishment under pressure.

When players have the opportunity to see others fail, it creates a safe zone, and those who are less sure of themselves will begin to volunteer. When the time comes and coaches see all players willing to volunteer, they have accomplished the goal of helping kids develop bravery.

Coaches should be hesitant to have players do things that may embarrass them, though.

PUTTING PLAYERS IN POSITIONS TO SUCCEED

"I think what coaching is all about, is taking players and analyzing their ability, put them in a position where they can excel within the framework of the team winning. And I hope that I've done that in my 33 years as a head coach."

– Coach Don Shula, Football

Preview – Coaches should find ways that give players the best chance to perform well.

"I put you in right then because I knew you could handle the situation."

– Coach to the player after the game

When I batted lead-off or second in the batting order, I felt the coach's faith in me. Batting down in the batting order did the opposite.

I have worked with many hard-throwing ballplayers who wanted no part of pitching. Their decision not to pitch is usually much to the chagrin of the coaches and parents who think they would excel at it. The pressure of being the one with all the eyes on them is too much for them, so they refuse to try it. Every athlete's mindset is different. You must match players' mental and physical capabilities to determine the game spots and playing positions that are best for them.

The best-case coaching scenario is when coaches have players who are all *"gamers."* A gamer is a sports term for players who are gritty, unafraid, and give it their all. Unfortunately, that rarely, if ever, is the case. Most teams consist of all types, from gamers to casual players.

A familiar coaching phrase in sports is, *"We put players in positions to succeed."* That coaching philosophy is essential for youth coaches, too. Playing athletes in spots they are not mentally ready for can turn them into kids who don't want to play anymore. Some athletes relish being in the tight spots and positions in games; others do not. Coaches may be able to avoid putting timid players into stressed game situations until they are ready for it. That coaching strategy can help keep anxious players engaged over the course of time.

To Help Put Players in the Right Spots, Coaches Can:

➢ Learn each player's strengths so they can play to them in the right game situations.

➢ Read athletes' body language in different circumstances. A player's facial expressions and energy level are often the best indicators of confidence levels.

➢ Talk to players one-on-one to gauge their state of mind. Players' mental states change over the course of the season.

➢ Only play players in places they've rehearsed enough to feel comfortable. Avoid putting low confidence kids in the key positions that may hurt their self-esteem and future in the sport.

➢ Set lineups where players feel most comfortable and can use their respective strengths.

➢ Know which players love to be in clutch situations and which ones cringe away from those.

➢ Get players out of spots, when possible, when all confidence goes. When coaches can see players do not want the action to come their way, they should consider a position move before embarrassment sets in.

➤ Help the players with less assurance build the courage to try things they were nervous about before. That process begins at practice, and gaining confidence takes different amounts of time for each player. As players gain experience, they learn to trust themselves under demanding circumstances. As a player's confidence builds, you can put them in more challenging roles.

➤ Speak in the plural as much as possible. Statements like, *"We'll figure it out,"* and *"We will do better the next time,"* helps children relax, so they feel like it is not all up to them.

➤ Give players mental tips in practice so they learn to stay relaxed during intense game situations.

➤ Tell stories about players who overcame a lack of belief in themselves and ended up having flourishing careers.

Final Thoughts

Sometimes coaches have no choice but to keep players in vulnerable spots in games. At those times, coaches must be careful about over-encouraging the player. Even though coaches have the best of intentions, too much attention adds strain. Saying, *"You can do this,"* too often builds pressure and may be worse than remaining silent. Coaches may want to ask parents to limit their encouragement of struggling kids, too.

Coaching displays of disappointment after mistakes make it worse for athletes the next time they are in the same situation.

CHAPTER 12

Creating a Learning Space for All

"Coaches must learn how to work with different personalities. The first step is getting to know the players. The more they learn about a player's makeup, the easier it is to find ways to motivate them."

This is a letter I receive from a parent, which talks of one of the many player issues that coaches have to deal with.

Coach,

The pressure my son puts on himself to succeed in baseball is TREMENDOUS. Which means that not only during games is he driven to succeed, but he is even during father-son practices on an otherwise empty ball field or batting cage. If he's not hitting the cover off the ball or throwing laser-accurate throws to 1st base, he gets SO down on himself. He wants instant answers - tell me RIGHT NOW how I missed that ball or overthrew the first baseman. He gets so frustrated at even the most routine baseball tasks when he doesn't perform. In a nutshell, the pressure he's putting on himself to succeed is taking the joy out of how he experiences baseball. If you have anything you can share with me, any guidance you can give me to help my son, I would be forever grateful

GREGG POPOVICH

Gregg Popovich of the San Antonio Spurs is another coaching luminary who has figured out many of the keys to coaching. Popovich has united players from different countries into champions and consistent contenders. With his matter of fact manner, he doesn't feel the need to be real demonstrative. He is a master in keeping egos in check, a central aspect of coaching at all levels.

Gregg Popovich said to Eric Freeman of Ball Don't Lie, *"Because you were born to these parents or this area geographically, or this situation, you deserve more than somebody else?...That's the most false notion one can imagine."*

"But I think a lot of people forget that. They think that they're entitled to what they have...So we talk about those things all the time. You have no excuse not to work your best. You have no reason not to be thankful every day that you have the opportunity to come back from a defeat because some people never even have the opportunity."

I love it when Coach Popovich says they talk about things like entitlements all the time. He feels it's essential to speak about who athletes should be, and that this should be done more than once. Gregg also believes in a line I often use with athletes – *"Figure it out."* Sometimes, the coach has instructed enough, and it's up to the players to execute.

He preaches about the importance of constant player communication on the court. Player interaction is vital in competitive action. It gives players a feeling of ownership that they have a direct say with how they compete.

Lessons Learned from Coach Gregg Popovich:

1. Athletes are not entitled to things just because they are better than others.
2. Game collaboration among players is essential.

3. Athletes have no reason not to work hard.
4. Players should show gratitude for the opportunity to play.
5. Coaches should talk to athletes about who they are and how they act.

DODGING THE FALSE PRAISE AND ENTITLEMENT

"Some people are born on third base and go through life thinking they hit a triple."

– Coach Barry Switzer, Football

Preview – Coaches must recognize what false praise is and know the dangers of it. The result often creates *"a feeling of entitlement."*

"You were awesome today."

– Coach to a team that played with little effort

I've had many players start out the season well as a result of their physical gifts. But they become complacent after a while, as everyone tells them how exceptional they are. It comes easy to them, but they improve little, if at all. I've also seen less talented athletes who develop through consistent work. No one tells them how much talent they have, but they praise their work ethic and improvement. Often, it's the talented players who quit sports young because they never learn to deal with setbacks.

As much as I believe in a positive coaching style, it can be misunderstood. Praising youth is vital, but it has its limits. Many coaches are afraid of hurting players' feelings, self-worth, and confidence. They'll give praise to avoid this, regardless of what the players' effort levels were. False praise is telling kids they played well when they didn't. It tells players they have a lot of talent, despite the fact that they exert little.

False recognition gives athletes the wrong sense of identity and security. Athletes begin to believe they can do no wrong. They think they contributed a considerable amount even when they didn't play hard. Misleading tributes result in players who do not accept challenges. It limits their ability to improve and figure things out on their own. Too many unwarranted accolades cause kids to fail to assess their actions honestly. They do not learn a solid work ethic, either. The messages of resiliency, humility, and reality are lost when coaches praise all the time.

Little growth comes from telling kids how wonderful they are. At some point in their life, someone is going to be honest with them. Those players handle that adversity poorly because they only heard how valuable they were for so long.

The most dangerous form of false praise is when kids are given a sense of entitlement, when they feel they have the right to something without having to work for it. Athletes begin to believe they deserve gifts and notoriety just because of playing, who they are, or how well they play. Their arrogance can cause problems.

Coaches and organizations create the privileged mindset by giving players things for no reason. Awarding trophies just for playing – participation awards – has added to our age of entitlement. On the surface, this does no harm. If it makes kids feel proud of participating, then the intent of the award is OK. Unfortunately, it may give kids a sense of unwarranted achievement because trophies suggest accomplishment.

When groups have reserve money for awards, it has a better use. Leagues and teams should decide what that use should be. One alternative to trophies is T-shirts that say something like, "*I am proud to have given my all to my team or league.*" T-shirts are worn out in the community and display a sense of pride. Excess money can also go to a local charity. A donation can make people feel terrific about an organization, not to mention it can give players a real understanding of what it means to have compassion.

Damaging forms of entitlement exist, usually involving the superior athletes. The elite players receive handouts and praise to the point where they can easily develop a "*What's in it for me*" posture. Colleges, sports agents, and national sports organizations cater to the best and foster entitlement. Privilege is the opposite of what athletes should learn.

Getting things without earning them is not an accurate picture of the world. Kids should learn to work for things. A sense of entitlement can cause many young players to turn into apathetic athletes. They only play hard when the stakes are high enough. Additionally, other players dislike the elite athlete's manner, which can hurt team chemistry and performance.

Coaches can avoid false praise and motivate in the following ways.

Coaches Should:

> Not tell players how well they did unless it's the truth.

> Deliver the most praise for energy spent, not for results or talent.

> Give honest evaluations of effort to players, even when the honesty may hurt their feelings. There is a time and place for honesty, though. Right after games and in front of others is not the time or venue to put players on the spot. Giving critiques in a helpful way is best, instead of blasting a player's effort.

> Teach kids the value of hard work and exemplify that with your own actions.

> Have players earn their spots on the field and positions in the lineups.

> Evaluate each player's strengths and weaknesses, and set realistic expectations for each athlete.

> Explain that the real winners are the players who are better at the end of the season than they were in the beginning. Tell everyone improvement is not a given for just having played

> Give players areas of direction with short- and long-term ends to reach. Some adjustments have to do with mental changes and some have to do with the physical ones. Adults should explain that it takes time to change skill and mindset and players should not expect overnight success.

> Use mid-season report cards to check for the stated objectives and progress.

➤ Have an end of season report card to assess each player's progress. Report cards can be oral.

➤ Give off-season suggestions to help prepare for the next year.

➤ Not give gifts of any sort for outstanding play, joining a team, or just for playing.

Final Thoughts

Coaches must always take into account the age of players when making evaluations and giving analysis.

Giving praise for hard work is never false.

Coaches must be prepared to provide and back up assessments of players to their parents.

COPING WITH LEARNING DIFFERENCES

"Treat each player as your own son/daughter if you can... the parents have invested in you."

– Coach Hank Iba, Basketball

Preview – Coaches need a coordinated plan to deal with players with learning differences.

"What the heck are you doing?"
"What did I just tell you?"
"Where is Billy?"
"Quit playing in the dirt."
"Go sit down if you can't get along."

– Disgusted coach

Inexperienced coaches find themselves saying these things a lot. My earliest encounters with athletes with learning differences and behavioral challenges were frustrating. I could not figure why players would not:

- ✓ Pay attention
- ✓ Sit still
- ✓ Integrate with other kids
- ✓ Stop daydreaming
- ✓ Stop playing in the dirt
- ✓ Ever look at me
- ✓ Stop asking what time it was, where their parents were, or when we were going to do something else.

Most annoying was the boldness of some players, and how they failed to do what I asked them to do. Players who seemed to disrupt the flow ruined my days. I took it as a personal affront and let it affect my coaching. Before long, I found myself asking them, *"Do you even want to be here?"* Then I began to ignore them, or I would sit them down for a while. My tactics created bad feelings for all. In time, I became more aware of players with learning differences, and realized I could do better. Making the effort to become better at handling all type players became one of my most rewarding teaching experiences.

Working with players who have focus issues can offer significant challenges. But it can also turn into a satisfying experience. Demonstrating a competent way of dealing with kids who need more can be a valuable educational experience for players, parents, and other coaches, too. Coaches who can handle players with learning differences will generally earn the admiration and respect of everyone involved with the team.

Here are tips to help with athletes who have learning differences.

Coaches Can:

> ➤ Ask parents to inform you about any learning differences or behavioral issues. Some parents may be hesitant at first, but assure them

that it's best if you know so you're better equipped to help their child. When coaches know a player cannot sit or stay attentive for long, it helps with coaching patience and practice plans.

➤ Get advice from parents about working with their child.

➤ Ask parents who else they're comfortable with knowing about the situation. Some parents may prefer other players not be told, even when the child's issue is usually apparent. If the parents are comfortable with it, you should review the situation with the coaching staff and team. Getting input from others and having a coordinated plan is a start to helping the player and situation.

➤ Read a little about any diagnosed disorders online. The more knowledgeable about the difference, the more prepared you'll be to help the child.

➤ Make sure everyone grasps that a learning difference does not make one a bad kid.

➤ Show patience with the player for all others to see, as that helps others relax.

➤ Not allow others to show disgust with players who seem to do their own thing.

➤ Discuss actions with the player when their behavior becomes dangerous or takes enjoyment from others. A learning difference does not mean you need to allow rude or irreverent behavior, either.

➤ Keep parents informed about what you're doing and let them know that the coaching staff is doing what they can to help.

Final Thoughts

You must hold all players accountable for their actions, but they should also realize some situations are works in progress.

Coaches must remain on the lookout for qualities they can build on in all players and bring those out of them.

When players are out of control and dangerous to others, coaches must have a conversation with the player's parents. Any discussion about removing a child from the team should be a last resort, and only when the child cannot maintain self-control.

Coaches should never ignore, nor give an inordinate amount of time to any player. Finding the right amount of attention to give harder-to-manage players takes the time to figure out.

HELPING THE LOW- OR NO-CONFIDENCE PLAYER

"All coaching is, is taking a player where he can't take himself."

– Coach Bill McCartney, Football

Preview – Many coaches suggest that athletes are mentally weak. That talk is one of the most unhelpful things coaches do.

"It's all in your head."
"She gets psyched out."
"He gets so nervous."
"He just freezes up."
"She is not aggressive."
"He doesn't want it."

– Common adult analysis about struggling players

A friend asked me about how important mental toughness is in a ballplayer and whether it can be taught. I answered that it is a necessity, and ensured that players can attain it. He mentioned he thought it would be an interesting article that could help athletes. I know he's correct because, in my many years of teaching the game, one of the main concerns parents have is about what's going on in their child's head, especially in games. Typical statements like the above ones attest to their way of thinking.

All of the statements address the notion that something crazy is going on between their child's ears, which is causing them to perform poorly. After all, *"They can do it in practice, but not in games,"* is just another statement that implies it must be in the player's head. These statements generally refer to some mental block and a lack of confidence on why athletes struggle. Usually after observing the struggling player, I find incorrect fundamentals as the reason for ineptitude. Things have only become psychological because others have convinced them of that.

Players can change from mentally weak to strong by improving their skill mechanics. However, once adults convince players they have a mental impediment, that turnaround is harder. Any statement like, *"It's mental,"* or *"It's all in your head"* harms a young player's athletic development. Little is more damaging to athletes than thinking that they have *"head problems."* Once they are self-conscious about their issue, trust and improvement prove to be more difficult. Even worse news, the insinuation stays with players for a long time.

These coaching moves can help kids get out of slumps and start to believe in themselves.

Coaches Should:
> ➢ Never mention a lack of steady play as a mental thing.
> ➢ Convince players that improving their fundamentals will solve their struggles. Fundamental flaws are more controllable than psychological ones. Physical actions are things players can work on to change in the near future. Believing habits are the source of problems keeps it from being in a player's head. Improving the basics with hard work is the best chance of limiting the length of a slump.
> ➢ Give mechanical tips, which can give players the hope they need to play with some measure of confidence. Even when coaches don't know what a player is doing wrong, technical suggestions may help. Providing skill tips is better than letting players go on with no clue about what is wrong. Having hope, when self-assurance wanes, is a key to a turnaround. *"Willing things to happen"* rarely works when there

are mechanical inefficiencies. Faith in one's abilities can return in time with the improvement of actions.

➢ Help teams focus on proper execution, which brings group confidence back.

➢ Add extra work. Often, players get away from the basics, which then leads to bad habits and a drop in performance. Extra work may break the bad habits and bring timing back. Hard work solves most issues and allows players to relax, knowing they have done all they can to get better. Balancing enough rest with additional work is necessary, so fatigue doesn't set in.

➢ Address other aspects of the game too, so as not to make the slumping area as obvious. It never helps when people fuss too much over a rough period because sometimes, things have to run their course. Working on other parts of the game helps players get their mind off of struggles for a spell, and other talents can rise to the top in that way. When players gain confidence in another aspect of play, it can help build it in the struggling areas.

➢ Help players learn and work on visualization skills. Often, the ability to see one performing well in the mind carries over into success.

➢ Remain optimistic. A coach's pessimism will not improve a player's trust in themselves, whereas encouragement gives hope.

➢ Keep players relaxed and focused as much as possible in games. Learning to display confident body language helps bring back self-reliance, too. Looking defeated often results in poor play.

➢ Suggest outside coaching help when players appear completely frustrated.

➢ Give players time off when nothing else seems to work. Getting away from the playing for a day or two may allow players to relax and start with a new outlook.

➢ Point out the quality things players did in other areas of play.

Final Thoughts

A strong mental game only goes as far as one's mechanics can take them. The better the fundamentals, the better chance a player has of succeeding.

The result of doing things "right" is confidence, a desire to work hard, and fun. Everyone will notice how a player's mental game improves when their fundamentals improve.

Once players feel mentally strong, they have the confidence and the willingness to compete, no matter the circumstances. They accept challenges, when in the past they would rather let their teammates handle the tough situations.

Coaches must never lose patience and faith in struggling athletes.

Having an "*all fun day*" team practice is an excellent way to relax kids.

The best result of struggle is that players usually learn to better handle their next downturn after working through one. Developing resiliency helps athletes deal with troubles, a necessity in both sports and life.

PROCESSING THE TEENAGE PLAYERS

"I'm not buddy-buddy with the players. If they need a buddy, let them buy a dog."

– Whitey Herzog, Baseball

Preview – Coaches of teenage and high school athletes have an added challenge.

"Tommy was the sweetest, nicest boy around, but now he seems to look at me like I'm the enemy?"

– Coach to another adult

I asked a parent how their coach, a friend of mine, was doing. *"Not good,"* was the reply. *"He's not having fun, he and his son are fighting all the time."* *"That's a shame,"* I responded. Having dealt with both for many years, I know the parent and child are kind hearted.

It becomes comical in a way, but it's predictable. Kids who were quick to listen and laugh before, now look at me like they never knew me. My best jokes that once got roaring laughter now receive nothing but a cold stare from the same players. In my early coaching years, I thought I must have gotten on their wrong side in some way. In time, I grew to understand it – they are now teenagers.

Coaches will begin to notice a big difference when athletes reach their teenage years. Once-joyful players may become unsmiling and appear to be less coachable ones. It's important to understand that the changes really have nothing to do with you as a coach, but more to do with the fact that puberty has hit. Coaches of teenage players must adjust to maturing kids and prepare for defiance that may seem hostile toward adults.

Teenagers are eager to display their independence and may want less to do with adults. Even the most avid athletes can turn into bold and less interested students for a year or two (or forever). You must recognize that life changes are the reason for unresponsive athletes, and special handling is critical.

The keys to dealing with teenage athletes include the following.

Coaches Should:
> Prepare for the bored look, but remember it doesn't necessarily mean they're really uninterested.
> Not take changing player attitudes as a personal affront.
> Never allow players to feel like they're getting the best of you to the point that you're showing frustration.
> Not treat players like little kids, but rather as burgeoning adults.
> Stay away from the *"You have to"* statements. While it's a standard coaching phrase, *"You have to"* is one of the most non-motivating

phrases you can utter to an athlete. "*You have to work harder*," or "*You have to do it the way I showed you*" turns teenagers off fast. Young players may listen and try what coaches suggest. But teens, when told they *have* to do something, can become defensive and want to prove they can do it their way.

➢ Avoid giving the "*Do you want to be here?*" speech too often.

➢ Bring the enthusiasm – players will favor the coaching passion even when they appear uninterested.

There are several ways you can treat players more like adults. Explain at the start of the season that they're not kids anymore, and that responsibilities come with this. Coaches should explain that these things are now expected from them.

Players Should:
➢ Be on time.

➢ Work hard during training and in the school classroom.

➢ Hustle on the field.

➢ Be a dependable teammate.

➢ Be receptive to coaching.

➢ Follow all team policies and understand the consequences of breaking rules.

➢ Treat others with respect.

➢ Use social media wisely. This sentiment probably must be repeated throughout the season.

➢ Speak up for themselves rather than having parents do it for them. They must figure out that no longer being a kid means they can't rely on mom and dad to do everything for them anymore.

Coaches should also explain what the players can expect from the coaches.

Coaches Will:
➢ Be open and honest with players and give fair evaluations.

➤ Expect athletes to deal with the coach's assessments.

➤ Give options. Words like, "*You may want to give this way a try*" offers players a choice. Most players tend to disengage when they hear "*Do it this way or else.*"

➤ Use depth charts, so players know their standing at each position.

➤ Discuss the roles of each player, so players have an understanding of the expectations and goals you have for them.

➤ Explain that players represent more than just themselves and their team. They represent the sponsor, school, organization, or city.

➤ Set up a small group of players who report to the coaches about any serious issues team members may have. This system gives the team a voice and stops problems before they arise. This process also reinforces their maturing positions.

➤ Set up a plan for extra training for any players interested.

➤ Give a clear end-of-season report card to help players know the areas of their game that need improvement.

Final Thoughts

Some teenage players may seem like they actually want to upset adults. Coaches must do their best to avoid getting into an adversarial relationship with them.

You may have to use disciplinary measures more with this age group. As long as you're fair, you'll most often maintain respect in the end. Once players have served their punishment, they should be given a second chance. A player's admiration for his or her coach may come if the coach always uses fair treatment and then acts as if nothing happened after any chastisement.

Many coaches think that becoming friends with players is the way to go. Earning their regard is best, and that may mean a friendship or not. Acting buddy-buddy with players may mean the player has control of the relationship.

Coaches should talk about the dangers of alcohol use, performance-enhancing, and recreational drugs. You must emphasize that winning and achieving full potential are only praiseworthy through legal and ethical means. Teenagers get that message at school too, but it is an excellent message to be reinforced by their coaches as well. Discussing stories of drug and alcohol abuse in the news by famous athletes is an opening for that talk. Touching on these issues with younger athletes is OK, too.

APPRECIATING THE HOT PLAYER

*"**What you lack in talent can be made up with desire, hustle, and giving 110% all the time.**"*

– Coach Don Zimmer, Baseball

Preview – Dealing with players who are in the zone requires coaching skill, too.

"Hey, no one touch Bobby. He is on fire!"

– Familiar words about the athlete who is playing flawlessly.

I recall coaches who would go days without talking to me. You might think that was a bad thing, but it was OK with me. Coaches have a different tactic when players perform at a higher than average level.

There is no player I look forward to working with less than the one who has 15 hits for his last 18 at-bats. My thought is, *"Can't improve on that; I can only screw them up."* Success is a tricky area. When you see a player in the groove, it's best to stay quiet and let the groove play out. When you give advice or verbally recognize how well a player is doing, you risk a change in habits before their hot streak would have ended. It's best to let an athlete keep going without bringing to their attention how well they are doing.

These are some coaching suggestions for dealing with *"On Fire"* athletes:

259

Coaches Should:

- ➤ Stress the basics. Hot players tend to think things come easy and dismiss the basics after a while. Often, exceptional times turn into struggling ones because players begin to take the little things for granted.
- ➤ Make sure players don't over work. Flourishing athletes know their efforts pay off, so sometimes they figure doing more will produce even better. However, overdoing it tires the body and mind. Maintaining the exact routine, no more or less, is best.
- ➤ Be sure to not mention a hot streak in front of the player. When players are in the zone, don't mention it. Sometimes it only takes a mention of the hot streak to change a player's mentality. Once they become conscious of how well they're doing, it can be enough to take them out of the zone. When the groove begins to leave, players press, and before long they may struggle.
- ➤ Have the players increase their emphasis on other parts of the game to keep their mind off a hot streak.

Final Thoughts

Ignoring players is generally never the way to go, but in this instance, it can be the exception to the rule. During these stretches, coaches can give more of their time to struggling players.

SURVIVING THE KNOW-IT-ALL AND THE BOLD PLAYER

"Make sure that team members know they are working with you, not for you."

— Coach John Wooden, Basketball

Preview – Earning the appreciation of mouthy and hesitant-to-listen players is another coaching challenge to embrace.

"This is the way I do it"

– Player statement with a look of leave me alone

I've had many youth baseball players who had little interest in listening to what I told them. That surprises me because I have a major league baseball background. All coaches must prepare for the hard-to-coach athletes. Good coaching can get players to change their attitude after a while. Few feelings are better for a coach than gaining the admiration of a player who once showed you no regard.

First, you should try to have an understanding of why some players may not listen.

Players Resistant to Coaching May Have:
- ✓ Had success doing it their way.
- ✓ A parent or another coach showing them one way, and they are not interested in changing.
- ✓ A resistance and stubbornness to any instruction.
- ✓ The belief that they are doing it the way the coaches are telling them to do it.
- ✓ An independent streak that makes them want to figure everything out on their own.

It's most annoying when athletes don't want coaching and they challenge you with backtalk and sneers. These bold players may have little parental guidance in their lives and a general distrustful perception of adults. They like to show their teammates how tough they are by not taking instruction from the coaches. Their antagonistic conduct and actions disrupt the team, to their pleasure. Many brash athletes may have behavioral issues that have nothing to do with the coaches.

The cocky, rude players are the hardest to get through to, but you can try these tactics.

Coaches Should:

➤ Look at the hard-to-coach athletes as a chance to influence a player's life; try not to see them as an un-coachable kid.

➤ Greet them daily by name, even though they may snicker back. Sometimes, killing them with kindness turns them around over time.

➤ Ignore their brash manner as much as possible and don't take their insolence to heart.

➤ Never give them the satisfaction of demoralizing the coaches. Sassy players hope to do just that.

➤ Not punish them with extra physical activity or offer the *"Have a better attitude"* line too often. Those actions can drive an un-repairable wedge into the situation.

➤ Spend as much time instructing them as every other player, even though that may be difficult.

➤ Praise them when they do things right – all youth deserve positive re-inforcement.

➤ Admonish them when they are disrespectful to others. They hope to intimidate and want control of things, and coaches should not allow them to do so.

➤ Inform parents of any promising actions. That can help the players who have tension with parents and those who may only play because of their parents' desires that they play. Upbeat talk may help ease the situation.

➤ Not placate athletes. Allowing a player to get away with continuing their rude ways, even though it may seem like the easy way out, is not OK. After a while of trying to coach them, there may be no alternative but to leave them alone for a spell. Remind players that you believe in them, even when they give the impression they do not care.

Final Thoughts

Many of the tactics that work to reach these types of players are the same as those used when coaching teenage athletes. Sometimes it's helpful to begin discussions with *"The way I see it..."* – it's the perfect phrase to open up conversations with people. It doesn't accuse anyone of anything, but it states an observation from the outside. In that way, people see it's a view and not an indictment.

Talking to players one-on-one is always a good option. Once players recognize a coach's willingness to listen, they may change for the better.

A patient, fair, and consistent stance gives players a chance to change. When players decide the coach cares about helping them, they may change their ways and learn to show respect.

CHAPTER 13

---~---

Creating a Mindset That Accepts and Adapts

Coaches must be willing to change and adapt to every player, instead of trying to change them into who coaches want them to be.

Here is a short story which shows that coaches can change. They may just need a little prompting from the right person.

One of my baseball students seemed to be in a better mood than usual one day. I asked him how things were going, knowing that he didn't care much for his coach. "*Great!*" he answered. "*Cool, what's up?*" I asked him. He told me that at a recent game, the coach's father walked out in front of the team at the post game talk. The father had just watched the game and said to his son:

"You have turned into the coach you hated to play for when you were young."

The player told me that time froze for a few seconds, but ever since then, the coach has had a much more positive tone with the team.

PAT SUMMITT

Another marvelous coach was the University of Tennessee's Pat Summitt. Coach Summitt sometimes coached in a style that youth coaches should not. She pushed players beyond the point they thought they could go. At the highest levels of sports, this method can work with the right type of athlete. At the lower levels though, her style isn't one that youth athletes will be ready for, and it could be detrimental in the long-term. There is no question, though, she was a remarkable leader and had many attributes that are exemplary for youth coaches.

According to author and speaker Molly Fletcher, Coach Summitt admitted she wanted to control every aspect of play at first. She eventually changed, believing that reaching potential came when players made some in-game decisions. She learned that coaches could only provide the instructions. Players had to come to know the game calls and plays on their own. Pat Summitt learned that letting go of total control was not easy, but over time, she recognized that over-coaching did not work.

Coach Summitt also encouraged feedback from players after praise and criticism. Her system had players respond with *"2 points"* after hearing approval, or *"rebound"* after criticism. This method served 3 intended purposes.

1. Players had to listen to catch those words. When they did not, the coaches would identify the player who was not listening.
2. Players knew that they could get rewarded, not just chastised.
3. The word rebound was beneficial for keeping players resilient. They learned the importance of bouncing back from criticism.

Coach Summitt also understood that progress does not come from silence. She taught players that keeping things inside took away from the necessary communication. At the lower levels of sports, coaches shouldn't expect too much player feedback, but they can encourage them to ask questions, and listen to get a sense of their feelings. Pat Summitt also wanted teams to confront their weaknesses. Summitt accomplished this by having players involved in deciding daily goals. Like many excellent coaches, she felt players give more when they have input on what they practice. Of course, coaches should never shy away from the things players don't like doing, either. Instead, they should find ways to make the monotonous things more exciting.

Most elite coaches borrow from John Wooden's philosophy, and Pat did the same. She believed in fair treatment for all, even though she may have treated each player differently.

Lessons Learned from Coach Pat Summitt:

1. It doesn't pay to over-coach athletes.
2. Players are accountable for listening.
3. Constructive criticism is something coaches can help players learn to accept and rebound from the next time.
4. Communication among all helps teams avoid unrest.
5. Fair treatment earns people's admiration.

TURNING AROUND THE NEGATIVE PLAYER

"Difficulties in life are intended to make us better, not bitter."

– Coach Dan Reeves, Football

Preview – Negative athletes think the worst is coming and often bring the whole team down with them.

"I told you I was not going to do well."

— Pessimistic player

I couldn't believe I heard that statement because it came from the best hitter on the team. He went out and performed well, but was mad after, thinking he should have done better. I just shook my head before beginning the long trail to help.

Some athletes use glum thoughts to motivate them. It may work sometimes, but it doesn't work for long or for most. Plus, it only takes one negative player to bring the entire team view down. Downbeat thoughts or actions usually have one of two possible outcomes. They either talk players into inefficient play, or they leave them unsatisfied even after doing well. One cannot win, at least in their mind. The coach's biggest concern is that *"downer"* players drag teams' satisfaction level down. That situation is most likely when it's one of the better players. Often, players will follow the lead of others, and when one gets negative it could become a team-wide occurrence.

Here are some of the actions that coaches must look for and act on.

Coaches Should Look for Players Who:
- ✓ Talk themselves into bad play by thinking they'll fail.
- ✓ Show disgust by swearing, throwing things, arguing, pouting, whining, or making excuses.
- ✓ Have wandering minds and lose attentiveness when things do not go their way.
- ✓ Have unrealistic hopes and want constant and immediate results.
- ✓ Are never satisfied and take the blame for losing.
- ✓ Only want to rehearse the things they do well.
- ✓ Cannot picture the long-term goal.

Coaches must attempt to turn draining attitudes into more hopeful athletes and people with these methods.

Coaches Should:

➤ Never allow gloomy thoughts and actions go without mentioning it to players. Asking the player to smile is one solution, even though they may not do it.

➤ Teach players to be hopeful. Athletes can learn to focus on happy thoughts, memories, and cues when they begin to think pessimistically.

➤ Explain that cheerful gestures bring about desirable ends and gloomy thoughts produce unwanted ones.

➤ Teach what positive visualization is. Athletes must learn to remember their successes and review those in their minds.

➤ Inform players that it's never advantageous to show the other team that the situation is getting the best of them.

➤ Explain that it's not just about them, but it's about the whole team.

➤ Ask players to recognize the productive things they do. I tell players who get mad every time they fail, it's only fair they express happiness when they do well.

➤ Help players develop long-term targets, instead of placing constant expectations of productivity on each outing.

Final Thoughts

Distrustful thinkers are not conscious of the detrimental effect they have on themselves and the team.

Some players are cynical in every aspect of their lives. Changing them into optimistic kids is more challenging. Coaches should know that frames of mind do not change overnight, but continual reinforcement of a healthy outlook helps in time.

AVERTING THE STAR PLAYER TREATMENT

"Talent is God-given. Be humble. Fame is man-given. Be grateful. Conceit is self-given. Be careful."

– Coach **John Wooden, Basketball**

Preview – Coaches should be careful of giving players the star treatment. They are the ones who gain the sense of entitlement.

"Let it slide, after all, where would we be without him?"

– One coach justifying a rule break to another coach

Following is an example of a letter that many coaches receive at some point.

Dear Coach,

I cannot believe you dropped our daughter from the starting line-up. She has been the best player on every team she has ever played on. If that continues, we will look for a different team for her.

I know of many players labeled as professional prospects quitting even before reaching high school. Those talented young athletes who were always told how awesome they were fizzled out when adversity arrived.

Many people fall into the trap of giving superior players the star treatment. They dole out over-the-top adulation and privilege to the best athletes. Parents are the biggest culprits of that, but coaches often fall into the trap, too. At the highest levels of sports, star players receive special treatment. When youth receive special privileges and treatment, it leads to problems. Primarily, those athletes may end up believing they are better than others and deserve special handling.

269

When players get the star treatment, they learn to shy away from tests when things do not come easy for them. They have never experienced ineffectiveness before, so they become upset and retreat from working hard. They become apprehensive and lack the mettle to reach beyond themselves. Also, the increased pressure of believing they have to live up to being the best overcomes them. Most will end up quitting the minute others outplay them.

Coaches have to walk a fine line with players' self-images. They should not treat the best players as too special. At the same time, they should not diminish their achievements, either.

Here are the things you can do to maintain balance with your top athletes.

Coaches Should:

➢ Resist telling a player how remarkable he or she is too often, especially in front of others.

➢ Not dwell on how exceptional a player is with the athlete's parents. Although nice to hear, parents know they are good and already have or develop grand illusions about their child's prospects. Often, those beliefs are unreasonable and can lead to enormous strain on the young one.

➢ Use other players as models of proficient play, not just the star player.

➢ Not give unique handling to the best players.

➢ Praise their effort to others, when they deserve it, rather than saying how incredible they are.

➢ Reinforce the value of "*team*," making sure not to make it about any one or two individuals.

➢ Put an end to cocky behavior at the earliest sign of it. A typical sign of that behavior is boastful and arrogant conduct.

➢ Find ways to challenge them more. Explain to the better players why they may be tested differently from others.

➢ Help kids embrace hardships, so they do not fear them. Explain to them that it takes courage to continue when things don't come so easy for them.

➢ Make it clear that hustle is essential because other players think highly of them. Teammates will resent those who are lazy or act like it is easy for them, even if they are the most successful players.

➢ Never allow the better athletes to show disgust with other players' performances. They must learn and understand that not everyone can do what they can.

➢ Describe the word humility and why it's a desirable trait.

Final Thoughts

Coaches should talk about the importance of school work to all players, especially the stars. The unique player may slack off in school, thinking they have their future made in the sports world.

Coaches should not allow themselves or others to expect too much of the above average players, either. Athletes should not get the "*You have college or professional talent*," talk before their high school years.

Coaches should be careful of developing the "*star team*" way of thinking, too. Some coaches think their teams have an edge by acting superior and arrogant. Humbleness and class are best.

As implied, coaches must be sure not to go too far in the opposite direction either. Never praising the star players or failing to recognize their contributions is going too far. When the star player has a rooted work ethic, you can use the player to show that effort pays off.

AIDING THE UNUSUALLY HARD ON THEMSELVES PLAYER

"Do not let what you cannot do interfere with what you can do."
– Coach John Wooden, Basketball

Preview – Some kids are way too hard on themselves, a frustrating thing for others to experience.

"Don't worry about it. If it were easy, everyone would be a star."

– Coach to a player who hangs their head over every little mistake

---

I had a player who wasn't hitting, and he was beside himself with frustration. At the next practice, I told him I wanted him to field a hundred ground balls. His response was, *"But I'm not hitting."* *"I know,"* I came back with, *"If you aren't going to hit, we better make sure you can catch the ball."* I was partially joking, but not completely. I wanted this player to relax, realize it was not the end of the world, and a little humor did that.

I learned early in my professional career never to make the games be about my performance only. One should not feel too elated with a productive individual game after a team loss. That display does not sit well with teammates or coaches. Likewise, displaying sad feelings after a victory is a no-no at the highest levels. It's not like winning has to be that important in youth sports or that personal satisfaction is not OK, but both reactions give the impression you're only playing for yourself. Realizing that displaying too much satisfaction is not best is a hard lesson for some athletes to learn, but it's best to learn it at a young age. Coaches can inform players to remember to consider the team when they show too much elation from personal accomplishment.

Of more concern to coaches are the players who show extreme frustration over every poor moment. Their behavior drags others down with them and demoralizes everyone. Athletes are competitive by nature, and it's natural to show frustration when they fail. But when it leads to immediate and constant disappointment, it's a problem that you must address.

The hard on themselves player is different from the negative player. This brooding player is optimistic, whereas the latter one is pessimistic. Those hard on themselves pout the second things do not go as well as expected.

Once irritated, players usually remain mentally down for the rest of the time. Pouting players aren't able to see their self-centered manner.

Coaches must hold players accountable when their conduct drags others down. Allowing pouting players to feel sorry for themselves can lead to a glum atmosphere. As a coach, you should help them see how they come across to others around them. You can help your players learn to deal with frustration in a better way.

Coaches Should:

> Not scold players for feeling disappointed, but point it out and try to limit how often it occurs. Tell players you appreciate how much they care. Inform them that they have 3 seconds to sulk after failing. At the end of that period, they must forget about it and move on.

> Never try to placate them by telling them how well they played when they struggled. Often, that's the last thing they want to hear. Also, pleading with high-intensity players to, "*Just have fun,*" is not a solution that will work.

> Ask players to commit to the team goals and not just to their own play. Reinforce the idea that each member is part of something bigger than themselves.

> Talk to players and see if they will express what makes them so upset. Letting them get it off their chest right away may help. Some kids may not have any real reasons for never feeling satisfied, or they may just not know what those reasons are.

> Not embarrass players by bringing up their sulking ways in front of others. Talk in general terms with the whole team about the dangers of thinking of only oneself. Explain how the "*Woe is me*" mannerism appears to others.

> Help players get the message that inconsistency is the nature of sports. Players must learn that no one excels in every game and that coaches do not expect perfection from them.

➤ Explain that a never-satisfied outlook may give temporary motivation, but it takes a toll after a while. Help players learn to enjoy the journey, which includes some heartache.

➤ Enlighten kids by letting them know that they can learn more from mistakes than efficiency.

➤ Give players ways of turning doubtful thoughts into helpful ones. Giving players a short, upbeat saying to repeat when things go wrong can work. For instance, RBI stands for **R**elax, **B**reathe, **I**mprove. Instead of beating themselves up after outs, players learn to say RBI, an obvious baseball term for runs batted in, so it's an easy thing to remember. Immediately thinking: *relax, breathe, improve* helps a player prevent the negative energy from getting them too upset after a failure.

➤ Remind athletes there will be another day and their day will come.

➤ Try to get players' minds off of their disgust as soon as possible by talking about something else. *"What class is your favorite in school?"* is one I might throw at them when I see them get too upset at practice.

➤ Explain the danger of burnout that can come from a never-satisfied attitude.

➤ Use a sense of humor to try and ease the tension.

➤ Ask the player's parents to miss a game to see if the player's outlook changes. Some player's internal pressure comes from wanting to please mom and dad so much.

Final Thoughts

One of my most-used coaching phrases is, *"It won't be the last time you mess up"* that states the nature of sports to kids.

The common expression, *"There is no I in team,"* is directed at the pouting player.

The easily-frustrated player is often a perfectionist, another trait that is not always bad, but in sports, it can be somewhat detrimental.

Sometimes, the sulking athlete is the *"Crier."* Try to be patient with them, as crying is not usually what they *want* to do, but some kids can't control the tears. Coaches shouldn't let others tease crying players. They should praise them in front of others for their caring ways.

ENCOURAGING THE UNINTERESTED AND FEARFUL PLAYER

"Nobody who ever gave his best regretted it."

— Coach George Halas, Football

Preview – Fear can destroy an athlete.

"Do you want to be here? You have more talent than anyone else on the team, so it's beyond me why you won't apply yourself."

— Coach to the indifferent athlete

Those are familiar words of the dumbfounded coach. I had to learn the hard way, just as all coaches do, that not all kids have the same levels of interest and desire. Some children are not willing to try hard, and no matter what a coach may try, they won't change. I recall talented players, even at the professional level, who never reached their potential. No matter how much the coaches pleaded with them to give more, they never would exert themselves.

Some young players have an intense fear of injury to the point where they shy away from the activity. Although frustrating to see, adults must give these players time and space to work things out. Calling them soft or putting them in spots meant to toughen them up will probably dishearten them more. Coaches should not draw attention to a player's trepidation of getting hurt in front of others. Once others perceive someone a certain way, they may become the object of ridicule. Scared kids get a label that is hard for them to shed.

One of the most frustrating athletes is the gifted one who just goes through the motions. They show little energy or desire and act as if they are too cool to exert themselves. They appear to be noncompetitive and act as if they would rather be doing other things. Other less-talented athletes play hard and outperform them.

On the outside, it looks like these players do not want to be there with their lazy mannerisms. But, often overlooked is that they may have a high fear of failure. They don't commit because they believe they cannot meet their own, or their parents', expectations. By giving less than their best effort, they have an excuse for not coming through. The usual response to these players is to tell them how talented they are and that you think they're wasting that talent.

Sometimes, lazy players result from *"helicopter parents"* – parents who are always around. They don't let their child do anything on their own. They believe in making everything right for their child. The problem is that kids whose parents do too much for them, often display less motivation. Additionally, the players often lack confidence and are always looking to their parents for affirmation. Coaches may not be able to do a lot to change parenting behaviors, but at some point, they may have to disclose to parents that their actions may be the cause of their child's laziness and low interest level.

Coaches should not let their frustration over lethargic players allow them to give up on the athlete. A lack of interest affects their growth in the sport, but they are not beyond hope. Many uninterested athletes will come around with an excellent education environment and patient coaches. Exciting workouts that accentuate learning and growth can help.

The thing to understand is that the lazy and fearful players do not see themselves that way. Coaches should not dwell on a player's low energy levels and fear because that does not help the situation. Here are the keys to developing interest and effort.

Coaches Should Teach:

- ➤ **Focus**. You can explain that hesitation and nervousness are normal reactions, but they have the ability to focus despite those feelings.

- ➤ **Courage and Resilience**. The dedication to hard work will not come until players know that it's OK to mess up. Tell kids not to play just to prove anything to others, but that they owe it to themselves to give more effort. Coaches should preach the importance of accepting challenges.

- ➤ **Support**. It's natural for coaches to show frustration and get on players from the beginning. But that display of disappointment is what lazy players get from everyone else in their lives. Once the coach does it too, the player will likely lose appreciation for them, too. Calling them out for a lack of effort is not a useful plan. Once players lose trust in the coach, it rarely returns. Players who do not feel judged in the beginning may change, relax, and start working hard. Coaches should never allow anyone to ridicule and nag players who don't try hard.

- ➤ **Self-image**. Coaches should describe player actions in ways that do not attack their desire levels. Saying, *"Be more aggressive next time"* is better than saying, *"You have to want it."* The ability to say things to players in a matter of fact voice is best. Saying, *"I know you can move faster,"* is better than screaming, *"Come on, quit being so lazy."*

- ➤ **Praise**. Mentioning a player's good effort in front of their parents can help. Anxiety often corresponds with distress over letting mom and dad down. Reassuring words from the coach to parents may ease some of the tension for athletes.

- ➤ **A plan to commit**. Coaches should talk with players one-on-one about setting realistic goals for themselves. They should ask lackluster players what might work to help them feel engaged. Their answer may help coaches come up with a plan for motivating them. Also, it may wake kids up to the fact that they are *"loafing."*

> **A feeling of competency and progress**. Coaches should jump at any skill upgrade with these players. Little else can inspire interest as much as feelings of achievement can.

> **Daily aims**. Coaches and players should decide what things to do on a regular basis. Narrowing the objectives helps keep athletes on task. Practice is the time to begin to develop a fearless mindset.

> **Accountability**. Kids should learn not to rely on their parents for things they can do for themselves. Coaches should explain that players are responsible for their gear and carrying their bags. They can have all players help with the equipment and cleaning up after sessions.

> **Value of activity**. Lazy players become bored sooner than others. Coaches should include a wide variety of activities and drills to keep all players busy.

> **Inspiration**. Give kids ways to practice at home. Homework tells kids that you care they improve and will not give up on them.

Final Thoughts

Some athletes engage when they feel their role is vital to the team. A bigger role on the team or a chance to play a better position than usual may spur them.

Coaches should explain and point out examples of what playing hard means. When a lack of hustle occurs in games, coaches must do something. Instead of yelling all the time to hustle, you should explain what you mean. Taking players out of games for a short spell and ask them if there is a reason they are not playing hard is a last resort.

All types of fear diminish with the proper preparation, and increase with the threat of punishment.

Coach free practices, when coaches just watch kids in situations when they play on their own are important. Kids may play hard when not judged or pushed by adults. When a change is evident, coaches can ease their attention with that athlete.

Successful athletes have a way of using fear as motivation to work hard, but have the ability to throw that fear away when playing.

Coaches must ask players not to look to their parents for advice during games and practices. If kids continue to do that, you should ask parents to watch from a further distance away.

When they feel unhappy, ask players to talk to you.

As a last resort and in a one-on-one conversation, this question may work with an older athlete, "*What are you afraid of?*" The player response will likely be "*Nothing.*" At that time, come back with, "*Maybe, but it appears to me you are scared of working hard.*" This reaction may spur the player to give more effort and entice them not to be so "*cool*" and afraid to exert.

CHAPTER 14

~

Creating the Final Touches

Subtle coaching techniques help motivate athletes and come in handy over the long season.

Below is a letter I wrote to a coach of a youth team I have worked with for a few years. Having players who want to play for you year after year should be a goal of all coaches.

Coach,

Congrats on your tourney win. I could tell in the first 2 innings how much improved the guys are in all phases of the game. It's a testament to you and your patient coaches who allow the kids to be themselves and have fun. No wonder you have been able to keep the same team together all these years. Keep up the great work. Jack

PHIL JACKSON

Another of the winningest coaches of all time is pro basketball's Phil Jackson. Phil earned the nickname the Zen Master because of his belief in mindfulness, and his spiritual and holistic approach to coaching. Something must have worked as Phil Jackson led his teams to 11 NBA championships.

Phil coached some of the greatest stars and was a master at getting even elite players to buy into a team atmosphere. He had a way of thinking outside the box to get inside the minds of every player on his team. At different times he had his teams practice with the lights out and had silent practices to add variety and intrigue into his training techniques.

Like coach Wooden, Phil Jackson had a way of saying things that make a lot of sense. You may just have to think a little bit about Phil's words to figure them out. Following are some of the quotes from Jackson and my take on them.

1. *"The strength of the team lies within the individual. And the strength of the individual lies in the team."* A neat way of saying that the team and individual will get nowhere without each other.
2. *"Wisdom is always an overmatch for strength."* This quote attests to the powerful nature of the mental side of sports.
3. *"You can't force your will on people. If you want them to act differently, you need to inspire them to change themselves."* Motivation comes from the athletes themselves with inspiring assistance from the coach.
4. *"If you have a clear mind…you won't have to search for direction. Direction will come to you."* Cluttering players' heads with too much information messes them up more than it helps them.
5. *"When the mind is allowed to relax, inspiration often follows."* Kids with patient, kind-hearted coaches figure things out in time.
6. *"No one plays this or any game perfectly. It's the guy who recovers from their mistakes who wins."* Coaches must teach players the reality of sports and how to deal with adversity.

Lessons Learned from Coach Phil Jackson:

1. Check your ego at the door; it's about team.
2. The mind is a powerful thing when not cluttered.
3. Sometimes coaches should just sit back and watch.
4. Practicing in different ways is an effective way of engaging players' attention.

SHOWING THAT START TIME MEANS THAT

"The absolute bottom line in coaching is organization and preparing for practice."

— Coach Bill Walsh, Football

Preview – Starting workouts with a bang is worth it.

"We went over that in the beginning."

— Coach to the parent of a player who arrived after the stated start time

I know many high school coaches lock the gym doors at the stated practice time. Late players miss out. Professional coaches inform players if they are five minutes early, they are late. That strategy is unreasonable in youth sports because kids have little control over arrival time. But, it's frustrating to start practice, only to have to repeat everything when others come late. Also, seeing players unaware of where they should be once you begin drills is an organizational hassle.

After I became a coach, I discovered why some of my coaches were so unhappy with late arrivals. When coaches wait to begin until all the players are there, valuable time is wasted. If they go ahead and just start on time with explanations of what they will cover that day, confusion will soon follow and they'll end up repeating their instructions for late arrivals.

To combat kids showing up late, I begin practice at the stated time. When the start time is four o'clock, I begin it at four, or as close to it as possible. To entice players to show up on time, I make the beginning appealing and memorable. I love it when late arriving players show up, and everyone is laughing, working, or excited. The tardy players will try to come earlier the next time. Fully using the time to the utmost potential is only possible when players get there on time.

With the following procedures, coaches can entice players to show up on time.

Coaches Should:

- ➤ Have someone send a time-reminder notice to players the day before practices.
- ➤ Get there early enough to be ready to begin on time. The appearance of organization is a sign of integrity and dependability. It shows that you want to use every minute to give to the kids.
- ➤ Begin at the designated time, from the opening day of workouts, whenever possible.
- ➤ Begin each session with something exciting. Competitions, races, and amusing stories are thrilling ways to start practices.
- ➤ Have all coaches instruct during warm-ups.
- ➤ Explain to players and parents that correct warm-ups are essential because they provide the repetitions and exercise to improve and prevent injury. The beginning of practice is the time for gaining the basics, getting loose, and bonding with the team.
- ➤ Explain the day's agenda after some initial work, when all have arrived. That way you won't have to repeat everything or deal with unaware kids.

Final Thoughts

Coaches get satisfaction when they hear that children urged their parents to get them to practice on time.

It also helps to finish practice at the designated time because many parents have tight schedules, too.

Sometimes, arrival times are beyond anyone's control. Ask parents to alert coaches if they'll be late whenever possible.

After using the above method, coaches notice less late arrivals and wasted time.

ESTABLISHING THE NO BEACH RULE

"Without self-discipline, success is impossible, period."

— Coach Lou Holtz, Football

Preview – Coaching fatigued athletes is not pleasing or fair to the coach.

"He had a sleepover last night, and he just came from a basketball tournament."

— Parent comment to coach

To this day, I remember sitting at home on beautiful summer days while my friends were at the local beach club. I felt like my social life suffered because of our coach's *"no-beach-on-game-days"* rule. But as a coach now, I recognize the importance of his request.

Tired players are a drag for coaches to deal with, and they're not the real measure of a kid, either. Even one exhausted player can be a disruption to everyone. Their lack of effort and bad attitude is evident to all. Worn out athletes have little energy, do not listen, and cannot focus.

Kids are often busy with many activities, from other sports to outside interests. Coaches know that kids have more diversions in their lives than ever before. That is all the more reason for coaches to have some simple, reasonable guidelines for teams. Having a team policy that limits over-scheduling players is useful. People may not follow the regulation, but by providing the guidelines, you've done your job of holding others accountable. Because most parents want effort, they come to understand the importance of rested kids and may not over schedule them.

You can try these suggestions to try to avoid getting the exhausted child.

Coaches Should:

> Not over schedule teams with games, tournaments, and training sessions. Entering tourneys that play at ridiculous times is not right for the young players, either.

> Understand the effects of the heat or cold and account for it in the best ways possible.

> Encourage parents to avoid having kids playing two sports that overlap a great deal the same time of year.

> Discourage sleepovers the night before games. You should reinforce the importance of a good night's sleep before, and rest on game days.

> Encourage parents to have players come to practice and games with something in their stomachs and the necessity of eating healthy foods.

> Ask players to avoid spending too much time in the sun on game days.

> Have players relax in cool areas between games on very hot days.

> Make sure players hydrate with healthy drinks before, during, and after games.

> Explain the dangers of over exerting before games. Many parents have kids practice before they go to games but don't realize they are wearing them out.

> Be careful of overworking players during warm-ups, especially if they have more than one game that day or it's a hot day.

Final Thoughts

Parents have to find the line between too much and not enough activity.

Even though video game playing has some drawbacks, one positive is it limits physical activity. On the other hand, parents don't want kids to sit around playing video games all day either. They may have to come up with other activities to keep kids busy without too much time in the sun. You can suggest a sports-related book for athletes to occupy some of their down times.

DEVISING PRACTICE MOTIVATION

"Nothing will work unless you do."

– Coach John Wooden, Basketball

Preview – This motivation technique works to build practice enthusiasm.

"It is not only how much you do; it is how smart you do it."

– Coach to the team

The opening 30 to 40 minutes of my baseball camps had kids just playing catch. Most players tire of playing catch after just a few minutes, but no campers complained. The key was the competitive drills. Kids enjoyed it without even thinking about the amount of time spent on it. Coaches were happy because players were working on their skills.

Athletes are competitive by nature. Contests keep concentration levels high and they are excellent ways to motivate. The incentive to win keeps players involved and hungry to improve. Trying to upgrade their performance and win the next round drives kids to work hard.

This coaching method helps players prepare in a productive way.

Coaches Can Have Players:

➢ Begin with a contest and keep players' scores.

➢ Announce and compliment the winner.

➢ Set up drills that have players do the same actions.

➢ Finish that segment of training with the same, original contest.

➢ Compare players' scores to the opening round.

➢ Congratulate the winner and the players who show the most improvement from round 1 to 2.

With young players, having a little prize for the winners may raise the excitement level. Coaches do not need to tell players what the winning criteria is beforehand. For instance, you can give the award to the winner of the first contest. That's a sign that players are the best in the beginning or that they worked on a skill at home.

Another time, you can award the player who wins the second challenge, after the drill work. That award signifies improvement and that the drills worked. Finally, you can award the player with the highest increase from the first to the second measurement. Using these different criteria for winning the contests ensures players try each round. In this way, there are different winners from round to round, which adds to the excitement.

Solid drills and techniques between contests should lead to better play. You can have group competitions in the same manner by having players or coaches pick sides to compete against each other. The ultimate goal of the matches is to show players ways of practicing to improve.

Final Thoughts

Some players may show little or no increase in future rounds. Coaches should point out that this is the nature of sports, but that work will pay off in the end.

It bears repeating that having ways to measure production spurs motivation, energy, and player development.

This type of motivation technique helps coaches find the drills that work the best, too.

PROMOTING HOME WORK

"Your biggest opponent isn't the other guy. It's human nature."

— Coach Bobby Knight, Basketball

Preview — A key to player evolvement is repetition away from the team. A system of measurement at home helps players improve.

"I didn't have time to practice."

— Player to coach

Coaches should prepare to hear the above statement, but it's not one any coach wants to hear. I figured out early on in my coaching career that little time exists to help every player. Some players have further to go than others to be competitive. Furthermore, muscle memory takes a long time to change. A coach can only do so much in the allotted training time, so at-home work helps. Motivating kids to do some work at home is the challenge. I learned that the best way to entice practice is by having ways of creating a test and measuring performance.

Coaches love when players practice on their own. The problem is that often this at-home practice has players performing things the wrong way, which can hurt players' progress. The results can be worse game performance, which leads to less desire to keep practicing.

The best chance of enticing players is by making it exciting. An effective way to motivate is through self-competition. Getting players to strive for their *"personal best"* helps.

Similar to the at-practice measuring system contests, coaches can give players ways of measuring their moves at home. Measurements help players dedicate, have specific points to reach, and remain engaged. Giving players challenging, stimulating, and productive methods of training at home inspires them to do just that.

Coaches Can Encourage Athletes by:

➢ Showing players a system of accurate measurement. With some sports and movements, this is easier than others.

➢ Measuring the amount of correct actions of the particular action or skill that was worked on before leaving practice that day.

➢ Assigning the same skill work to measure at home.

➢ Having players keep a small journal of their at-home sessions that show the work days and their results.

➢ Explaining the 80% rule. The player's goal is to get to the point of doing something correct at least 8 out of 10 times. This rate can change bad habits into good ones over time.

➢ Engaging in the same competition and quantifying process at the next practice. This check usually shows which players practiced. Most players will show improvement, which was the goal in the beginning. This increase in production spurs many athletes, and may motivate the ones who failed to train.

Final Thoughts

Coaches can only provide the means and motivation for players to work out, but actually doing it is up to them.

It's better to do something correct a few times than it is to work incessantly not using correct form or technique. Without a coach on hand, kids won't know if what they are doing is correct unless a measuring system is employed. This system helps players to practice smart, take their time, and strive for perfection. Once a skill is consistently done correctly at a consistent rate, it's more likely to happen successfully in games.

Pleading with athletes to practice on their own usually does not work. Only the more dedicated athletes will do it. Part of the problem is that practice by oneself is not a lot of fun or tension-filled when done with mom or dad. With the measurement system, coaches should tell parents they can score for players but should remain quiet unless asked for advice.

RECOGNIZING THE VALUE OF ROUTINE

"Great effort springs naturally from great attitude."

– Coach Pat Riley, Basketball

Preview – Routine helps motivate athletes.

"Mom, I thought we had practice today."

– Player question to parent

I was not a superstitious player, but like most players, I kept a routine when things were going well. When things began to click, I wanted to do the same things each day. Once I was out of the groove, I looked for another pattern.

Successful athletes like predictability. They will often wake, eat, workout, and go to bed at the same times every day. Some athletes take it further. They insist on dressing a certain way, eating certain foods, and talking to the same people. They listen to the identical music and leave for games at the same time each day. When one thing changes, they feel like it will affect their performance. There are reasons beyond just being superstitious that exist for consistency. A regular schedule can motivate and provide self-discipline. The mental game is vital to athletes, which make daily habits worthwhile.

People are creatures of habit, and a consistent schedule motivates them. Routine is an often overlooked source of motivation for young athletes. Uniformity creates will-power and self-control. You can help use the power of routine as a motivational force.

Here are some ideas that help.

Coaches Can:

➤ Consider playing on the same days and times each week, when setting up the schedule.

➤ Have the same location, hours, and days for workouts each week.

➤ Inform players at the beginning of each session what the sequence of events will be for the day. That information helps players feel more comfortable and mentally prepared. Providing an agenda helps anxious and young kids the most.

➤ Help athletes develop their individual routines that are comfortable to them daily, before games and the next play.

➤ Keep the same routines after well-played games and alter them after poor play.

➤ Encourage players to get into a regular training schedule at home, too.

Final Thoughts

Keeping players engaged, believing in, and enjoying the journey regardless of the results are central to coaching success.

Coaches should consider the age of players and the team's philosophy before setting up a plan. Having just the right amount of games and practices requires careful thought.

A regular schedule helps parents get kids where they need to be each week, too.

Some sports have a weekly game on the same day, making it easier to get into a set pattern of activity. Of course, some scheduling options are beyond a coach's control.

BROADENING SKILL DEVELOPMENT

"What to do with a mistake: recognize it, admit it, learn from it, forget it."

– Coach Dean Smith, Basketball

Preview – This coaching technique aids players' insight.

"Stop right there, don't move."

– Coach to an athlete

I've scared many ballplayers with that statement. As a baseball coach, I try to catch players in the act of both right and wrongdoing. I wouldn't be doing my job if I let flawed actions occur or failed to help kids understand when they are precise. You have to break the mechanics down to the smallest detail. Stopping players at opportune times helps them learn the missteps *and* dead-on moves.

Most movements in sports occur fast. Because actions happen so quickly, it can be difficult for athletes to know what they are doing. Often, what players do and what they think they are doing are different things. Even upper-level athletes have trouble figuring things out.

An initial stage of learning skills begins with getting a feel of the movements. Halting play in the middle of action gives players a chance to both see and feel what they're doing. Otherwise, coaches just *say* what's wrong, and a player may not fully comprehend.

The "*stop, look, and check*" strategy works well. This coaching process may seem obvious, but many coaches fail to use it or only use it once, thinking that's enough. It may seem a time-consuming and tedious process, and truthfully, it is. But the benefits outweigh the extra time, and kids learn faster with this coaching method. By stopping, looking, and checking what is going on, players begin the discovery process.

Video analysis is another excellent coaching tool, but time can prohibit the constant taping. In-game video is most useful, because what players do in games and practice may differ.

No mystery exists for using this coaching method.

Coaches Could:

➤ Catch players at the moment with *"Freeze right there!"*

➤ Ask the player why you halted play. It may be to point out correct or incorrect actions, but players must learn to recognize both.

➤ Explain how what they are doing is either correct or incorrect.

➤ Place players in the proper positions before reenacting the action.

➤ Set up drills that force the right moves.

➤ Have players perform things slow at first. Once better at it, more and faster repetitions lead to progress.

➤ After a while, ask the players why you stopped play and explain what they can do to correct incorrect moves.

Final Thoughts

Often, it takes many stoppages before players figure it out. Still, coaches should not hesitate to stop play until awareness comes.

Video analysis is valuable for showing players what they do. Coaches should use it from time to time as it can speed up player comprehension. But you must be careful of over using video. The use can lose its effect after a while because kids tire of seeing themselves doing things wrong.

ENGAGING WITH SHOW-AND-TELL

"Practice doesn't make perfect. Perfect practice makes perfect."

– Coach Vince Lombardi, Football

Preview – An educational tool in school, show-and-tell, is an excellent sport educating procedure, too.

"Tell me, I'll forget; show me, I'll remember; involve me, I'll understand."

– Old Chinese Proverb

I am often surprised at which athletes learn. The ones who look like they know and maybe are best at something, often do not. To help, I turn players into the coaches and let them teach. I find they learn and remember things so much better when they have to explain them.

It's not mandatory that players know what they are doing. However, it helps for making adjustments and for getting out of slumps. Knowing and doing are two different things, but each helps the other.

Coaches should never assume that just because players prosper, they'll know why or how they did so. One solution to helping players learn a skill and strategy is the show-and-tell coaching method.

Following are some ways coaches can use this technique.

Coaches Can:
  ➢ Ask players to bring a sport-related item to practice with an explanation of what it is and why it relates. Online pictures with short explanations of what is going on would serve this purpose.
  ➢ Have groups prepare something where each player explains an aspect of the play. The group project promotes teamwork and accomplishment.
  ➢ Grade players on any presentations and give them ways of improving them the next time.
  ➢ Pick individuals or groups to execute a particular training exercise or play. Each player, one after another, must come up with a different drill or reason for something. This tests players who are at the end of the group even more.

➢ List drills and let players choose which one they want to explain and show.

➢ Give individuals or groups a game scenario to figure out and then let them explain it to the team.

➢ Ask players to watch a game on TV and report back on what made the most impression on them. A terrific way for kids to learn is by watching higher level play.

➢ Encourage players to come up with questions about other player demonstrations. Kids may hesitate to ask coaches questions, but may be more willing to do so with other players.

➢ Have athletes interview someone who knows the sport and report to the team about the experience.

Final Thoughts

The show-and-tell possibilities are endless. Coaches can use their imaginations to come up with ways of using it. You should add information to what players explain.

This teaching technique builds players' confidence and game knowledge.

WORKING WITH PERSONAL COACHES

"A coach is someone who can give correction without causing resentment."

— John Wooden, Basketball

Preview — Today's athletes often have *"their team."* This group can include physical trainers, nutritionists, and a sport's psychologist.

"Her other coach told her to do it differently than how you're saying, and we pay a lot of money for the other coach."

— Parent warning to the team coach

A big reason I stay busy instructing is that players often become confused when several people are telling them what to do. I become another person telling them new things. I frequently feel sorry for players because they have to decide who to listen to among the sources of information.

One of the biggest changes in youth sports over the last many years is the use of personal coaches. Elite players almost always have them, and some non-competitive level kids do, too. Sometimes even athletes as young as 6-years-old have personal coaches now.

Confusion from having to listen to multiple coaches can be disheartening for athletes. Along with the confusion, they are in awkward positions. When told by different coaches to do things in a variety of ways, they have to decide who to follow. That decision isn't easy when they know one of their coaches may not be happy with what they decide.

It's a new age and team coaches must deal with this reality. Instead of insisting things be their way, coaches should be willing to work with others. Parents may be spending a lot of money for private coaching, so team coaches should not blow them off as quacks. They should never demand *"their way"* or that players disregard another coach's advice. In that way, players benefit and are not put in the position of upsetting one coach or the other. All coaches can co-exist in a beneficial way with open, honest, and compassionate communication.

Here are other things coaches can do for the benefit of the player:

Coaches Can:
- Ask parents to inform them when players have a private coach.
- Make sure the entire coaching staff is aware when players have outside help.
- Tell athletes that the coaching staff will not insist on their way, but will suggest ideas based on what they observe. With that, parents and players can report information to personal coaches without offending anyone.

➤ Make it known that you're open to discussing things with other coaches.

➤ Use tact when dealing with players and appreciate that all mean well and are out to help players. Say things with the other coach in mind. For example, saying, "*You will never be any good with that style,*" is inconsiderate. Saying, "*Ask your coach to address this, because I see this happening,*" is better.

➤ Talk with another player's trainer when serious differences of opinion seem to stifle development. However, parents must approve this interaction and may have to be the go-between. Checking in with other coaches is time-consuming. Spending the time to do so can be the last resort, and only when a player struggles over an extended period.

➤ Explain that often coaches are saying the same things with different terminology.

Final Thoughts

When more instruction is necessary than coaches can give, they can suggest outside help to an athlete's parents.

It's natural for team coaches to give less attention to players who have other coaches. That said, ignoring players because they have another instructor is not acceptable

AVOIDING THE SLEEPLESS NIGHTS

"Things turn out best for those who make the best of the way things turn out."

– Coach John Wooden, Basketball

Preview – After a tough day on the field, coaches may have to try this before trying to sleep at night.

"I am not sure I want to keep coaching if things like this are going to keep happening."

– Coach to spouse

I've heard coaches say that they never took their work home with them. They must have been award winning actors because this is just about impossible. Even after 27 years of coaching, I still have the occasional sleepless night. Even after feeling like I did the right thing at the time, sometimes I cannot get things off my mind. After trying to sleep for a long time, I often just get out of bed.

People say, *"It's only kids, and it is all about fun,"* but that's really just wishful thinking. Youth sports are intense, and it's never easy handling situations in the moment. Sometimes it's a parent who is a pain in the neck. Other times it's a player, or an arrogant coach. Most coaches will have days that make them wonder if coaching was the best decision for them.

As a coach, you must develop ways to deal with adversity, just as players must. Exercise, meditation, prayer, and talking to others may help. Those are not always enough to remove your constant thoughts.

A fantastic way to handle your frustration and rid yourself of sleepless nights is letter writing. Putting the issue and possible solutions to the problem on paper works to ease the mind. This note is just for you, not for sending. At the very least, it can help you calm your mind, move on from the situation, and sleep. Also, you'll be better ready for a similar situation the next time.

In This Letter, Coaches Can Answer These Questions:
- ✓ What or who is bothering me so much?
- ✓ What action did I use and was it the best way to go about it?
- ✓ Why am I taking it so hard and am I over reacting?
- ✓ Does the situation need more consideration or is it best to let it go?

- ✓ What are other possible ways of fixing this situation and dealing with it the next time it occurs?
- ✓ Is there anything else we can do in our coaching methods to avoid the same thing from happening again?

This letter writing provides a clearer picture of the situation. The following day, you should reread your letter and see how you feel about things.

Final Thoughts

Any time coaches believe an issue will continue to affect people, they must draw up a plan of action. A meeting with the involved parties may be the next step.

When coaches lose too much sleep about decisions that cost the team a win, they are taking things too hard. Remind yourself – this is not professional sports. Coaching youth is about the relationships and maturation, not triumph. Your personality should not change over game decisions and losses. If this happens often, coaching may not be right for you.

Postscript

As mentioned in the beginning of this book, you'll not be able to do everything written here. Nor will every reader agree with everything I've stated, but the key is to consider things carefully, and to remember to always put the kids first. All of this information may seem a little intimidating, but I hope it inspires you to do more. One right move can forever influence young athletes in a positive way.

I'm sorry about the number of times I used the word "*should*." I could have substituted "*could*" or "*might try*" more, but ultimately, coaches should do many of the suggestions here. There's no way around it if you're going to be the best you can be and create that *season to remember* for everyone.

Of all the concerns in today's games written about in this book, the trend towards youth sports becoming exclusionary should be of concern to all coaches. Ways of making all sports affordable and still competitive must come. Funding sources that allow children from all areas access to every sport must become a priority. Businesses, big and small, must step up to the plate to aid struggling communities to ensure all kid's the same opportunities. Also, coaches can help leagues to employ an easy waiver process that allows low income families a chance to enroll their kids at lower or no cost.

Hopefully, solutions come, so no child loses out on the opportunity to play their activity of choice. A movement in that process is The Aspen Institute's Project Play Report, titled ***Sport for All, Play for Life: A Playbook to Get Every Kid in the Game.*** It details 8 areas that can help communities allow every child to have the opportunity to play sports. Every youth sports organization should read the report and encourage their coaches to do the same.

As Coach Vasko wrote in the foreword, *"Our youth are counting on it."*

Other solutions may include incorporating many of the features of the current travel system into local community play. Things like adding games and in-season tournaments into the local leagues may help to revive the non-travel sports. With that plan, the best players would not look outside the area for the most competitive teams.

Some people may disagree with the use of a few quotes from Coach Bobby Knight. I felt they were important to use to show that even intimidating type coaches may have the right message, but the wrong way of delivering it. With that in mind, I'll leave you with one more coaching quote that attests to how you can make a difference.

"Always keep an open mind and a compassionate heart."

– Coach Phil Jackson

About the Author

Former major league player, Jack Perconte, has coached and taught baseball and softball for 28 years. A greater thrill than playing at the highest level for "Coach Jack" has been helping all involved with youth sports further their potential. He has aided ballplayers with his hitting manual, *The Making of a Hitter*, and parents with his book, *Raising an Athlete*. Here, in his third book, he shares his experiences and expertise with a step by step guide to help coaches. Visit www.baseballcoachingtips.net to follow Jack's playing and coaching advice.